THE DANGER AND THE GLORY
Irish Authors on the Art of Writing

Hedwig Schwall
Editor

To Pete & Kate,
with
congratulations
on your
50th anniversary!
Hel & Hedwig

ARLEN
HOUSE

The Danger and the Glory

is published in 2019 by
ARLEN HOUSE
42 Grange Abbey Road
Baldoyle, Dublin 13, Ireland
Phone: 353 86 8360236
arlenhouse@gmail.com
arlenhouse.blogspot.com

Distributed internationally by
SYRACUSE UNIVERSITY PRESS
621 Skytop Road, Suite 110
Syracuse, NY 13244–5290
Phone: 315–443–5534
Fax: 315–443–5545
supress@syr.edu
syracuseuniversitypress.syr.edu

ISBN 978–1–85132–206–0, paperback

Typesetting by Arlen House

Cover artwork by Rita Duffy

LOTTERY FUNDED

CONTENTS

Acknowledgements

The publisher and editor wish to acknowledge and thank the Department of Foreign Affairs and Trade, and the Embassy of Ireland, Belgium, for their help in realising this project.

 An Roinn Gnóthaí Eachtracha agus Trádála
Department of
Foreign Affairs and Trade

The support of the Arts Council of Northern Ireland is deeply appreciated.

Over the past ten years the European Federation of Associations and Centres of Irish Studies (EFACIS) has steadily been developing activities throughout Europe and beyond. I am grateful to the EFACIS Board that they gave me carte blanche to start this new initiative of *Kaleidoscope* (https://kaleidoscope.efacis.com/writers).

When asked *What is the nature of your art to you?* Irish fiction writers were invited to write their own version of John Banville's essay 'Fiction and the Dream', and it is no doubt due to the strength of the 'model text' that so many authors responded. My sincere thanks to the author for giving us the freedom to be creative with his essay. I am also deeply indebted to the sixty-one writers who responded, so generously sharing their honest views on the dangers and joys the writing process may bring.

I also want to thank all the writers and colleagues who helped me to get in contact with the participants: Anne Enright and Lia Mills, Éilís Ní Dhuibhne and Janet Dunham, Caroline Magennis and Dawn M. Sherratt-Bado.

The next step in the production was done by Carlos Solis Reyes who made the texts available on the *Kaleidoscope* website: a big thank you to our master of web revels.

The main milestone in the process leading to this book was of course Alan Hayes. *Reading the Future*, the beautifully varied anthology he made to celebrate 250 years of Hodges Figgis, had impressed me; we met and Alan agreed to publish *The Danger and the Glory*. Not only did he generously share his contacts with me, he actively supported the project and took infinite care with the publication. If ever I met a man with a heart for literature, it is Alan – he eats, drinks and sleeps the stuff.

A very special word of thanks also to Rita Duffy who especially designed the cover, kaleidoscoping references to Ireland's North, South and beyond. Ever the bridging and combining one, Rita mixes verbal and visual art, with a nod towards Anna Burns' latest novel.

Like most EFACIS initiatives, this writers' project is the product of cooperation between Irish writers and young volunteers from all over the world. Ciarán Byrne took the lion's share in coordinating the project; proofreading was done by Dylan Ó Loingsigh and the interns from Cultural Studies at KU Leuven, Harry Thorrington and Stella Cheng.

Books and websites cost money and we are deeply indebted to the support provided both by the Department of Foreign Affairs and Trade and by the Arts Council of Northern Ireland. Our sincere thanks also go to the Embassy of Ireland in Belgium and to the Northern Ireland Executive in Brussels. Without their support this initiative would never have come about.

Finally, we want to dedicate this anthology to the memory of Clare Boylan and Eileen Battersby, two admirable critics and writers in their own right, who constantly opened up new worlds, new passages between cultures. Both had so much more to give but were stopped in their tracks when one died of cancer (16 May 2006), the other in a fatal accident (23 December 2018). This book is a tribute to them, in gratitude to their enormous work and in the hope that in the near future many more good writers will be picked up by perceptive, open-minded publishers, critics, translators, scholars and book clubs in Ireland, its diaspora and way beyond.

Fintan O'Toole

FOREWORD

'A poet', claimed W.B. Yeats in 1937, 'writes always of his personal life, in his finest work out of its tragedy, whatever it be, remorse, lost love, or mere loneliness'. And then in the way that everything in Yeats always swerves away from itself, he added: 'he never speaks directly as to someone at the breakfast table, there is always a phantasmagoria.' This is of course the perennial tension in the creative process. To be real, art must spring out of personal life – remorse, lost love, mere loneliness, but also reconciliation, found love, mere contentment. But to be art it must be phantasmagoric. A phantasmagoria, in its original usage in English, was a magic lantern show, an exhibition of optical illusions. Artists are always involved in a kind of performance, always projecting their personal light from behind the screen that separates us from them. They talk to us, but not as they would do over coffee and toast. Even if they seem to be chatting intimately and mundanely, that is just another effect, another image thrown up by the magic lantern, another optical illusion.

And yet art is real too. One of the *Oxford English Dictionary*'s definitions of a phantasm is 'A thing or being which apparently exists but is not real'. But artistic creation turns that around. A poem or a novel, a story or a play (to think only of the literary arts) is a thing which apparently does not exist but that is nonetheless real. It has or acquires a presence in the world. Derek Mahon, in 'Tractatus', begins with Ludwig Wittgenstein's definition of reality: 'The world is everything that is the case' but adds that

> The world, though, is also so much more –
> Everything that is the case imaginatively.

Writing turns the imaginary into a 'thing or being', an objective occurrence outside of the writer's consciousness. But it also does the opposite. It turns the things and beings – the physical and personal circumstances of life – into imaginative presences, the process that Eoin McNamee calls in this intriguing collection, 'this suborning of people into fiction'.

These essays are the responses of Irish writers to the great question of how they 'negotiate the boundaries between inner and outer world'. Responses, that is to say, not answers. Who knows where, in the making of fictions, exactly at what point the personal becomes phantasmagorical and vice versa, how what is merely the case becomes what is the case imaginatively? Who knows how what Yeats calls 'the bundle of accident and incoherence that sits down to breakfast' coheres into the opposite of accident, which is art?

Not the writers themselves. If they did know, they probably wouldn't tell us. They would accuse us, as Hamlet does: 'You would play upon me; you would seem to know my stops; you would pluck out the heart of my mystery'. They would guard that mystery with their lives, lest we pluck out its heart and kill it. But they don't know.

There is a lovely image here from Wendy Erskine of the old arcade game Penny Falls. You put your pennies in a slot at one end and you could see them moving along the line and accumulating tantalizingly towards the tipping point at which a load of them would drop out through the chute at the other end: 'Mostly the new penny causes no movement but sometimes it sets up an unexpected chain which causes a cascade down the metal chute.' Writers are the people who can't help themselves – they know the game is rigged, that the pile of coins always seems like it is just about to fall towards you if only you put in one more penny. It is a mug's game. In Anne Enright's words here, 'The pay is often poor. The book is always terrible. It does not make you feel better. And back you go to do it again.' They can't walk away from the tantalising illusion. They keep going until, sooner or later, the cascade happens.

There is always, in charting this process, the danger of reduction from the sublime to the ridiculous. As McNamee has it 'the steps you take towards beauty are unlovely'. And as John Banville puts in relation to his own translation of dreams into work, 'cracking the code is not important, is not necessary … in a work of art, the code itself is the meaning.' There would be no great point in a book like this if it were merely an exercise in code-breaking or of reverse alchemy, turning the gold of art back into the base metal of life.

But that is not what it does. These are artists, after all, storytellers. So they tell us artful stories. And they are all, in a sense, ghost stories. 'Sometimes', writes Rosemary Jenkinson, 'a voice from plays or short stories cries out to me in the night like a teething child'. Or images are drawn, in Joseph O'Neill's phrase, from the 'emotional well, bucket by bucket'. The night is dark and so are the depths of the well. In order for things to emerge, they have to have been submerged. They have to have gone dark. Known experience does not become the material of successful fiction until it has first become unknown, drifted down from the conscious into the unconscious mind.

And then, when it reappears, it is a revenant. It is striking how often the writers here talk of dreams, about how, in Kevin Barry's terms, 'Writing is all about trying to get to the place where we dream while we're awake.' It is a hard business because ordinary life demands that most of us must keep high the walls between the night world and the day. For writers, on the other hand, 'the boundaries between inner and outer world' are ragged and porous. Between dreamtime and the waking world, there is a shifting, evanescent, haunted landscape populated by the phantasms, the ghosts, the after-images of what was glimpsed in the peripheral vision that is the writer's way of seeing. This book is an absorbing map of that terrain.

Hedwig Schwall

INTRODUCTION

The Danger and the Glory is a celebration of Irish fiction writing in the twenty-first century, and an offshoot of the EFACIS project *Literature as Translation*. The first initiative, *Yeats Reborn* (2013–2015) celebrated the 150th anniversary of the poet's birthday with translations in over twenty languages (still available on Yeatsreborn.eu) or in a bibliophile edition. The second translation project (2016–2019) focuses on texts by John Banville. This garnered translations in forty languages, but writers were also invited to react to Banville's essay 'Fiction and the Dream', in which he described what the nature of literature, and writing, is to him. We received magnificent contributions from major authors such as Claudio Magris, Corin Braga, Carmen Boullosa, Paul Claes, Georgi Gospodinov, Philippe Le Guillou, to name but a few, and published them on the website johnbanville.eu.

Finally we invited Irish fiction authors to write an original text on the art of writing. Along with Banville's evocative text I had sent a list of questions to the participants to pick from:

- What, to you, is the nature of literature?
- In which conditions does your writing come into being/flourish? Does mood play a role?
- Which conditions are detrimental to the right concentration?
- Does writing need a room (physical, mental, emotional) of its own?
- What place does writing have in your life? How does it interact/interfere with life, or does life interfere with writing?
- Is the literary translation of life into stories/poetry/drama somehow an unceasing commitment? Could you give an example of how that works?
- Does the unconscious come into play, and if so, how? Could you give an example of how something gestated over a certain time? Do the best passages come (un)intentionally?
- What exactly can a wo/man's specific ways of perceiving bring to writing?
- What is your favourite genre and why?
- What is the purpose of writing for you?
- What should your writing do to the ideal reader? To society?
- What is an ideal sentence to you and why? Are there any metaphors which are central to your perception/work?
- If you were to describe the act of writing in one scene, would that be a curse, a relief, bliss, a struggle, all of these?

There was no pre-set format nor any restrictions in content: any kind of text was fine, whether a short essay, a few aphorisms, a fictional scene, a (fictional) diary entry, a dialogue, a few paragraphs with observations, or a combination of these. The perfect size for essays was set between 1000 and 3000 words; if the arc of the argument or the meditation would go beyond 3000 words that was fine.

This project involved mainly prose fiction and offers a snapshot in time of answers to lasting questions. The snapshot character is reflected in the project's three consecutive names. The original working title was *writers@work*, echoing the series of writers' interviews

Clare Boylan had done on the topic of writing in the 1990s for *The Guardian*. Writers@work would be published as the first instalment of the website *Kaleidoscope* through which EFACIS wants to enhance the interaction between Irish artists and readers abroad, both diaspora and non-Irish. But the charm of a hand-held book is that it can be cherished in long-term use, so we decided to publish *The Danger and the Glory*, in reference to Banville's essay on the writing of fiction, 'its significance, its danger and its glory'. Danger indeed: the contributions show how authors put themselves at risk, going deep into their own darkness to spin a fictional construct from this which may say something about our common humanity; they may invest years in this, and find it does not work. The glory bit is less obvious, yet many writers talk enthusiastically about the phase in the creative process when the writing takes off. So after the risk may come the ride: when the fiction 'works' writers surf on their sentences.

So twenty-five years after Clare Boylan's *The Agony and the Ego* asked both British and Irish writers about their creative process I consciously focused only on writers working from Ireland – North, South and diaspora, English and Irish speakers. While the website version (kaleidoscope.efacis.eu) offers fifty contributions this book adds eleven more voices, twenty-four men and thirty-seven women). There are gaps, of course: some authors were deep into other projects, others were ill; yet the book offers a reasonable range of young and old, established and starting authors.

A final question may be, why should we focus on fiction in our age of social media? Rita Duffy's book cover answers the question in a graphic way. While both local rumours and global social media intimately interfere with people's lives and numb their ability to think for themselves, this girl reads novels, keeping a healthy distance from all too mimetic behaviour. Especially when bombarded with strong impressions, articulation of our self is not a matter of vanity but of sanity, both on the personal and the political level. Let's read our world more closely, these writers seem to say, have we listened to voices different from the usual ones? It is of vital importance that we listen to other cultures, other mores, other ways of representing urges, emotions and values. As Joyce famously put it: 'the way to Tara is via Holyhead'. Indeed, like this Irishman who saw Ireland more clearly from the continent, students who read and translate Irish literature become more aware of the riches of their own language; and we hope that the readers of this book will find themselves enriched by these sixty-one contributions which are so honest, so fresh, and so generously sharing their deepest concerns.

THE DANGER AND THE GLORY
Irish Authors on the Art of Writing

John Banville

Fiction and the Dream

A man wakes in the morning, feeling light-headed, even somewhat dazed. Standing in the curtained gloom in his pyjamas, blinking, he feels that somehow he is not his real, vital, fully-conscious self. It is as if that other, alert version of him is still in bed, and that what has got up is a sort of shadow-self, tremulous, two-dimensional. What is the matter? Is he 'coming down with something'? He does seem a little feverish. But no, he decides, what is afflicting him is no physical malady. There is, rather, something the matter with his mind. His brain feels heavy, and as if it were a size too large for his skull. Then, suddenly, in a rush, he remembers the dream.

It was one of those dreams that seem to take the entire night to be dreamt. All of him was involved in it, his unconscious, his subconscious, his memory, his imagination; even his physical self seemed thrown into the effort. The details of the dream flood back, uncanny, absurd, terrifying, and all freighted with a mysterious weight – such a weight, it seems, as is carried by only the most profound experiences of life, of waking life, that is. And indeed, all of his life, all of the essentials of his life, were somehow there, in the dream, folded tight, like the petals of a rosebud. Some great truth has been revealed to him, in a code he knows he will not be able to crack. But cracking the code is not important, is not necessary; in fact, as in a work of art, the code itself is the meaning.

He puts on his dressing gown and his slippers and goes downstairs. Everything around him looks strange. Have his wife's eyes developed overnight that slight imbalance, the right one a fraction lower than the left, or is it something he has never noticed before? The cat in its corner watches him out of an eerie stillness. Sounds enter from the street, familiar and at the same time mysterious. The dream is infecting his waking world.

He begins to tell his wife about the dream, feeling a little bashful, for he knows how silly the dreamed events will sound. His wife listens, nodding distractedly. He tries to give his words something of the weight that there was in the dream. He is coming to the crux of the thing, the moment when his dreaming self woke in the midst of the dark wood, among the murmuring voices. Suddenly his wife opens her mouth wide – is she going to beg him to stop, is she going to cry out that she finds what he is telling her too terrifying? – is she going to scream? No: she yawns, mightily, with little inward gasps, the hinges of her jaws cracking, and finishes with a long, shivery sigh, and asks if he would like to finish what is left of the scrambled egg.

The dreamer droops, dejected. He has offered something precious and it has been spurned. How can she not feel the significance of the things he has been describing to her? How can she not see the bare trees and the darkened air, the memory of which is darkening the very air around them now – how can she not hear the murmurous voices, as he heard them? He trudges back upstairs to get himself ready for another, ordinary, day. The momentous revelations of the night begin to recede. It was just a dream, after all.

But what if, instead of accepting the simple fact that our most chaotic, our most exciting, our most significant dreams are nothing but boring to others, even our 'significant others' – what if he said to his wife, All right, I'll show you! I'll sit down and write out the dream in such an intense and compelling formulation that when you read it you, too, will have the dream; you, too, will find yourself wandering In the wild wood at nightfall; you, too, will hear the dream voices telling you your own most secret secrets. I can think of no better analogy than this for the process of writing a novel. The novelist's aim is to make the reader have the dream – not just to read about it, but actually to experience it: to have the dream; to write the novel.

Now, these are dangerous assertions. In this post-religious age – and the fundamentalists, Christian, Muslim and other, only attest to the fact that ours is an age after religion – people are looking about in some desperation for a new priesthood. And there is something about the artist in general and the writer in particular which seems priest-like: the unceasing commitment to an ethereal faith, the mixture of arrogance and humility, the daily devotions, the confessional readiness to attend the foibles and fears of the laity. The writer goes into a room, the inviolable domestic holy of holies – the study – and remains there alone for hour after hour in eerie silence. With what deities does he commune, in there, what rituals does he enact? Surely he knows something that others, the uninitiates, do not; surely he is privy to a wisdom far beyond theirs?

These are delusions, of course. The artist, the writer, knows no more about the great matters of life and the spirit than anyone else – indeed, he probably knows less. This is the paradox. As Henry James has it, we work in the dark, we do what we can, we give what we have, the rest is the madness of art. And Kafka, with a sad laugh, adds: The artist is the man who has nothing to say.

The writer is not a priest, not a shaman, not a holy dreamer. Yet his work is dragged up out of that darksome well where the essential self cowers, in fear of the light.

I have no grand psychological theory of creativity. I do not pretend to know how the mind, consciously or otherwise, processes the base metal of quotidian life into the gold of art. Even if I could find out, I would not want to. Certain things should not be investigated.

The dream world is a strange place. Everything there is at once real and unreal. The most trivial or ridiculous things can seem to carry a tremendous significance, a significance which – and here I agree with Freud – the waking mind would never dare to suggest or acknowledge. In dreams the mind speaks its truths through the medium of a fabulous nonsense. So, I think, does the novel.

The writing of fiction is far more than the telling of stories. It is an ancient, an elemental, urge which springs, like the dream, from a desperate imperative to encode and preserve things that are buried in us deep beyond words. This is its significance, its danger and its glory.

Kevin Barry

ON CRAFT AND CONSCIOUSNESS

In which conditions does your writing come into being/flourish? Does mood play a role?

I don't think I require specific 'conditions' as such. I'm writing all the time. I don't struggle to make a start in the mornings. I'm not necessarily always writing well, of course, and it may be that there are times of the year when the words are coming more smoothly, maybe in summer ... When there's more light and you can swim in the lake, you're a happier animal, and maybe you're in a physical and mental condition where you're more attuned to your work.

Which conditions are detrimental to the right concentration?

The presence of the Internet. To write well, you need to be in a very concentrated frame of mind, and being online is the antithesis of that. When you're online, your brain is hopping around like a demented little flea, and this is not a good place to be if you're trying to write.

I've convinced myself of two things: 1) that there's a God; and 2) that he has a big lever to turn the Internet on and off and he only turns it on at 1pm in the day. I try, religiously, to keep away from the online world when I'm writing in the mornings.

Does writing need a room (physical, mental, emotional) of its own?

Well I do have a room ... or a shed, more specifically. It used to be a holding cell for the prisoners who were held at our house, which used to be a police barracks, dating back to the 1840s. Sadly there isn't the ghost of even a single tortured Fenian. I like to write in this place but I don't need it ... I write in cafes, on trains, in hotel rooms, I'm not precious about it.

What place does writing occupy in your life? How does it interact/interfere with life, or does life interfere with writing?

I've been lucky enough to write fiction and drama full-time since my first book of stories came out in 2007. I don't teach or do anything else. And after a while you find that writing stops being the thing you do, and it becomes the thing you are. All of your life is turned towards the object on the desk, and how you transform the materials of your own life and experience into fiction.

Is the literary translation of life into stories/poetry/drama somehow an unceasing commitment? Could you give an example of how that works?

One of the peculiar things about it is there's a kind of time lag ... It takes a long while before the events and emotions of your life start to surface in your stories and scripts. I find that often a story or a play will be inspired by something that occurred maybe ten or eleven years ago in my actual life. You just have to be patient and not strike too soon or not force it. Often the inspiring material has to sit back in your unconscious for ages before you're sufficiently embittered to start writing.

Does the unconscious come into play, and if so, how? Could you give an example of how something gestated over a certain time? Do the best passages come (un)intentionally?

The unconscious is the place where fiction and drama happens. The only thing in life that is close to writing is dreaming – they both come from the unconscious. And when you think about it, we are all brilliant storytellers when we dream ... the dialogue is perfect, we conjure great cinematic scenes, there are plots with their own dream logic. Writing is all about trying to get to the place where we dream while we're awake. That's why I like to write first thing in the morning while I am still (as Don DeLillo nicely put it) 'puddled in dream-melt'.

What is your favourite genre and why?

I try to read as broadly as possible across the genres ... so I read what's referred to as 'literary fiction' (a phrase that makes the soul shudder), and crime fiction, and 'popular fiction' and graphic novels and essays and memoirs and poetry. Above all, actually, I think the daily or nightly reading of poetry is essential, not just for your development as a writer but for your development as a person.

What is the purpose of writing for you?

To keep me going. I'd be fucked without it.

Sara Baume

FIVE FORMATIVE SCENES

one

I am six or seven. The mobile library bus parks at the school gate every second Thursday at noon. It is yellow and black. It smells like stale paper and furniture polish and old carpet. One Thursday, on the noticeboard between the shelves and racks there's a poster advertising a short story competition. The topic is *Animals are our Friends*. The prize is a free pass to Fota Wildlife Park. I decide I will write a story about a marmot. A marmot is a North American rodent, also known as a groundhog, a woodchuck, a whistlepig. Marmots are stubby of stature, stout of build, woolly of tail. Their coats are yellow-brown, grey-brown, white-brown. They form large family groups and dig labyrinthine burrows. In summer, they forage for flowers and eggs. In winter, the beating of their hearts decelerates and they sleep through until the spring. There are many nice Irish rodents I could have chosen to write about – red squirrels, wood mice, pygmy shrews. But no, I decide my protagonist is going to be a foreign species none of my classmates has ever heard of, and better still, I decide I am going to write in the voice of a marmot; that I am going to *be* a marmot – even though I know practically nothing about them, because the Internet hasn't been invented yet and my parents don't happen to own an encyclopaedia which covers the letter 'M'. These small matters will not discourage me.

I am going to be a marmot.

I am a marmot.

Sheltering beneath a cottonwood tree, frolicking in the ryegrass, defending my burrow against weasels and skunks, whistling dementedly into the Colorado wind.

two

I am eight or nine. A black, circular plastic box – a pocket-sized set of solitaire – turns up beneath the tree on Christmas morning. A gift for the whole family, even though it can only be played by a single person at a time. Beneath the lid, a fat cross of small holes, each fitted with a yellow peg, except for the one dead centre. The object of the game is to make a fixed number of strategic leapfrogs in order to remove pegs – every peg leaped over can subsequently be removed. At the end of the game, only one peg should remain – the central one which was originally empty. Around the fireplace – with a succession of Christmas specials flickering on the TV screen, a bumper tub of Roses open on the coffee table – everybody in the family takes their turn. Everybody in the family narrowly fails. Everybody in the family cheerfully gives up. Except for me. I am the youngest – logically the most likely to come last in every competition. But I am also the only one who refuses to surrender to pocket solitaire. All the way into the new year, I play and play, leapfrogging the pegs – carefully, angrily, frantically – offsetting my natural disadvantage with hours of obstinate effort.

In the closing days of the Christmas holidays, I finally conquer it.

The last yellow peg jumps the second last yellow peg and lands dead centre.

three

In the moment following the moment that I am flushed with the joy of victory over pocket solitaire, I realise that my achievement is of no consequence to anyone but myself. Nobody has been watching me play, and so there is no way of verifying that I have won honestly. And even if I could prove it, who would care? There are many different definitions, I realise, of what constitutes an accomplishment. Most are incomparable, and therefore impossible to measure.

Success, I realise, has the colour and consistency of condensation.

four

I am ten or eleven. We live in an old house at a rural crossroads. Every St Stephen's Day, Easter Monday and on occasional bank holiday weekends, I watch from my bedroom window as the members of the local fox hunt begin to gather outside – parking their jeeps and livestock transporters, saddling their horses and ponies, releasing their scent hounds. I am on the fox's side, and so the fact that the hunt assembles here infuriates me. I make a banner for my bedroom window. BAN THE HUNT it spells out in screaming red letters, above a gory painting of a bloodied fox. I prop it up on the sill, leaning against the glass, and wait for the next hunt. My grandma is mortified. My sister is teased by her school friends. My mum explains to me that she is on the fox's side too, and that it's ok to have strong opinions, but it's also ok to preserve traditional rituals, to dress up and gather together and parade around in stupid costumes every once in a while. The horses have a good time, she explains. The hounds have a good time. The fox rarely gets caught, and even if he does, maybe that serves him right for eating all the farmer's chickens.

It's ok to have strong opinions, my mum explains, so long as you can also see the other sides – so long as you weigh up all conceivable consequences before you go ahead and act.

five

I am just eighteen, and just finished school. My first real summer job is as a line worker in a factory which packages processed food, mostly microwaveable soup. Cream of mushroom and tomato, beef broth and chicken noodle. But I only know this from the labels – I never see any real soup. My line deals with the lids and labels; the cartons arrive already sealed. The labels are attached by the first machine; the lids are secured by the second machine – all that is required of me is to lift the cartons from the crates and place them onto the conveyor belt, upside-down. The factory is located in an estuary on a small island where almost every inch of land is occupied by a factory or a warehouse or a car park, where the shoreline is crusted by industrial effluent.

I wear a mop-cap, a blue smock and polythene gloves as if I am a surgeon. I lift and place the soup cartons for six hours a day.

And at the end of every day, I look back, at all those hours embodied as plastic cups, measured out in millilitres of watery soup – soup I would not serve to my worst enemy; soup I not would drink if I was starving to death.

Sam Blake

FINDING THE STORY

Way back in 1999, my husband went sailing across the Atlantic for eight weeks on the Atlantic Rally Cruise race. It was November and the evenings were long and dark, and I found myself sitting at home on my own. I had no children then, but I had an idea for a book. It was called *The Poison Tree* and was based loosely on the poem of the same name by William Blake, one of my favourite poets and coincidentally my now pen-namesake. I started to write it longhand as I didn't have a computer at home, going into the office in the evenings and at the weekends to transfer it to the screen. Like all first time writers, I was *completely* convinced it would be a bestseller. It wasn't. I had made every rookie writing mistake possible, and on top of that, I sent it out the moment the last full stop went down. Thankfully, it was rejected by every publishing house I sent it to, all over the world. But the bug had truly bitten and I took the advice of a great friend, author Sarah Webb, who told me to 'just keep writing'.

So I did.

The ideas for novels arrive in a myriad of ways. Some take years to form, some come in a flash, others float into my head as disconnected parts and I have to write my way into the story to find out what it's really about. As writers we hear snippets of conversation or read something in the paper and the germ of an idea forms. One 'light bulb' moment bounces off another, and then another, and then the story grows. Stephen King talks about a great story being the collision of two unrelated ideas, and this is the key, story is the synergy created when those ideas meet.

Four (unpublished) books later, the 'unrelated ideas' that fed what was to become my debut novel, *Little Bones*, collided one sunny Sunday afternoon as I was driving back from a Readers Day that Sarah Webb and I had programmed at a hotel in Dublin Airport. I had spent the day listening to internationally successful novelists discuss process and as I got into the car, I switched on the radio to a documentary about Kerry-born playwright, George Fitzmaurice. Fitzmaurice is best remembered for a play *The Country Dressmaker* staged by the Abbey Theatre in 1907. It saved the fortunes of the theatre but despite its success, Fitzmaurice died destitute in a room in Capel Street, aged 86. He had no will and few personal belongings, but on his bed lay an old suitcase containing a copy of every play he had ever published. That suitcase caused the collision of ideas which resulted in a bestselling novel.

Many years previously I had watched an RTÉ TV documentary about an unmarried twenty-three-year-old Irish girl, Belinda Agnes Regan, who, in 1947, was living in lodgings in Manchester. She had left Ireland knowing she was pregnant, but terrified of the disgrace it would bring, had concealed her condition. She went into labour in the middle of the night and delivered the baby herself, incredibly, in a room she shared with a younger girl, her landlady's daughter, who apparently slept through her ordeal. Covering the baby with a blanket 'so Shirley would not see it,' she crept to the bathroom.

When she returned, the baby wasn't breathing.

Wrapping the body in a blue frock and brown paper, she hid it in a suitcase under her bed. She went home for Christmas, and while she was in Ireland the body was discovered. On her return to Manchester, Regan was arrested and was one of the last women in the UK to be convicted of infanticide. The image of Belinda's suitcase had always stuck in my head, and these two stories, linked by old suitcases but heard so far apart, came together on the drive home. I started wondering about dressmakers and what would happen if the bones of the baby had ended up in a different dress – a wedding dress – the crucial thing that Belinda Regan had perhaps yearned for, for nine long months. At that point I had no idea who had owned the dress, or how the bones got there or why ... But I started writing.

I knew the wedding dress in this story, then called *The Dressmaker*, was in a cottage in Dalkey, the home of an artist with a very troubled past (and present). After writing a few chapters about Zoe and her grandmother, I realised someone needed to find the bones to get the story started. That was when Detective Garda Cat Connolly, in the middle of her own personal crisis, arrived on the scene with her gym bag and boxing gloves in the back of her Mini. Cat Connolly guided me through the story. Despite hours of research looking for an explanation, investigating baby killers, it was only as I wrote the scene in which a key witness is giving a statement to Cat and DI Dawson O'Rourke, that I found out, with some relief, exactly what had happened and why. The true story of the bones came to light, and then it all made sense.

I've always read crime. I'm fascinated by puzzles and what goes on behind closed doors, about why people keep secrets and what those are. When I started what became

Little Bones, I didn't think it would be a police procedural or the start of a series, but by the end of the first book the characters weren't finished with me. When my agent sold it, I found out that the publisher wanted a three book series, so I was lucky enough to follow Cat through several cases, all of which test her.

For me, building successful characters is all about understanding their motivation, trying to get inside their psyche to see what makes them tick and behave the way they do. It's essential to me, in order to make my characters feel really real, to uncover the factors that contribute to their behaviour. Motivation is key.

As a writer you draw on everything around you to create character. I have a friend who keeps fit with kickboxing, and Cat is very like her in many ways. I wanted Cat to be fit and fast in her day job, but also to have something to focus on outside of the Garda station to give her a personal life and depth. The sport conditions the way she thinks; she's fierce and feisty. I love, as a reader, to learn about worlds I'm not familiar with – I didn't know anything about boxing when I started and I wanted to bring that to Cat Connolly.

I'm very interested in blurring the edges of fact and fiction so that the world that my characters inhabit feels completely real. It's important to me that if a police officer reads one of my books, that it feels as true to him as it does to someone who knows nothing about policing. I write faster when I can clearly visualise a scene, and to do that, experiencing them is invaluable. I visit the locations, whether that is an elegant house in Monkstown or a wooded path in the Dublin Mountains; I want to hear and smell and experience what my characters feel. One of my favourite writing quotes is 'As a writer, words are your paint, use all the colours' (Rhys Alexander). I try to do that on every page.

To get Cat right, and to give her fight scenes the ring of truth, I needed to talk to a kickboxing champion. And doing that, I realised that Google can't tell you everything – it can't tell you how your muscles burn after a training session, how they stiffen up, and it can't tell you what it feels like, after a really tough hour in the ring, to be sweating so hard that you cannot see. I only found *that* out by taking up kickboxing myself. I'm fit, I go to the gym, but nothing can prepare you for the effort and energy used in a full-on kickboxing training session. And to write Cat's fight scenes I needed to know exactly how they unfolded, that she's right-handed so she needs to lead with her left, that you need both incredible flexibility and balance to be a champion in this sport. Going to classes was the best thing I could have done for Cat and for the books; my only problem was that, apart from being about twenty years older than everyone else and the only woman, I hate actually hitting people – but, fortunately, Cat Connolly doesn't have that problem. The incredible Maeve Binchy, whom I was privileged to know, always said 'write what you know' – I can't say I've killed anyone recently, but I *have* spent a lot of time in the ring ducking punches.

One of the wonderful things about writing a series is that the characters feel like those close friends that we all have, but rarely see. When you do meet up again, you pick up right back where you left off. My fourth book though, *Keep Your Eyes on Me*, is a total departure from the Cat series, a standalone that required a whole new cast. It is still at the editorial stage and I know I don't have it quite right yet, but all the components are there. As I write this, one of the key characters is still eluding me. I know I'm missing a part of her make up, but she's slowly becoming clearer.

One of the earliest lessons I learnt when I started writing was that writing is rewriting. Once the first draft is written, the words are on the page and you can work with them, change scenes, develop or delete characters, begin to shape the story. And that story can change. Despite being a plotter who needs to know roughly where my stories are going before I start, the published ending of my third book, *No Turning Back,* is completely different to the first draft. I realised in the final round of edits that it just didn't work and changed it completely.

Recognising when something isn't right, listening to your gut instinct, and having the courage to change it is something that comes with experience, and is a vital part of the process. Much of fiction writing is learning to tune into your subconscious, and the times when I've got stuck, when I can't write, I've discovered are the times when my subconscious is putting on the brakes – I've invariably made a wrong turn somewhere, a character has said something out of character or made a comment about something that they couldn't know. Once I go back to where it wasn't working and find my mistake, it all flows again.

Any writer who has a day job (I have several) and/or children (I have a couple of those too) knows that getting away from it all is sometimes essential to getting a book finished. I have quite a busy mind and the only way I can turn off and focus on a story is to plug in my earphones and get away from the office (which is at home, to further complicate things). Music is the key to accessing the creative part of my mind and freeing it from the everyday clutter. I created a soundtrack for Cat Connolly, chart music she loves to listen to. When she's pounding a punch bag in the gym and focusing on a case, like me, music is vital to drown out the noise in her head.

I've created a totally different soundtrack for *Keep Your Eyes on Me* – it's set in Bloomsbury, London, in New York and in Dublin, and one of the key characters is an ex-ballerina, so this time it's classical music she loves. Because I run my own businesses I don't have a nine to five working day (more like nine to eleven, six days a week) so I've learned to write anywhere, anytime. Once I've plugged in my earphones, I'm in my character's world and immersed in the story. Even if it's six o'clock in the morning and I'm on a plane to the Frankfurt Book Fair or early for a meeting in a city centre hotel.

When I'm working on a book, I aim to get at least a thousand words written a day, they might be total nonsense but I know I will go back over them and polish them before I start writing the next thousand words the next day. The hardest words to write are always at the start but it gets easier once the story starts to roll. With *No Turning Back* I was under pressure to start in order to meet my deadline, and I had lots of bits of plot but I wasn't quite sure how they connected. I took the advice of a writer friend, Alex Marwood, and 'wrote the stuff'. She sometimes writes forty thousand words of 'stuff' to find her way into a story. In many ways it's liberating to know that you're not writing the finished story, but the 'stuff', and I literally wrote my way into the first draft. Lots changed in subsequent drafts but I had the words on the page.

Writing fiction is something I love doing. It's my hobby as well as a job, and when I'm not writing I feel like a part of me is missing, as if something is empty. I'd write even if I wasn't paid for it, but I have definitely put in Malcolm Gladwell's ten thousand hours, writing four full-length novels and I don't know how many partials before *Little Bones* found a home. Pinned up over my desk I have this quote: 'The worst thing you write today is better than the best thing you didn't write'. Hold that thought.

Dermot Bolger

A WRITER'S LIFE

I recall sitting with a handful of my classmates in Beneavin College, in the working-class Dublin suburb of Finglas, in May 1977 as our English teacher, Colm Hewitt, gave up his Saturday morning to help those of us who were doing the higher level English paper to study Yeats' poem, 'Among School Children'. It is the poem where Yeats described his feeling when walking through a class of children who gaze in wonder at a 'smiling sixty-year-old public man'.

Across the gap of more than forty years since that day, I can recall the beauty and linear strength of Yeats' words, but also what for me back then was the impossibility of imagining what it must ever feel like to be sixty years old. Yet in February 2019 this was the milestone that I reached. Recently I walked through a classroom of children gazing up at me as I gave a talk and I realised how – although obviously I am not in any way a public figure like Yeats was – I had suddenly become the sixty-year-old man inside his poem.

Yeats' poem has stayed with me since 1977 although its depth of meaning has subtly continued changing in my mind as my life has changed. This is true of many of the poems that I didn't fully understand when I first encountered them at school but which have since become signposts to my adult life: their lines re-emerging in my memory from across the decades to often help me survive moments of personal trauma.

At twelve I decided I wanted to be a poet. My primary teacher, the late Michael Donnelly, read us a poem by Francis Ledwidge that was not on the school curriculum. Years later, when I tracked it down, I realised that it was one of Ledwidge's weaker poems, but to someone like me with a stammer, subjected to sporadic bullying, his words about being excluded were mesmerising. I walked home that day with a friend whose ambition was to join the Irish army. I shyly confessed my new ambition to be a poet. He was not unsympathetic but said that to be a poet you needed to go to university and as neither of us knew anyone from Finglas who had attended university he suggested that maybe it might be wiser to become a soldier instead.

We were wrong on two counts. Firstly, many Finglas people went on to university: one girl a few doors down from me became an esteemed medical doctor, and one lad I kicked a football with behind the shops later became a physician who was knighted in Britain for his research into the molecular pathogenesis of human obesity. Secondly, you needed no degree to become a poet. The great freedom of poetry is that you need nobody's permission – all you need is just a pen and paper and the courage to go wherever your imagination leads.

I still treasure a copy of Patrick Kavanagh's *Collected Poems* inscribed to me by Frances Barron, another teacher in Beneavin College. While many poems in this volume remain lodged in my memory, it is Kavanagh's 'Author's

Note' that most resonates now. He wrote in it: 'A man ... innocently dabbles in words and rhymes and finds that it is his life', saying how, if he hadn't discovered poetry, 'I could have been as happily unhappy as the ordinary countryman in Ireland'.

I don't know what Kavanagh's Monaghan neighbours made of this ungainly and (in his later years, when in ill health) occasionally cantankerous man, though I loved the observation of one Monaghan neighbour – stunned by how many national figures descended on Inniskeen after his death in 1967 – that 'locally his funeral was the making of him'.

If Kavanagh had not decided to dabble in words then it is no foregone conclusion that he would have remained all his life living in his native Inniskeen, working as a small farmer and shoemaker and being remembered now – if at all – as merely an erratic Gaelic football goalkeeper for the parish team. Intellectual wanderlust or clumsiness (his father told him, 'you broke everything on the farm except the crowbar. And you bent that') might have seen him disappear into the Irish diaspora in London. Any such fate might have given him a more financially secure life than the one he actually led, where – again quoting his 'Author's Note' – 'I literally starved in Dublin. I often borrowed "a shilling for the gas" when in fact I wanted the coin to buy a chop'. But a less precarious life in a secure job would probably not have seen his statue erected on Dublin's Grand Canal or a literary centre honouring him in Inniskeen.

I return to Kavanagh's 'Author's Note' because I love his phrase about how someone 'innocently dabbles in words'. It sums up the problematic alchemy of poetry: something which I have now written for forty-five years, spending the past thirty-five of these years making a precarious living from just the thin sliver of my imagination. Poetry is not like fiction in that no novelist 'innocently dabbles in words'. They sit for hours slowly coercing characters to allow themselves to be summoned up from within the novelist's imagination.

But poetry is a more mysterious kettle of fish. You can no more summon up a poem than hurry one along. Poems write themselves in your subconscious, then ambush you at unexpected moments, when you are walking the dog or washing dishes. Yeats said that from the quarrel with others we make rhetoric and from the quarrel with ourselves we make poetry. Because human nature is conflicted, there is always a quarrel in our mind with contradictory thoughts. Occasionally, one thought sparks into life with a jolt of electricity and we know instinctively this is a poem's opening line. We also know that if we don't write it down immediately it will disappear and we can no more summon it back up than last night's dreams.

Poetry has never made me rich, but thankfully my ability to diversify into novels and plays means that, unlike Kavanagh, I'm unlikely at this stage to starve. But just like him, my innocent dabbling in words has brought me on two extraordinary journeys. Firstly, a physical journey where I have read poems in a blizzard on a stage in a Beijing park or led two thousand Irish soccer fans through Stockholm as Grand Marshall of a St Patrick's Parade or performed in venues as diverse as New Delhi, New Brunswick, New York and Newcastle West. And, secondly, on an imaginative journey where at unlikely moments – sitting upstairs on a 16 bus in Dublin or having to lie sprawled in a Manhattan hotel corridor (to the consternation of other guests stepping over me) to scribble words that came from nowhere and would have vanished if I didn't catch them – I'm constantly surprised by the words I innocently dabble in.

It is a career where you never retire. Indeed calling it a career seems extreme when, in the main, it earns a writer so little money, but then again calling it a vocation sounds rather pretentious. So maybe it is best to term it 'a calling' because at unlikely times words do come calling to you. Those words are linked to emotions and because we each experience emotions differently a poem that touches one reader will leave other readers cold. Poetry cannot be foisted on everyone. But because poems are often crafted from the rawest grief or the height of love or other deep human emotions, I'm convinced that there is nobody alive who, at some tumultuous moment in their life, could not pick up some particular poem and feel a shock of recognition at how someone else has captured the emotions they are feeling.

My impulses, experiences and work practices as a novelist, a playwright and a poet are all radically different. The theatre is a more collaborative and convivial workspace where (even though you must begin the process of writing alone in an isolated room) you wind up seeing the phantoms of your imagination being brought to life, day by day, through the work of talented actors in a rehearsal room and learn so much in advance of the opening night by watching those actors unselfishly give you all their commitment and energy. Because you are constantly learning just by seeing the play being rehearsed, the text of any play is always still a work in progress. When Picasso was once asked 'When is a painting finished?' he replied, 'When the gentleman from the gallery comes to hang it.' As a playwright I have discovered that a play is only finished when the gentlemen and ladies from the newspapers come to hang the playwright.

On one level theatre is the most engaging and exciting of all disciplines because, as theatre is live, anything can happen on any given night. On the opening night in Dublin of the production by the Abbey Theatre of my adaption of Joyce's *Ulysses* I watched the audience intently during the first act, not sure if they would go with the text.

Even when it got a great reaction at the interval, I was still too afraid to allow myself to relax until we reached the fifteen-minute mark in Act Two by which time the audience were so engrossed that you could hear a pin drop. I breathed a sigh of relief and felt we had made it. Then at that exact moment I saw a movement in the audience and a former World Middleweight professional boxing champion stood up, cradling the body of an old actor in his arms. The old actor had just passed out unconscious and the boxer could only carry him to the nearest exit to get urgent medical attention by, quite rightly, striding across the playing area of the stage, leaving the cast standing there, dumbstruck, and then having to pick up the pieces of the play and try and rebuild the spell they had been weaving until that moment.

Not every night is quite this exciting, but every performance is different because of the constantly changing dynamic tension and interaction between the cast and audience. For a solitary creature like a writer, there is a great immediacy in seeing a live audience of several hundred people engage with your words, whereas, in contrast, a novelist rarely encounters his or her readers in these numbers or this way. But within minutes of the last curtain call on closing night, the carpenters are at work demolishing the set before the audience have even left the building and you know that no other audience may ever get this full experience of the play back unless a new director and a new cast are prepared to take the risk of mounting another production of this same play in another city on some future date over which you have no control.

In contrast to this, even if a novel has been left sitting untouched for years on a library shelf, having fallen out of fashion, an individual new reader who stumbles across it, ten or twenty years later, can still fully imaginatively engage with the characters in a fresh and original way. The forgotten drama text, however, has to wait for a theatre company to rediscover and add it to their repertoire before a new audience can experience the text of that play properly.

For that reason, the novel is the most special and intimate of forms for me because, even when a novel ceases to be widely read, it is still always lurking there between the cover waiting to be stumbled upon by chance by a new reader who will bring the characters to life in their own minds. The thought that this can happen at any time is a very special privilege for a writer.

There is a notion of novelists as omnificent masters of invented universes and that we pull the strings of puppets in fictional characters who dance only to our tune. Some novelists do work in this way and at times both I and my bank manager wish that I did. Indeed, if I did so, I would probably still have hair, but there again my imaginative life would be less interesting. Or to put this simply, if I knew what was going to happen next every time I sat down at my desk to write fiction, I would be so bored that I would probably never bother sitting down.

This is a point I often make to aspiring novelists: sometimes the less we know about what is going to happen in a work of fiction, the better off we are. The more we know about what happens next, the more we close off the possibilities of the unexpected, the less chance we have of allowing our subconscious minds to speculate and probe down to the awkward truths that we need to express instead of the glib things that we initially thought we wanted to say.

If we already know what we intend to say in a novel we are going to learn nothing by saying it. Only when we allow our imagination the space to catch us by surprise, when we sit back and stare in bafflement at words that suddenly start appearing on our screens, do we find ourselves to be truly writing. Only then can we honestly say that we are being brought – often by the seat of our pants – on imaginative journeys into the unknown. Suddenly we have left our comfort zone behind and start to discover things about ourselves, often in the guise of writing about some character who seems utterly different.

Therefore, in my experience, good writers very rarely talk much about whatever novel or short story they are currently working on. A work in progress is a private affair, because it is an unfinished imaginative voyage into the dark. You may often know instinctively from quite early on exactly how the novel will end, but not how to reach that ending – because if you get too far ahead of yourself mentally, the imaginative curiosity that drives you on may die.

I am now the author of fourteen novels, yet the process of writing a new novel remains as uncertain as when I wrote my first book. Writing my first one was probably easier, in that I felt under no pressure because I never believed that it would ever be published. What held me back at first was a supreme lack of confidence, the inability to understand that everyone's life is of equal importance. I now believe that, if written properly with the right engine of curiosity, what fascinates me about a character will hopefully fascinate unknown readers, provided that I commit my heart and soul to this character, that I believe in the world I am making up with sufficient conviction to allow others to believe in it too.

Poetry may be a sprint and a strong adrenalin rush when inspiration strikes and words fall into place (often at unlikely moments). But novel writing is like marathon running. Novels are not written with inspiration – although they need bursts of inspiration. Novels are primarily written through boring, repetitive routine. They are ground out in slow paragraphs on boring wet Tuesdays. They are the culmination of writing sessions when words turn to muck in your mouth and of other writing sessions when you start to filter through words that had seemed uselessly inadequate yesterday and find a way to mint fresh language from them.

Writing a novel is like opening up an imaginary hotel for the phantoms of your subconscious. You cannot be guaranteed that guests will turn up on any given night, but you need to have the light on and the door open just in case. I have been lucky enough to write my novels in some unlikely places. Two were written in the watch room of the Baily Lighthouse. Passengers flying into Dublin may have thought that the light flashing on and off at Howth Head was to warn shipping, but it was frequently me trying to find the right light switch on my way out.

But you don't always need a physical room or a full day of doing nothing else. Writers work in short bursts. If embarking on a book or memoir, what you need is to take your ambition seriously and insist that others close to you respect those rules. You need to partition off part of each day for yourself – even just one hour when you lock yourself away, when people know you are not to be disturbed, when you open that imaginary hotel in your mind and see who turns up.

I have learnt perseverance and patience and that a huge amount of writing takes place in your subconscious mind. It is being formed by your inner thoughts before you become aware of it. It may physically need to be written during snatched moments if you are juggling numerous responsibilities. But it is also being written in the hours when you are not writing it. Your subconscious mind is toying with it and it will come to you – like a forgotten name or the clue to a crossword puzzle – when you cease thinking about it.

Writing a novel is daunting, but less daunting when written one page at a time. If you wish to not get swamped, you need to break the book down into achievable mini-summits, to focus not on finishing the book but on finishing each chapter. You need to know when to push ahead and when to backtrack and restart. Starting again does not mean that there was anything wrong with the original words, but it means that characters change as a story changes. When you start writing a book you think you know your characters, but as the book evolves they evolve too and after fifty pages they have subtly become different from the characters you had on your first page. There also comes a time when you need to go back to the start and readjust things before the characters you are now writing about become too detached from the characters you started with.

When a novel is finally finished then, as a novelist, you send it out into the world hoping it may find a reasonably-large readership and maybe foreign translations or even film rights. There is a launch, press interviews and a small cluster of reviews in newspapers to give the process a minor sense of occasion. However as a poet, when you send out poems into the world, it is like you are dropping the tiniest pebble into the deepest well. The astonishing thing I've found after four decades is that, years later, you finally hear the tiny splash it has made when, to your surprise, you meet a reader somewhere who has kept that particular poem by their bed because your words captured something of the essence of their experience. Such rare encounters make the hours and months of reshaping poems worthwhile because you find you've touched someone in a deeply personal way that neither of you can explain. Those are the encounters and moments that send you back to your desk the next morning knowing that, in the end, the English language will always defeat you, but that just perhaps on this particular day you will win the smallest skirmish with it.

It does not always happen but, just occasionally, I emerge from whatever room I am working in, feeling that perhaps I may have come up with a line or a phrase or a verse that would have captured the imagination of the eighteen-year-old boy whom I once was, sitting in a Finglas classroom, just about able to comprehend Yeats' 'Among School Children' but feeling that surely I would never be able to comprehend the impossibility and implausibility of attaining the age of sixty.

Lucy Caldwell

WELLS, WAVES, CROSSROADS, STARS

One evening in November, two years ago, I gave a reading from a recent story in a bookshop in Belfast. It wasn't a good story, but it felt an important one. Writing it, I had obsessed over balancing it exactly; 926 words, as it worked out, in each half. The story needed to balance because that was how I felt: I'd reached one of life's fulcrums, and couldn't yet tell which way things would tip.

That autumn I'd had two miscarriages; then a play, my long-dreamed-of version of Chekhov's *Three Sisters*, slaughtered by the Belfast critics. I felt I might never write, or indeed create anything, ever again.

I stood at the front of that bookshop and talked about feeling at a crossroads. In just over a fortnight, I would (officially, implausibly) be already four weeks pregnant.

To be hollowed out; to be replenished.

For almost all of my writing life, when explaining to students, others, how creativity works, at least for me, I have used the image of a well. You drain your resources and then somehow have to believe that slowly, the well will fill again. You may not notice the slow seep of it; the moment when the groundwater's ebb becomes flow. But it does happen; drop by mysterious, precious drop.

I'd had a surge of creativity after the birth of my son, two years earlier. He'd been very ill shortly after birth, and for some weeks we hadn't known if he would survive. That experience unlocked or unleashed something deep within me: I felt emboldened, I felt fearless. I didn't care what people thought of my work. I suddenly felt, as never before, the imperative to do it. I'd written, in the space of a year, what I considered my best work to date: my short story collection, *Multitudes*, about life in 90s Belfast, and a life lived between Belfast and London since; and my adaptation of *Three Sisters*, set also in 90s Belfast. They came from the same time, the same place, in so many ways; they felt like sister-works.

I'd written them furiously, in whatever scraps of time I had; my son's nap-times, evenings, the two sacrosanct writing mornings which were all I had in a city where we couldn't – still can't – afford childcare.

I'd ridden the crest of that wave, and crashed in exhaustion on some far shore, with no idea what to do next.

And it was more than the usual sort of depletion. I knew I'd used up everything I had to say about Belfast, and my life there, but I didn't know how to move on, or whatever to write about again. Maybe I'd written the story to explain this to myself, or to psychically work it out; to nudge things on, or force them one way or the other; at least that's what I think now. It hadn't worked, and I stood there, ashamed of the story, fraudulent, unable to articulate any of it.

Halfway through the reading, I gave up on my story, and read someone else's, better, words, instead.

There is a poem I love by Louis MacNeice called 'Star-Gazer'. In it, he remembers a starry night from his boyhood, forty-two years ago, and how he darted from side to side of a railway carriage trying to see all of the stars. He remembers marvelling then at the fact that the light he was seeing had left them 'long years before I was'; now, he thinks that the light that was leaving them then, forty-two years ago, 'will never arrive/In time for me to catch it.' I have been thinking of it as I write this.

Six months pregnant with my son, I'd had dinner with Lennie Goodings, the legendary Virago publisher. We talked about Enid Bagnold's *The Squire* (first published in 1938 and reissued by Virago in 1987 and by Persephone in 2013). It was one of the few novels I'd read about motherhood and we talked about this, too; wondered at the paucity of fiction about motherhood.

Write us some new stories, Lennie said, and I demurred and laughed, gestured at my bump. I have to get through this bit first I think, I said.

It is a peculiar state, the passive-receptive phase. I love the wide casting-of-nets at the start of a project, where you can read with abandon, everything and anything that might be of use, and have licence to go places, talk to people, with no obligations but the vague notion of 'research'. I love the feeling when something starts to take shape, and you're carried along on the currents of it. Most intoxicating of all is the brief phase which can come towards the end of a project, a sort of terminal velocity, where you seem weightless: the words come easily, inevitably, and everything makes a perfect sense. You have to be careful what you read, watch, listen to, where you go, in this phase, because everything seems relevant, has a tendency to seep in. It is the opposite of the passive-receptive state where your instincts seem to hibernate. And there's nothing you can do, beyond just simply trying to be – be kind to yourself, be trusting that deep down things are resting, or settling, or accumulating; preparing for something new.

I had my tarot cards read recently by a writer friend, who is also an art historian. One card that came up repeatedly was *La Temperanza*. The tarot card of Temperance, she told me, as depicted in the Rider-Waite deck, shows a winged angel figure, one foot on a rock, the other in a stream, pouring water calmly between two golden cups. The angel represents the importance of balance, moderation, patience, control. In some modern tarot decks the card is called *Art*. She is not the devastation of being struck by lightning, or the raptures of the Lovers; she's not even the playfulness of the Fool. She's the virtue of staying grounded, of not rushing, not hurtling; of equilibrium. She's the opposite of everything that I thought that 'art' was supposed to be, until I had children.

The burst of creativity I had after my son was born feels now like a last hurrah – the intensity, the urgency of it. The after-image of something flaring bright on the retina just as it is lost; of something suddenly apprehended, or finally understood.

With two small children, work is much more plodding, much more mundane. When my designated writing hours are up, that's it: there's not going to be any more time until the following week. I've had to learn patience, and to trust the value of incubation; that my subconscious will keep whatever I'm working on alive. But when my publishers asked recently to contract a second collection of stories from me, I was surprised to realise I'd finished half a dozen. The stories are a departure from anything I've written before, in setting and in style. They are almost all about motherhood. Those precious mornings filled with new sentences, new stories, not in any great rush, but drop by drop by drop.

As I write this, that night in the bookshop in Belfast is two years ago to the day. My daughter is 15 months old, my play had a triumphant production by a Chekhov specialist company in the USA this summer, and just yesterday I signed the new deal. The seasons, the cycle, the cosmic dance.

I didn't know, that evening, what I would do or write next. The seeds of everything were already there.

Jan Carson

IDEAS COME TO ME LIKE BIRDS

'Ideas come to me like birds that I see in the corner of my eye.'
— Patricia Highsmith

On Tuesday morning she is sitting at the breakfast table, hand hovering over the expensive cafetière her parents gave her for Christmas last year. She is counting out one hundred and eighty seconds in the usual fashion – *one thousand, two thousand, three thousand* – measuring out three properly-paced minutes before she depresses the plunger. She likes medium-strength coffee. She is, in general, a moderate person, though prone to spending exorbitant amounts of money on bold – some might say garish – items of jewellery.

She is almost one hundred and fifty thousands in, when a flicker appears in the corner of her left eye. Something is falling, or rising, or perhaps hovering, in front of her kitchen window. She has a vague sense of it dragging on the periphery of her vision. It is mildly irritating, like a twitch or a trapped sneeze. She wipes her eyes with the back of her hand. It's early and she's still a little befuddled with sleep. She wonders what it could be. An insect? A branch? A bird most likely, for she lives three storeys up and there are no trees on her side of the building. She has hardly any interest in this fluttering thing. But surely, there's no harm in taking a closer look, perhaps even putting a name to it. She turns her whole body so she has an uninterrupted view of the window. There's nothing there. The window is blank and blue as an untroubled lake. She shrugs and returns to her cafetière.

As she pours her coffee she notices the flicker creeping back into the corner of her eye. She is curious now, not desperately so, but intrigued enough to rise from her seat, coffee mug in hand, and slide round the table to peer through the window. There is nothing to the left, nothing to the right, above her only sky, the thought of which brings to mind that one, famous John Lennon song. *'Imagine all the people.'* She hums it as she returns to the table, temporarily distracted from the distraction in the window.

As soon as she's seated it begins again. She tries to ignore the incessant tickle of it, sliding up and down the side of her sightline. She adds milk to her coffee and, forgetting that she's decided to cut out sugar, two heaped teaspoonfuls of the white stuff, stirring until she can no longer feel the grains gritting against the mug's sides. She tries to concentrate on this morning's crossword. Crosswords are another of her new resolutions. She is trying to be more present; to cut out distractions and focus on being a simpler, more balanced individual. Her sister's loaned her a mindfulness CD. She's been listening to it in the bath. With candles. The box says mindfulness will help her pay attention to her thoughts and feelings without judging whether they are right or wrong. Right now, she is struggling to pay attention to anything but the mysterious creature flitting about outside.

She sets the newspaper aside and returns to the window. It's an old-fashioned sash type, stiff and heavy. She puts her shoulder to the glass and shoves hard. Once open she sticks her head through the gap. She glances up and down, left and right. She's sure she's looking for a creature of some sort; a bird most likely. The third floor's too high for cats. Though the open window affords her an extra degree of perspective, she can't see anything of significance. She has the distinct, and slightly disturbing, feeling of something narrowly avoided; a car, for example, or a chance encounter with an ex-boyfriend. She closes the window sharply, relishing the dull thuck of timber settling into old timber. She returns to her coffee. Her coffee is cold. The thing continues to twiddle about in the corner of her eye. It is becoming increasingly irritating.

She takes a shower. She's running late now and hasn't time for a bath. In the shower she thinks about the distraction. She puts wings on it, feathers and a pointed beak. She colours it red, and once it is red in her mind, finds it impossible to believe she's seen anything but red feathers, blurring frantically. She knows this is impossibly exotic for Belfast, in October, but she tells herself that she's seen it and therefore it must be possible. When she leaves the bathroom, wrapped in a damp bath towel, she expects to see a red parrot, or some other tropical bird, hovering outside. She sees no such thing. Only the sheet glass and the curtains dropping down either side of the window like an empty picture frame.

She leaves the house three to four minutes later than usual. She has to run for the bus. Her hair is still wet from the shower and, as she picks up speed, it begins to whip viciously around her face. She hasn't a lick of make up on. She's too distracted to notice. While running, she thinks about the thing outside her window, rolling the idea of it round her head until it is as clear and easily described as the shoes on her feet or the elderly lady who's always standing at her stop. She could swear the bird – for she's sure it is a bird – is still flitting about on the edge of her vision. But this must be her mind playing tricks. She's half a mile from home now. She can't imagine it's following her.

All day she's distracted by the thought of it. She sits at her desk, incapable of concentrating on her spreadsheets. She's sure she can see red birds blurring backwards and forwards above the office skylight. All she wants to do is recline the reclining part of her chair and stare at them. But she isn't paid to watch birds. She is paid to type numbers into spreadsheets, to add these numbers up, and occasionally multiply one number by another, which is more difficult and requires concentration. This morning she cannot seem to concentrate on anything but the thing hovering outside her window. She rearranges the biros in her drawer and the paperclips too. She doodles little red birds across a whole rake of Post-It notes and when the boss – who is a nice lady and not prone to placing undue pressure upon her employees – drops by to ask how the accounts are going, she snaps and says, 'I'm working as fast as I can. I've only got two hands.' She apologises immediately. 'I'm sorry,' she says, 'I have a headache.' The boss says she should take a break. 'Go outside, get some air.' The boss places a hand on her shoulder while saying this so she will appear firm, but also caring.

She takes a half-hour break from her desk. She walks across the street to the park next to Tesco's. The thing flickers along next to her. From time to time she swipes at it, trying to make contact. She never catches anything more substantial than cool air. When she turns it's always gone. People stare at her as they pass. She looks a little unhinged. Twisting. Jerking. Flailing her arms around her head. In the park she lies down under a tree. She sets her alarm for twenty-five minutes. As soon as her shoulders touch the grass, she realises just how tired she is. Thinking about the thing has sapped all her energy. She is almost immediately asleep. She dreams of red birds. Red birds flying. Red birds sitting on windowsills. Red birds pecking at little crumbs they've found scattered beside litter bins and downtown benches. She wakes suddenly when the alarm goes off and for a moment continues to see red birds fluttering overhead.

That evening, when she returns to the apartment with a microwavable lasagne in her handbag (she's far too exhausted to contemplate healthy eating tonight), the thing is still flittering about outside her window. She tries turning her back to it, closing her eyes and downing half a bottle of cold Chardonnay so quickly it gives her brain freeze, but the thought of it is almost more distracting than the actual flicker. About midnight, driven to distraction she opens the window and yells into the black, night sky, 'go away, leave me alone.' She imagines the neighbours will think her mad. She couldn't give a toss about the neighbours. The thing does not leave her alone. It continues to flit and stutter and duck out of sight every time she turns around. It has given her a migraine; the worst kind, with flickering lights.

Finally, with no options left, she begins flinging small items out the window, hoping to scare the distraction away. A coffee mug. A shoe. Her sister's mindfulness CD. A hardback copy of *Wuthering Heights*. A tennis racket. Two scatter cushions. A framed photo of her parents on their wedding day. The *Next* catalogue, which is quite hefty. It sails through the air like a greased missile, only stopping when it makes contact with something solid. She hears the clunk of one thing hitting another, somewhere, out there, in the impenetrable dark. This noise is both heartening and rather unnerving. She knows she's finally managed to pin the shifty thing down. She suspects she may have killed it in the process.

She dashes downstairs, taking all six flights in a handful of urgent strides. She's barefoot and doesn't care. Outside, the garden is like a jumble sale. All the items she's pitched through her window are arranged haphazardly across the lawn. She remembers, from A-Level history, that *defenestration* is the term for throwing an object or person from a window, but this seems too grand a word for what she's done; too precise and calculated. She finds the *Next* catalogue beside a rhododendron bush. There's a tiny smear of blood, like spilt jam, stuck to its corner. She wipes it against her pyjama leg. It leaves a stain. The bird is lying next to the catalogue, one wing open, the other folded in upon itself. Its head is bent back at an unnatural angle. It is quite clearly dead.

She fishes a tissue out of her dressing gown pocket and picks it up. She can feel the heat of it leaking through the thin paper. It's already beginning to cool. She takes a long look at the bird, using the screen of her mobile as a torch. It is not red or at all exotic. It's just an ordinary starling; greasy and mottled. There are dozens like it strung across the telephone wires. She turns its little body this way and that inspecting its legs, its beak, its tiny black bead eyes. She's lost all interest in the bird now it's dead. She feels bad about this. Should she feel bad? She's not the first person to kill a bird on purpose. She decides not to feel bad. She imagines there will be more birds to come; better birds with brightly-coloured feathers and enchanting songs. There's nothing to be done with the starling, especially now the flight has left it. She opens the wheelie bin and drops it inside. She closes the lid and returns to bed where she is almost instantly asleep. She dreams of birds, fluttering outside her window. She feels as if she's hardly slept at all.

Evelyn Conlon

TELLING TALES

I could no more define poetry than a terrier can define a rat.
— A.E. Housman

Often when writers talk about how they work they do so
blinking through a smokescreen. You can see it in their
eyes. Many of us do not know how we did it, and certainly
do not know how we will do it again. Indeed, for me,
looking too closely makes me uncomfortable. When people
ask about my discipline I cannot answer, but I must have
some, because I know how many books I have written. I
also know that my practice has changed.

I was around nine years of age when I decided I wanted
to be a novelist although I wasn't quite sure what that was.
I didn't know what the word meant and hadn't got around
to asking. I had learned the alphabet some time before
going to school. I remember vividly the day my maternal
grandfather's teaching made sense, the light of seeing
words had gone on, the gift of reading was almost there,
the leaving of ignorance had begun. I would soon be able
to sit anywhere turning pages – that is all I would have to

do to live in a thousand worlds. 'Novelist' seemed a mysterious word, and I felt that I might swap it with 'author', which came into my currency not long afterwards. I have a distinct memory of walking along a field and imagining the plan. I was on my way to get tea, going home from the farm that was a few miles from our actual house, the journey to and back giving plenty of thinking time if it was done alone, without father or talking sisters. I could have been in a Kavanagh poem, but I hadn't yet got as far as knowing his work and his nearby history.

So, finding ways of writing, following the impulse of the story is a way of life for me. I cannot remember a time when I didn't think that the reading and writing of books is portable magic, one that I wanted to watch and perform. Although, of course, at some times writing has to take a back seat. And that's not necessarily a bad thing. It gives time to process, to think of things beyond pages, to have some fun, to learn, to look out other windows.

Writers who are women with children have, by necessity, a different timetable, as Tillie Olsen told us well. When mine were young I wrote and re-wrote more in my head; I filled notebooks on the run. I don't have to do that so much now because time is less controlled by the needs of small others. I once wrote most of a book in a car, a Datsun 100A. I left the children to school each morning, but did not return to my desk because I would have become diverted by the myriad of domestics needing attention. (Some of the pile up was the result of my making our living from teaching at night). After leaving the school gates I drove to Sandymount beach, had a quick walk, returned to the car, to write longhand until it was time to pick them up. Funnily enough it didn't feel like hardship, just a necessary trick. I was more involved in the book than in the cramps I was creating in my back and neck. When I pass office supplies shop windows with their instructions on correct seating I always nod a salute.

I knew about Luisa Mercedes Levinson who had cultivated magic realism long before Gabriel García Márquez, and who, in 1955, had collaborated with Jorge Luis Borges to write the story 'The sister of Eloísa'. She took to the bed for months after becoming a mother in order to finish writing a book. Her daughter, Luisa Valenzuela, later wrote avant-garde novels such as *Como en la Guerra* and *Cambio de Armas*, experimental, powerful critiques of the dictatorship in Argentina – so watching her mother from the bottom of the stairs did her a lot of good. But it mightn't have. I was afraid to take to the bed.

Gazing too deeply seems dangerous for several reasons; possibly I'm afraid of it in the same way as I'm afraid of telling strangers my secrets. What an old-fashioned thing to feel. There has always been a wide open kind of writing *a la* Dorothy Parker. My friend Nuala O'Faolain was a mistress of it, but it doesn't sit well with me. Yesterday I read an interview with an Irish writer who had bared his soul and my heart was shouting 'Oh dear, you've told her too much, that's all they'll remember about you now'.

When I began to seriously write, my reading mattered above all else; I searched to find women who had been steamrollered into oblivion, buried in the foundations, bright women who had something to say to me. I was also interested in finding men whose views were expansive. I got caught in Ireland after I had children, but I could read away from it, an escape that allowed me to write, and still does. As does research beyond my daily life, although with all its drama, truth and lies, music, politics, love, tears and friends, good and bad, it has been the foundry from which I catapult, naturally. Some of my work has involved specific placed research, which I obviously chose because those subjects interest me in the way they relate to society, to memory, to how we live. Forgetting is part of memory, as I realised when researching *Not the Same Sky*. Choosing what to forget is a political act.

I visited Death Row in the US while working on *Skin of Dreams* and spent weeks on the road with anti-capital-punishment advocates. The sheer madness of all that lent an air of its own to the book; sometimes it didn't feel that it was me writing it, no more than it felt like me in the back of the bus we travelled in. Writing *Not the Same Sky* brought me to all sorts of places in Australia, some of which I'd already visited way back when I travelled all over it, working at everything from barmaid in a mining town to a compiler of entries for a geography encyclopedia. I had already gone there by ship when I was nineteen, so I didn't need to do that again in order to imagine the long boat journey. *A Glassful of Letters* was based more on my inner thoughts, slanted by the desire to be out of Ireland, while also thinking that perhaps occasional escape would suffice. I used the half-epistolary form in order to be able to argue things out – this was a time when it was almost impossible to discuss what was happening on a daily basis in the north of the island. Even naming the place drew opprobrium.

A few years ago when writing 'Dear You', a story based on Violet Gibson, the Irish woman who almost succeeded in assassinating Mussolini, I went to the convent in Rome where she had been staying, walked the walk she probably did and stood where she took aim with her Lebel revolver. I then went to Mantellate Prison, where she spent time before they shipped her off to the asylum in Northampton for life. I've gone to her grave there too, and seen how they wouldn't even oblige her in death by burying her in her desired ground. From Hiroshima I wrote 'Virgin Birth', a story I imagined about the first woman who deliberately became pregnant after the bomb was dropped. I'm fascinated by such optimism. And there had to be such a woman. And a man with her.

Some of my earlier stories deal with how the strictures of our society affected the ways we lived. Mine, and other similar voices that have taken on those topics, are not always flavour of the month. And yet it was interesting to be asked to record 'The Park' for *The Stinging Fly* as the present pope's visit was imminent. That story – about those who protested against the 1979 visit, those who ran away to 'pope free zones' – seems to come from a different age, but clearly it is seen to still have relevance. This brings me to political action and being a writer. I *had* to be involved in issues around how our lives were circumscribed. Because I am a citizen as well as a writer. Perhaps if I'd been a man I wouldn't have felt the absolute necessity to be involved in the contraception, divorce and abortion campaigns. Perhaps I could have said 'Well, let the women look after that'. I'll never know.

I've written before about the occasional tackling of the gender issue head-on in my work. 'Taking Scarlet as a Real Colour', the title story of a collection, ends with the speaker writing to Henry Miller, suggesting to him that men writing about sex may have got it wrong, may have suffered from a misunderstanding. Again a collection title story, 'Telling', is about a great male writer telling a roomful of women how to write about domestic violence. I had form here, having once, in fury, published an article in response to the portrayal of a woman suffering domestic violence. I had already expressed bafflement at the narrow view of what constituted a family. At the time I was myself a 'separated' mother of two young boys, living in a hostile environment. The factual pressure of that, and my watching the wonderful way my sons were negotiating their difference, dulled any pedestrian sense of humour I could have had around the issue. Initially I didn't have any intention of addressing the issue publicly (why should I? No one else would). But then I could bear it no more. The reactions of women who had felt silenced and who contacted me in their droves to tell me of their relief, suggested that I was right to do so. And yet, in some ways, I wish I had stayed silent. It's easier.

Of course I would prefer not to be angry. And mostly I'm not. Of course, I'd like to be considered polite. And mostly I am. I once stood up to gently ask if a speaker, in his mentioning of twenty-two Irish writers, might consider that perhaps only one woman gracing his mouth was a bit minimalist. As I began to formulate the dry-throated words my brain said 'Oh God, not me again'.

In my next collection I have three stories that could be in the voice of either gender, one from an academic who goes to interview that first woman who deliberately became pregnant post the dropping of the atom bomb; another from a child who sits on the stairs listening to its sister lose the run of herself over her upcoming wedding; and the third from a border dweller who has run up a tree. I've read these stories at public events, and it has been interesting, to say the least, listening to people explain how they know, with absolutely certainty, why the characters are male or female.

I don't think about gender issues when I'm writing. I merely observe what happens between women and men, or what happens to women and men. But no doubt the shade of the things I see is affected by the colour code of my knowledge of the world.

When Jenny Diski decided to travel, and think, she conducted her strange and wonderful journey by train through America with the smokers; their carriage already earmarked for consignment to history, even as they were tossing about conversation on their last legal drags. Anthony Cronin brought us to Paris and back with a suitably fascinating set of co-travellers, but I'm still worried that one of them, well entrenched in his literary maleness, went to borrow a fiver from Simone de Beauvoir not knowing who she was. Rebecca Solnit went into her head and out again. Dervla Murphy, the consummate, intelligent travel writer went everwhere. Joe Brainard decided to remember, and how.

Biographies, even short ones, have their own particular difficulties. Some are straighforward, others fraught with uphill catastrophes from the minute they are imagined, let's say that of Ted Hughes. I wasn't surprised to read that Carol Hughes, Ted's widow, took serious issue with Jonathan Bate's unauthorised life story of Ted. The book had begun its life with the cooperation of the Hughes estate but, Bate claims, that was mysteriously withdrawn when he was well into his research. It may have been that Carol Hughes discovered that there would be a bit too much biography in the biography. And it's all in how you tell it. After publication she was particularly offended by the description of the funeral journey from Devon to London. Bate wrote of 'the accompanying party stopping, as Ted the gastronome would have wanted, for a good lunch on the way'. Since Bate himself wasn't there someone told him this, and a lot hangs on what you consider to be 'a good lunch'. Are we talking an edible pub sandwich here – or a proper afternoon outing? In my family life, once when we were bringing our Aunt Mary's coffin from Dublin to Bawn Cemetery in Co. Monaghan we stopped in McEntee's pub in Shercock to have tea and toast, but if anyone had seen the hearse parked outside who's to say what they would have made of it. There's enough history around our house to construct a right party out of that stop. Or the truth could be told, which was that her sister, Aunt Kitty, over from New York for the funeral, suddenly had to have a cup of tea before the stress of laying her sister down.

There is another daunting thing about describing this life. Most women and shy men who write have a problem naming themselves writers; it takes them longer than the other confident, brash and perhaps less talented variety.

And why can't one describe happenings other than work, and the answer, of course, is that writers *are* their work. They are incomplete without a pen, which is their breath. People are driven to labour at all kinds of things – scientific, physical, trade, medical – and some even to work merely for a living and to wring life out of the rest of their time. But there are others, like those in Tillie Olsen's *Silences,* whose being is all about transposing the thought onto the blotting paper that is a book. She was the first person I read who understood that this desire can be present even without the tools to understand it, that there are writers among the illiterate, those who have never been lucky enough to learn an alphabet, to find the solace that books, packets of hieroglyphics, give.

Gavin Corbett

FOUR CREOSOTED UPRIGHT POSTS

I become stupefied. I've read the thing so many times that
I stop seeing the good in it. I make interventions. I'm like a
hamfisted surgeon, and I don't care, my brain is that tired,
it's desperate, I'm following bad signals now. Maybe this
is just a little capillary that can safely be burnt to a close, so
no harm; maybe this carries the vital oxygenated blood for
the whole system and – whoops! – bye bye and boo hoo.
At some point the gore cannot be ignored and it's making
me ill.

I press Ctrl+A to highlight everything, then I hit the
Backspace key so that the 206 pages of text are replaced
with one blank one and a blinking cursor. I hear my laptop
sigh itself to sleep. I look out to the bright garden. There's
a structure at the end, inherited from the previous owners,
that I think might be called a pergola. What it is is four
creosoted upright posts holding a rectangular horizontal
frame seven feet from the ground with a sheet of
transparent corrugated plastic nailed to the top.

I wake my laptop. My empty MS Word page is still there – bled out, blanched, blinking disbelievingly – so I minimise it and go off on a Wikipedia dérive that takes me from Italian garden design through Capability Brown and on to Alexander Pope, the Loch Ness Monster and whatever else. When this important work is done I go out to the garden, and I leave the computer, folded to a close, on my barbecue under the pergola. I don't want to leave it directly on the ground because that would be going too far. And the corrugated plastic sheet above doesn't have any holes in it, so no chance of water dripping through. All the same, the pergola is open, more or less, on three sides (the back of it is up against a hedge), so there would be nothing to protect the laptop from squalls and driving rain. There is also the possibility that an animal might get at it. I sit out for a while beside the barbecue and the computer with a mug of tea and some biscuits and observe, overhead, a bullfinch cooling off in a water-filled gully of the transparent corrugated plastic. Bullfinches have beautiful cinnamon-coloured undersides. Then I go back indoors to change out of my pyjamas.

I set off about town like some half-alive, unthinking golem. The word 'golem' doesn't come to me then, only later – it's too writerly a word. I generally hold to the credo of John Shade, the poet subject of Nabokov's *Pale Fire*, that 'the hand supports the thought, the abstract battle is concretely fought' – in other words, that inspiration is more apt to strike when the writer is at work than when he is walking the streets or fields hoping for the Nine Muses to crawl down from their Greek hillside cabins. But on today's trudge, after the earlier slog at the desk, I'm not even looking to summon inspiration – at best I'm looking for restoration of my faculties. Life is just about tolerable when I'm not thinking of writing at a time when the writing is going badly.

But I encounter many people today who, nonetheless, make me think of writing. There are people in lines of traffic on their way home from offices or from construction sites; there are people behind counters who give me hamburgers and cakes; there are people behind chain-link fences in garden centres holding pots to their crotches and with small cypress trees extending to their chins; there are a fourth and further groups of people doing this, that and the other. These people don't make me think of writing the act, or of writing the art, but of the bed I've made for myself and in which I must lie. I think: how far removed I am from the world of the regular workplace, how difficult it would be to get back to that world, and how fucked I am for the mortgage and other foolish debts I have to pay. How hopeless, really, is my situation right now. I am a virtual unknown, and how is a writer with no profile and poor commercial prospects supposed to pay his way out of debt? My recognition that I'm complaining about this – my identification of this side of myself as a person-type I don't like – only, of course, increases my self-loathing.

What's worse, I must go home and write with this tempest of negativity in my head. Anxiety and self-doubt are strictures to my imagination, not fuel for it; the paradox of my praxis is that only when I am content can I fruitfully examine my discontent. If only I could get away from my thoughts for a while, from words, I'd be happy. What I have is a kind of word-sepsis, that's what I feel. But even the word 'sepsis' is suggested by 'praxis' – words are poisoning my thoughts, guiding them, pushing them, shutting them down.

I start to think that maybe there is a way back to a regular working life. I look at that man transporting plants in the garden centre. I think about working with my hands, far away from the world of books and writing, stacking tins of creosote on shelves and rolling plaster-cast gnomes around on their bases, and freeing my mind to dream and for words to swirl. Not only then would I be a more useful member of society, but perhaps the written word would become disassociated from agony and I would remember what so drew me in the first place.

I take a little time – counting the notes in my wallet at the bar – to consider what exactly it was that started my loving relationship with words. I remember that I liked words because I liked making things – and not merely things, but objects. I remember – and am remembering now, as I recall myself remembering – that I was never the boisterous boy at home, or in the class, who always had something to say. It was because I was exactly the opposite – that I had nothing to say; or, perhaps, that I'd no urge to say anything – that I liked words so much. What I wanted to do was to be left alone to make things, make these objects, the most perfect objects I could make. Modelling-clay or paint could easily have been my medium, but my preferred material just so happened to be words.

I don't know why. There was probably no 'just so happened' about it. Words just had these fantastic evocative qualities; it seemed to me that so many words mimicked perfectly the things that they labelled. A word like 'chocolate' – to articulate which was to conjure sweet clotted phlegm in the back of the throat. Or words like 'frilly' or 'rich' or 'tower' or 'flesh'. And then there were words that would make me laugh by the sound of them, even though the things they described weren't in themselves funny; words like 'chutney', 'upshot' and 'bunting'.

And right down to the elements too, the letters. (I'm smiling dumbly at people in the pub now). I liked how the capital B looked like a pair of pursed lips about to explode open and articulate its own sound. Or that O was a set of open-rounded lips. That S was a slithery snake. That V had something ominous about it – it was like a dive bomber; like those German dive bombers with Jericho trumpets attached to their bodies that made the sound '*vvvvvv*' when they took their terrifying plunge. And that the two horizontal strokes in the capital F, or even the one horizontal stroke almost meeting the curved cornice of the lower case 'f', suggested the top front teeth and the bottom lip partnering to make that '*fffff*' sound. My childish mind even thought of letters as gendered. Delicate L and humming M were the most feminine letters. L and M's guardians were K and N, the most masculine letters, which sat either side of L and M in a defensive phalanx. L and M were well shielded and swaddled anyway, sitting right there at the centre of the alphabet, at a safe distance from eager G and precocious F, and a mile from sleazy Z.

I want to go home now and be alone with my letters and my words and myself. I say that, but it's just empty words. I can't shake my despondency, so I stay for maybe one more drink. Well into the evening I remember upskirting that bullfinch earlier, and then I remember that I'd left my computer outside in the garden. I quit the pub, I get home, I bring my laptop in from the cold and I open it on the kitchen table. I bring up my blank MS Word document, which leaps to fill the screen from its minimised state. The cursor is still blinking: sorry- and sheepish-looking now. No – I'm sorry, I say. I click on the Undo arrow in the top toolbar. And there's my text again, after eight hours. Just to be safe, I go to insert my memory stick, but there's a small dry seed jammed in the USB socket.

Celia de Fréine

THE IMPACT OF *IMRAM*

Many aphorisms comment on the benefits of travel, imposing themselves on the person who has undertaken the journey as a rucksack might carve a furrow into that person's back. Some suggest that travel broadens the mind and the voyager returns home intoxicated by the experience whether the delights have been cultural, culinary, linguistic or whether the person in question has simply been 'blown away' by a different landscape. Statements, such as the one Richard Hugo makes in his essay *The Triggering Town*,[1] suggest that the experience causes the wayfarer-poet to write about her/his own home town as seen through the prism of distance.

In recent years I have written essays[2] and articles[3] and given interviews of a personal nature. I was never a diary keeper and, as a schoolgirl, wrote only journalistic essays, eschewing any subject matter that might have involved describing my family circumstances. Today my boundaries have shifted: it is no longer necessary for a writer to conceal his or her humble origins. My deprived background was more complex than that of most writers in that my parents, who were from Northern Ireland, had moved to Dublin when I was a child. My childhood involved regular visits to the North to spend time with my extended family. Each of these visits involved crossing the Border which added to the challenge of the journey.

During my adult life I have spent time abroad on family holidays and fun holidays with friends, attended conferences and readings at international festivals. Between the years 2006 and 2015 I availed of residencies in both Europe and the US. All of these residencies have impacted on my writing and, as a result of having my mind 'broadened' and of reacting in a way Hugo might suggest, caused me to write work which I would not have otherwise undertaken.

The first of these residencies was based in Koper/Capodistria and formed part of a Sealines project[4] organized by Literature Across Frontiers. A work was commissioned as part of the residency: I was to create something that would 'lift' the words from the page; a multi-media project that included images would fit the bill. I purchased a camera in Trieste and set about my task.

At first I felt guilty: wandering around the city and its hinterland taking photographs did not seem like work and the more I became involved in the project the more I wanted to write about my experiences in Slovenia. The country, a republic, was the first to have broken from the former Yugoslavia and declared itself independent fifteen years previously. However, the thought of keeping a diary or of writing a travelogue held no attraction for me. I did not want to write a political treatise on the aftermath of the fall of communism, nor did I want to write an account of my day-to-day tasks, what food I was eating, what gigs I was taking part in. And so I began to write a book of poetry that would become *imram : odyssey*.[5]

An *imram* is a literary genre in Irish.[6] In it the hero sets out on a great voyage, is faced with many challenges along the way and returns home older and wiser. The word itself means the act of rowing a boat, i.e., undertaking a voyage by sea. Many *imrama* are extant, the Voyage of Mael Dúin being probably the best known of them. An *imram* seemed an apt medium for conveying what I wanted to say: I had set off on a great adventure in which I was faced with many challenges, the one significant difference being that, in this case, the hero was a woman.

As the multi-media project was the commissioned work, my *imram* was written on the side. I was reminded of the years during which I wrote the TV soap opera *Ros na Rún*[7] when I might commit an act of subversion by jotting down a poem on the back of an envelope during a production meeting. Or as indeed monks would compose a pithy remark or a poem such as *Pangur Bán*[8] in the margins of the more important manuscript they were copying. In fact I discovered that this particular white cat had been immortalised in a monastery not far from where I was based. My poem 'cat : cat'[9] references the earlier feline and proves Hugo's statement, as does another poem in this collection 'talamh eadrána : no man's land'.[10] This second poem explores the no man's land between the borders of Slovenia and Italy: it asks who decides on boundaries and how do we respond to them? As I crossed into Italy to go to Trieste and buy my camera, I was reminded of my childhood journeys in Ireland crossing from one jurisdiction to another.

imram: odyssey is, from a sales point of view, my most successful book of poetry. It has been selected as one of the 'Top 50 Irish Contemporary Books' in the UCD Digital Platform for Contemporary Irish Writing[11] and in 2019 went into a second edition with a new introduction by Lucy Collins. I had already three books of poetry in print when I wrote it: *Faoi Chabáistí is Ríonacha,*[12] *Fiacha Fola*[13] and *Scarecrows at Newtownards*.[14] As the first two of these books are written in Irish only, their potential audience was limited and it soon became clear that it was necessary to translate my poetry into English if I wanted it to reach a wider audience. Translations of a selection of the poems from *Faoi Chabáistí is Ríonacha* were included in *Scarecrows at Newtownards* and have been well-received and positively critiqued.[15] *Blood Debts*,[16] the translation of *Fiacha Fola* brought the only book of poetry which deals with the Anti-D scandal to a much wider audience. Luz Mar Gonzalés-Arias has written extensively about this travesty;[17] she could not have done so had the book not been translated.

Which brings me to the thorny questions of which language I choose to write in and how and why do I move between languages? Máire Mhac an tSaoi mentions in her foreword to *Fiacha Fola* (translated by me in *Blood Debts*) that 'Celia de Fréine feels she chose Irish as a medium because of the natural surrealism in that language. I fully understand her.'[18] Irish, as a language, is indeed better suited to the surreal nature of my poetry. During the years when I was a member of the Thornfield Poets[19] I did not feel comfortable bringing in translations of Irish language poems to workshops, and began to write poems in English that reflected the spare architecture of that language. Many of these poems form the core of *Scarecrows at Newtownards* and include sonnets, a villanelle and sestina; forms that have come to be associated with English.

I had come late to poetry and it's worth taking a look at how and when I began to write in this genre. In 1985 I moved from the suburbs back to the part of Dublin in which I grew up and where, as a young adult, I had become involved in Irish language activities. The move prompted me to write poetry in Irish. However, as a result of negative feedback I believed I could neither write poetry nor write in Irish. Seven years later when I began to teach and had even less time to write I again began to tackle poetry, not least because a poem is such a small thing. Many of the poems came to me in Irish but I translated them into English before they reached the page. It took a further three years for me to publish poems in Irish. However, the initial rejection of my work was not a bad thing in that it forced me to create a system of moving between languages which was eventually reflected in my four bilingual poetry books.

The second of these, *Aibítir Aoise : Alphabet of an Age,*[20] inspired by the Polish alphabet genre, was written not as a result of any particular journey. It includes poems set in places as far apart as the US, Sardinia and Los Lobos and references many international artists. In Poland the alphabet book is a prose genre used to give accounts of the famous, the not-so-famous and the imagined. I adapted it to poetic form as it seemed an appropriate structure in which to house this disparate set of poems.[21] My second book, *Fiacha Fola,* had been a sequence with a narrative thrust and I had become enamoured of the idea that a volume of poems could form one cohesive unit. The alphabet framework also allowed me to celebrate friendship and to philosophise to a certain extent as in the book's title poem.[22]

My third bilingual book, *cuir amach seo dom : riddle me this,*[23] includes poems written during three residencies. Its title poem is the commissioned work I wrote while in Koper/Capodistria: it takes its cue from the riddle, a traditional Slovene form, and debates our attitude to the environment. The video I made to accompany it includes images of water on which the English language translation has been superimposed and also features the sound of water flowing, lapping and gurgling. As the audience can see the translation, I read the poem at public events in its original Irish only. The first time I did so was at the Vilenica Festival in 2007. More recently I read from it at the AEDEI Conference in Santiago de Compostela in 2018.

Manuela Palacios-González, Director of the Conference, shared an interesting comment with me afterwards:

> While you read in Irish, I noticed some people closed their eyes. Although I was first surprised because the English translation was on the screen (and the audience did not know Irish), I then thought of the importance of voice and rhythm, and of the enchanting power of a language.[24]

I have no doubt that the sounds of water added to the experience.

The book *cuir amach seo dom : riddle me this* also includes the sequence *Monsanto* which I wrote during a residency in Portugal spent in both Coimbra and Monsanto.[25] The central sequence in the book is inspired by the *Lady and the Unicorn* tapestries in the Musée Cluny in Paris and was written during a residency in the Centre Culturel Irlandais in 2011. While there, in addition to this sequence, I wrote an entire book (on the side, much like *imram : odyssey*) because, not only did I absorb the atmosphere of the city in all its splendour, I formed an attachment to one of its former residents.

Rainer Maria Rilke is best known for his poetry in German but he also wrote over four hundred poems in French. During my stay in Paris his name kept popping up: in the Musée Cluny, in Rodin's house, in local bookshops. I began to feel his presence everywhere I went. I bought a copy of his complete French oeuvre and was taken by one book in particular, *Migration des Forces*. As the weeks went by I responded to each of the one hundred and twenty five poems in it, questioning him on what he had said, at times suggesting alternate scenarios for the poems in question. I have now a very long manuscript, *I bhFreagairt ar Rilke : In Response to Rilke*, speckled with epigraphs in French, which needs to be culled before it is published in 2020.

Since then, quotes in French have continued to manifest themselves in other works. I have just finished *Ceannródaí,* the biography of Louise Gavan Duffy[26] and, as Louise was born in France, the book includes many quotes in French. Apart from this book and the play *Luíse*,[27] which is based on her life, phrases in French continue to inveigle their way into work-in-progress. This comes as no surprise: as my name suggests, and my DNA proves, I am partly of Norman descent. What is perhaps to be expected is that it took a period in Paris to introduce the inclusion of French into my work.

Although two of the poems in *Aibítir Aoise : Alphabet of an Age* are set in the US, I have also undertaken two major projects while based there. Both of these are in English, not least because time spent in the US had a different effect on me compared to that of my sojourns in Europe. One of these projects, *Threshold: Mark Gerard McKee & Celia de Fréine*, comprises twenty six poems written in response to the artwork of Mark Gerard McKee.[28] As McKee's work is painted on the backs of old doors, my poems reflect this unorthodox approach. The second project, *Lost in Shadow*, comprising a collection of poems written in response to the locale, its history and the people I met there, is forthcoming in 2019. The US landscape proved familiar: I was used to American food; the streetscapes and stock characters were familiar from TV; everyone spoke English. While the impact was less exotic than that experienced while visiting a country with an unfamiliar language, cuisine or landscape, the effect left its mark, nonetheless.

Travel may broaden the mind but it has broadened my oeuvre also. Had I not availed of these residences I would not have written four bilingual books or undertaken two American projects. Though the benefits have been enormous, I have not applied for any residencies since. I have my own bolt-hole in Connemara in which to tackle new work. When it comes to explorers, such as Beatrice Grimshaw, for instance, it is not so much that I envy them but admit to being in awe of their intrepid nature. I love the excitement of discovering new terrain but prefer it when a guide leads me to that terrain.

When I first began to write poetry seriously in 1992 much of the poetry being published then could be described as nature poetry. I wasn't deliberately trying to avoid writing it, I was responding to what I knew – life in both city and seaside town. It was, however, with *imram: odyssey* that my work began to move to the great outdoors. *Aibítir Aoise : Alphabet of an Age* includes many poems with a rural setting; *cuir amach seo dom : riddle me this* is set exclusively in the country; much of the 'Monsanto' sequence is set in a remote village; 'The Lady and the Unicorn' poems are based on a tapestry that reflect a rural idyl inhabited by a lady whose companions are animals and whose diet is one of fruit. *I bhFreagairt ar Rilke : In Response to Rilke* spans both urban and rural landscapes. Not only would I not have written these books had I not availed of these residencies; had I not travelled to the destinations in question, none of the work I might have written might have had a rural setting.

Since embarking on my many *imrama* I have crossed borders, absorbed new atmospheres and, at all times, been 'blown away' by new landscapes. It is true to say that many aphorisms could be applied to the results of these journeys. Travel has broadened my mind and its varied experiences have insinuated their way into my psyche. And yes, I have written about the places I know as seen through the prism of distance.

NOTES

1   Richard Hugo, *The Triggering Town* (New York, Norton, 1979).
2   Celia de Fréine, 'Becoming the Writer I Am', in Éilís Ní Dhuibhne (ed), *Writing For My Life* (forthcoming).
3   Celia de Fréine, 'Across the Divide', in Manuela Palacios-González, 'Stand Still: Photographs of Irish Migrating Women', in María Jesús Lorenzo-Modia (ed.), *Ex-Sistere Women's Mobility*

in Contemporary Irish, Welsh and Galician Literatures (Newcastle upon Tyne, Cambridge Scholars, 2016) pp 160–162.

4   The Sealines project involved exchanges of writers representing bilingual port cities. The other writers based in Koper/ Capodistria with me at the time were Pirrko Lindberg (Helsinki) and Egils Venters (Riga). I represented Galway.

5   Celia de Fréine, *imram : odyssey* (Dublin, Arlen House, 2010; expanded 2nd edition, 2019).

6   'Irish' in this essay can refer to the Irish language in the same way 'English' can refer to the English language.

7   Ros na Rún is a soap opera on TG4, the Irish language TV station.

8   Pangur Bán, translated by Seamus Heaney: https://www.poetry foundation.org/poetrymagazine/poems/48267/ pangur-ban.

9   *imram : odyssey*, pp 62–63.

10 *Ibid.*, pp 22–23.

11 https://www.irishcentral.com/culture/entertainment/top-50-irish-contemporary-books-will-make-sure-youve-always-something-great-to-read.

12 Celia de Fréine, *Faoi Chabáistí is Ríonacha* (Indreabhán, Cló Iar-Chonnacht, 2001).

13 Celia de Fréine, *Fiacha Fola* (Indreabhán, Cló Iar-Chonnacht, 2004).

14 Celia de Fréine, *Scarecrows at Newtownards* (Dublin, Scotus Press, 2005).

15 See Manuela Palacios-González, 'Of Penelopes, Mermaids and Flying Women: Celia de Fréine's Tropes of Mobility', *Estudios Irlandeses*, 12 (2017), pp 92–103. See also Luz Mar González-Arias, 'Impossible Returns: The Trope of the Soldier in Celia de Fréine's Poetry', *Irish University Review* (Winter, 2018).

16 Celia de Fréine, *Blood Debts* (Dublin, Scotus Press, 2014).

17 Luz Mar González-Arias, '*Blood Debts*: The Uneasy Combination of Hepatitis C and Poetry', 7th International Poetry and Medicine Symposium and Hippocrates Awards, 2016.

18 Celia de Fréine, *Blood Debts*, p. 12.

19 Thornfield Poets is a group who met regularly during the early part of this century. An anthology of our work, *Thornfield*, edited by Andrew Carpenter, was published by Salmon Poetry in 2008.

20 Celia de Fréine, *Aibítir Aoise : Alphabet of an Age* (Dublin, Arlen House, 2011).

21 See review by Glenn Shea http://www.celiadefreine.com/aibitir.htm

22 *Aibítir Aoise : Alphabet of an Age*, pp 14–15.

23 *cuir amach seo dom : riddle me this* (Dublin, Arlen House, 2014).

24 Email confirmation, 25 August 2018.

25 See review by Maria Irene Ramalho, Director, Poets in Residence Programme, University of Coimbra: http://www.celiadefreine. com/riddle.htm.

26 Celia de Fréine, *Luíse Ghabhánach Ní Dhufaigh Ceannródaí* (Baile Átha Cliath, *Leabhair*COMHAR, 2018), shortlisted in the An Post Irish Book Awards 2018, winner of the ACIS Duais Leabhar Taighde na Bliana 2018.

27 Celia de Fréine, *Luíse*, first produced by Umbrella Theatre Company, Scoil Bhríde, Ranelagh, September 2016.

28 https://ms17artproject.com/threshold-mark-gerard-mckee-celia-de-freine/

Danny Denton

(NOTATIONS FOR) MASS FOR WRITERLY VOICES

—

The Sentence, like life, begins
and ends; something happens
between the beginning and the
ending; it may or may not have
a consequence.

—

The body is a political
instrument, like it or not. It
moves toward and away from
the other entities that occupy
its sphere. To move toward or
away from entities that act is to
be political.

The idea is part of the brain,
or heart; the sentence is part of
the brain, or heart; the brain
and heart are parts of the body.

Ideas and sentences can be magic; the magic is part of the body; the body moves towards and away from the entities in its sphere; the body is a political instrument.

—

Some days, I am a better reader than on other days. From 2005 to 2007 I was in the form of my life. At times I read very well this year, though not always. Life gets in the way a little bit, sometimes. Distractions can be of a tune not harmonious with the reading.

Why do I read? I read to escape; I read to belong; I read to be instructed; I read to breathe; I read to investigate; I read to dream. What should my writing do? All the same things. I want to write the book I want to read, the book I'd dream.

And don't get me started on reading (and writing) as an act of resurrection …

—

The archaeologist is born into a childhood, and into dreams, and into living, and the archaeologist learns, through various jobs held as a teen, as an adult, both part-time and full-time, to turn up at the right time, to wear a uniform, to work hard, to learn from others, the joy of being paid. Then, usually, the archaeologist undergoes some formal education specific to archaeology. And then, one day, years later, having completed some preliminary research or notes (on the area, the history, whatever else), they find themselves on all-fours in the dirt, with a brush, brushing. And the brushing has gone on for eternity, and feels like it will go on for eternity. And the brushing brings little joy (though perhaps some joy in its rhythm). Until, *there*. Until *then*, there, right there, is a bit of something. A bone? A femur? The brushing becomes feverish then, until a tibula, until a skeleton (or part thereof), until a once-living being is uncovered (or part thereof), and the archaeologist is dreaming of the being's living, of its dreams and habits and breathing and movement. The archaeologist breathes it to life through her brushing and her dreaming. The possibilities realised as possible, they become boundless.

—

Ingredients:
- A pencil or pen
- Some paper

- A pulse
- A hard surface on which to rest (your head)
- Questions
- Problems
- A seat, or somewhere to place your arse
- An idea (if you can't find any, substitute with a notion)
- Scraps of whatever else you find lying around

—

Through words, you might *see*. Through words, you might imagine or live other lives. Many lives, many worlds. You could read the words, or you could write the words. Writing the words, you have just a little (just a little!) more control.

—

I found a frequency once, on a radio. It was an old radio and I had to tune it and listen carefully. I had to sit still and avoid other distractions for a few minutes, and once I sat still enough and listened not too closely but closely enough not to hear the outside stuff, there it was.

I later found that I could find it every time by just sitting and listening. And broadcast on that frequency was everything that ever happened in all of existence, and everything that could happen. Endless worlds of happening. And you can transcribe them if you want; all you have to do is sit still with the pencil and listen and write down what comes. I should tell you that it's not all good stuff that comes; very often it's shite that that radio speaks. But after a while you are able to filter the good stuff from the shite. Well, usually. I mean, if it's every sentence from every possible existence it's not always going to be interesting or good stuff, right?

—

Writing is a job, like any other. Writing can be a special job, in the way that many jobs can be special. Writing begets reading, and reading is a sacred activity. But outside of writing and reading and trying to get published (forever trying, always trying, never giving up), all sorts of really important things happen. Far more important things. Never forget that.

—

I used to be ok. I used to be normal enough, until The Sentence Machine. Now I can't answer my front door without wondering, *Will this person have anything for us? Will they have an interesting name, or an anecdote I can use, or some physical or personal tick or defect that I can feed into The Sentence Machine?* The Sentence Machine never sleeps. Literally. I wake up in the night to feed it a line or two (administered through a short blunt pencil and a hotel notepad I keep next to the bed). In the midst of an argument with my girlfriend, with my father, The Sentence Machine is listening and even doing some of its own transcribing. I used to be normal enough, until The Sentence Machine came into my life and started to feed, both on myself and on the lives of others.

—

In *Red Doc>* (Anne Carson), it is said:

'where you headed / bit further along the road / why you running / oh I often do / are you meeting someone / yes / who / a stranger / how will you recognize each other? / in a strange way'

—

The life-drawing class was great, because it forced you to look at different things in different ways. Sometimes you had ten minutes to draw the model in that particular pose, so that you had enough time to get into some detail, maybe even some shading. Sometimes you just did three poses in three minutes, so a minute a pose maybe, and then it was just vague dramatic lines and the shape of something, the outline of something. But it made me realise that a person has a million parts, ears, chins, bruises, limbs, bits of stubble, a crooked finger, flab, or not, all sorts of things that you never even look at: memories, fears ... So the class helped me to see better as much as draw better.

—

There is the existence we know and experience daily, and there are countless other parallel existences. You only need to imagine one thing, rather than experience it, for that statement to be true. There's a world in which you had toast for breakfast and not cereal. There's a world in which Harry Potter goes to school at Hogwarts. There's a world in which the Nazis won the war. Let's call them otherworlds and let's imagine them as on the other side of something: a doorway, a looking-glass, a plane of the unified field ... These worlds are endless in number and particularity, in infinite space, and through reading you can experience them. Through the words there on that page – there on that border – in the spaces that the writer must leave for you (space for interpretation, for visitation, for resurrection, for conjuring), you begin to see the shapes and postures and rhythms of another place, and real magic happens, and you cross over.

—

David Foster Wallace said: 'There is no such thing as not worshipping.   Everybody worships. The only choice we get is what to worship.' In my haughtier moods, I think of writing as a form of worship, of prayer. Reading too. What are we worshipping? The music of what happens? Being here? Being somewhere?

—

SCENE

A man (supposedly) comes into a low-ceilinged room, where there is a chair and an old rickety bureau. He holds a cup of tea. The chair is cheap, wooden, and has a cushion on it. The wooden compartments of the bureau are stuffed with paper and stationery and all the paraphernalia thereof; dust is general, though frequently disturbed by the movement of objects. Scratches and ringed teastains are general. Over the desk, on the wall, a blue-tacked patchwork of cuttings and photographs (or postcards): there is a coffee-stained government-issue envelope with the lyrics to a Tom Waits song typed on it; there is a yellow paper with an atom bomb drawn on it; the atom bomb has the word REPENT written along it; there is a photograph (bent, perhaps once folded) of two red traffic lights and a wet night street; there is an image of a deer with the head and blonde hair of a weeping girl; antlers come out of her forehead; there is a download coupon for an album; there is (pinned) the first page of *Gravity's Rainbow*; there is a newspaper cutting of a painting of the execution of Maria Camila O'Gorman. The writer sighs (a lot) and sits at the chair, pulling the cushion to support the lower back. Leans forward and pulls a copybook: A4, sum-lined. Bends forward to work. The tea will go cold.

—

Prayer is the contemplation of the mystery. Art's base, like religion, is faith, not reason.

—

Through words, I see.
Through words, I see.
Through words, icy.
Threw words, icy.
True words, icy.
True words. Eye. Sea.

Martina Devlin

RIOTS AND OTHER RITES OF PASSAGE

I was born in Northern Ireland.

In 1968, a civil rights movement began lobbying for equality of treatment between the Catholic and Protestant populations, influenced by Martin Luther King's campaign for black rights in the United States. Reaction against Catholic protests in Northern Ireland led to violence on the streets. In 1969, the British government drafted in its army to help the local police force to control rising tensions. The Troubles erupted and continued for almost thirty years until the Good Friday Agreement *in 1998. This text is about understanding how one is 'educated' by parents, community and state; about the lasting impact of childhood experiences.*

At a social event in England I find myself chatting to a hearty man, a grandfather, with Yorkshire's flat vowels and plain-speaking tendencies. He's a capable kind of person – the sort you can imagine taking charge in an emergency. When he hears my accent, he volunteers the information that he did four tours of duty in Northern

Ireland with a British infantry regiment. He was among the first batch to arrive at the start of the Troubles, back when the soldiers thought they were temporarily there as peacekeepers. They'd be in and out without getting their feet wet.

For quite some time, he said, the troops understood a military presence was destined to be short-term. Even when weeks stretched to months and the situation grew more volatile rather than less. But as for believing their role was one of maintaining the peace between warring factions – that misconception vanished like a snow flurry on the volcanic slopes of the political landscape. It soon became apparent that unionists saw them as their protectors, while nationalists regarded them as provocative.

'At first, when we went on foot patrol in Belfast in 1969, we only had batons – no rifles,' he recalls. 'They came later. Batons were useful for scattering people who shouldn't be congregating. We'd start thumping the batons against our equipment when the crowd was squaring up to us. They thought it was to intimidate them, to tell them to back off. But really it was as much for our own sakes. To keep our courage up.'

Why shouldn't people gather in their own community, I ask? And isn't it possible that a phalanx of soldiers in combat gear hobnailing up your street might increase the throng – and its antagonism? He shrugs. Not batting away my questions, exactly. But he doesn't have any answers. He's recounting his experience, not analysing it, I suppose.

I half-expect him to change the subject, or move away, but he seems to want to talk about Northern Ireland. It strikes me that perhaps such opportunities are scarce. There was a time when I wouldn't have met a soldier socially. And even supposing tectonic plates shifted and I did encounter one, he never would have discussed his occupation with someone like me.

The image of batons hammered on riot shields fills my mind. As a reporter, towards the end of the Troubles, I found myself in the middle of civil disturbances; behind protest lines as police in full riot gear formed into tight-packed lines, standing at the ready, intent – and charged. It was a terrifying experience.

Mentally, I add the beat of batons against riot shields. It must be an atavistic sound. A warlike drumbeat. Inevitably it pumps the blood.

I put another question to this former soldier drinking tea in front of me. Perhaps the sound of the batons incited people to riot? Wouldn't that thud-thud-thud incentivise them to let fly with bricks, or rocks or concrete slabs – whatever it was they heaved at the soldiers before the order was given to charge and people scattered?

We continue in this vein in a tone that's conversational, never tetchy. The man, let's call him Corporal Atkins, takes no umbrage at anything I put forward. He's reaching back almost fifty years into his memories. He must have been nineteen or twenty when he was posted to Belfast first.

As for me, I'm remembering my childhood in the town of Omagh, some seventy miles from Belfast and twenty miles from the border with the Irish Republic. Images swim through my mind. Companies of troops clattering past in armoured vehicles; soldiers on manoeuvres emerging suddenly from a field as I walked by, faces blackened and twigs sticking out of their helmets as camouflage; more soldiers, always more of them, rolling out razor wire to cordon off public space into no-go zones.

'When we'd go out on patrol into the Catholic areas, the women would bang bin lids to warn we were coming,' says Corporal Atkins. 'It brought people out onto the streets. They'd send little boys and girls to the front of the line to throw stones at us and we couldn't retaliate against children. The men at the back were passing up the stones to them.'

Was that when you realised you weren't independent peacekeepers after all, I ask?

'We got that within weeks,' he admits. 'And that one community felt very differently towards us compared with the other. We knew when we were in a Protestant area or a Catholic area. But we couldn't easily tell the difference between the two sides.' The people looked and sounded identical to the soldiers.

Troops must have been issued with rifles fairly quickly, I say. I don't remember ever seeing a soldier without one: the way they cradled them against their chests as they patrolled in single file, eyes on constant flicker. Those firearms fascinated my brothers and male cousins who grew adept at identifying the make of weapon and what it could do when fired. But they frightened me. I saw how adults reacted to them. How they stiffened, staring at the guns. Looking away. Eyes dragged back again. Rifles cleared a space between the person who held one and the person who didn't. I don't say any of this to Corporal Atkins. I simply point out that I never saw a uniformed soldier on the street without a rifle.

'They weren't prepared for what happened, the top brass,' he responds. 'They thought Northern Ireland would be sorted out in no time. Then when they realised it wasn't as easy as that we were given automatic rifles when we left the barracks on patrol. But they were too powerful, those rifles. Their bullets were able to go through the walls of a house – they weren't suitable for city streets.'

So innocent people would be killed, I suggest. Someone drinking a cup of tea, or lying in bed. Possibly children.

In fact, we know this happened – it was called 'collateral damage'.

He nods. There's a pause.

But most of the deaths during the Troubles were caused by the IRA, I add.

The corporal changes tack. 'When we arrived in 1969 we weren't properly equipped. We didn't have the right kit or anything. There wasn't even enough barracks accommodation for us. We were living in all sorts of unsuitable buildings, damp old barns of places. The best place was during the summer when they moved us into the student rooms at Queen's University.' The corporal smiles at his college experience. In another life, perhaps he might have been a student himself instead of a kid from the north of England who felt like the enemy on a Belfast street.

'I used to drive an armoured personnel carrier. You knew all about it if it was fired on – the noise ricocheted around inside the vehicle, much louder than it was outside. Once I pulled the hatch down a split second before a sniper's bullet hit it. I was that close' – he holds his thumb and index finger a millimetre apart – 'to being a goner.' Momentarily, with surprising stoicism, he considers the possibility of those unlived decades. Perhaps death never appears real until the instant it happens.

He goes on. 'The vehicle would be parked up in the Ardoyne and we'd be looking down on an area we called Catbone. I didn't stay inside the vehicle. I'd get out and try and talk to people. Not everybody wanted to talk to me but some people answered when I spoke to them. By and by, they got used to me and you could strike up a conversation.'

Ardoyne is in North Belfast, a mainly nationalist working-class area bordered on one side by the largely loyalist Crumlin Road. Conflict during the summer marching season has been a frequent occurrence there – the Orange Order insisting its parades follow traditional routes, the Catholic community objecting on the basis it finds them triumphalist.

Why Catbone, I interject?

He looks sheepish. 'Catholic bones. Anyhow, we'd get talking and sometimes people would give me little bits of information.'

For money, do you mean – as informers? Touts, in the local parlance.

He shakes his head. He didn't hand over cash. But he did hear crumbs: details about people, activities, places. Nothing outstanding if taken in isolation. But when I press him he says he passed on whatever he heard to his superiors who pieced it all together and found it useful. Corporal Atkins adds that the people who chatted with him didn't always grasp the significance of what they were saying.

If so, they were babes in the wood, I observe.

He doesn't answer.

Silently, I wonder if any of those people who let slip a random fact to the friendly young man in uniform of almost half a century ago – still pleasant today – paid for it with their lives.

I ask him what I think will be my last question. How do you feel about your time in Northern Ireland now, in hindsight?

Contempt settles on a face which has been genial until this point – even as we ranged from riots to ricocheting bullets.

'The politicians were muppets. Out of their depth. They should have struck a deal in the first year instead of letting it all spin out of control. Some of our commanding officers weren't much better. I remember one lad, fresh out of Sandhurst. I had to charge into the middle of a hostile crowd and rescue him by the scruff of his neck. He didn't realize he couldn't walk among them like he was doing. He hadn't copped they saw him as the enemy.'

The British Army was deployed in Northern Ireland from 1969–2007. Operation Banner, as it was called, was the longest continuous operation in British military history with more than 250,000 people serving across a thirty-eight-year span.

At first, the soldiers were welcomed with tea and biscuits by a relieved Catholic population whose demands for equality with their Protestant neighbours had met with repression or violence. But the mood soon altered when it became clear that the military's role was to maintain, by force, the bigoted practices of a sectarian state.

At the peak of the Troubles, in the 1970s, 21,000 troops were stationed in the region. Their role was to uphold British sovereignty and assist the armed local police force, the Royal Ulster Constabulary (RUC), now disbanded and reformed into the Police Service of Northern Ireland (PSNI). In addition, a new, locally-recruited infantry regiment, the Ulster Defence Regiment (UDR), was established.

It was almost wholly Protestant and, despite vetting, was penetrated by loyalist paramilitaries to gain arms and training; this has been proven by documents held in Britain's National Archives which also reveal political and military acceptance of collusion between serving soldiers and loyalist extremists. Corroboration is found in an intelligence dossier entitled 'Subversion in the UDR'. It includes a report noting the 'best single source of weapons, and the only significant source of modern weapons, for Protestant extremist groups has been the UDR.' The file estimates that between five and fifteen per cent of the regiment had close links with loyalist paramilitaries. Another document relates how Margaret Thatcher, as opposition leader, was warned in a briefing by Downing Street that the UDR was heavily infiltrated by paramilitaries.

The Provisional IRA, known as the Provos, waged guerilla war against the British Army, the RUC and the UDR. Some 1,441 serving personnel died during Operation Banner, half because of paramilitary attacks and the remainder from other causes, according to Britain's Ministry of Defence.

Northern Ireland's unionist government, which requested the armed forces' presence in 1969, was convinced heavy militarisation was essential and resisted any downscaling – even following the Good Friday peace agreement in 1998. For three decades, Northern Ireland became a security state and the population lived in what was effectively a war zone.

But here's the thing. All-pervasive security and a feeling of being safe are mutually exclusive.

He hadn't copped they saw him as the enemy. That phrase rang in my head after the corporal and I parted company. Hands up, that's how I regarded soldiers when I was a child, an attitude I absorbed from my community. No one said so explicitly. You gathered it from overheard snatches of adult conversation, the strain caused by the sight of them, the scrupulously-polite way any grownups I knew interacted with them – expelling their breath afterwards as though placed under exceptional strain.

Violence, I was given to understand, was wrong – my parents admired John Hume and the civil rights demonstrators. But it was clear that they resented the highly-visible military presence on the streets of our towns and villages, buzzing above us in helicopters, staking out the border between the North and the Republic with watch towers and listening posts.

Indeed, the Troubles presented a moral challenge for many nationalists: how to respond to blatant injustice by the State against its own citizens? How to press for reform without being sucked into violence by the savage response of the authorities to civil society campaigns? Bloody Sunday was a case in point. How well I remember the storm of emotions caused by that massacre of civil rights protesters in Derry on 30 January 1972.

Derry was the small city I associated with Christmas shopping. We'd travel there on the bus, thirty miles each way, my mother and sister and me, to choose presents and admire the lights. One year, maybe the Christmas before Bloody Sunday, I bought a ballerina angel for the top of the tree with my pocket money – I have her still, a little the worse for wear, like all of us.

Bloody Sunday ranks among the most controversial episodes of the Troubles, when soldiers opened fire on unarmed civilians taking part in a demonstration against internment without trial. Twelve days earlier, all marches had been banned in Northern Ireland for the rest of the year, meaning the protest was illegal.

The authorities were expecting rioting and had sent in paratroopers, known as the Paras (members of the 1st Battalion, Parachute Regiment), who had already gained a reputation for using excessive force. Six months earlier, in west Belfast's Ballymurphy estate, the Paras had been deployed to deal with unrest following the introduction of internment. Eleven civilians were dead by the end of a three-day period, including a mother-of-eight and a priest helping an injured man. Some were hit in the back running away, some were shot several times, no credible evidence was ever advanced that any of the victims were armed – but the army labelled the dead as gunmen and terrorists. No camera crews were present to capture what happened.

Now, the Paras ran amok again, this time in the Bogside. Some twenty-six people were shot, thirteen killed outright and a fourteenth died of his injuries in hospital. I sat with my family watching the footage on the news that evening. Probably, I had homework on the go, with the television playing in the background. News bulletins were a constant backdrop to my childhood and I didn't always pay much attention to them. But I know I stopped what I was doing on this occasion because of the shock caused by the reports. I'd have looked up, not quite understanding everything but catching the drift. The panic. The cries. The pandemonium.

The image of Father Edward Daly, crouched over, waving a blood-splattered handkerchief as a white flag, is not one easily forgotten. Two years later, by now Bishop of Derry, I would see him in mitre and robes conducting confirmations in our church a few streets away. Here on the news, however, he was leading a group of ashen-faced men carrying a dying seventeen-year-old youth. The handkerchief fluttered. The blood on it was scarlet – fresh. Soldiers in combat gear, rifles at the ready, flanked the party, watching them – conveying the sense that at any moment they might lift those weapons, take aim and fire.

Next, Father Daly had a microphone held under his chin. A reporter peppered questions. He kept insisting the shot teenager had been running away.

No, he wasn't firing at the army. No, he did not pose a threat! He was only a kid. He wasn't doing anything. People weren't even throwing stones at the soldiers. I know what I'm talking about – I was there when the Saracens arrived, he said.

Young as I was, I knew what a Saracen looked like. They were six-wheeled armoured fighting vehicles equipped with machine guns and portholes on the sides from which troops fired.

I remember my parents, grave-faced, tuning in to every news bulletin. Their whispered conversations. The overhanging sense of threat. The general mood was that the rule of law wasn't going to protect the nationalist community – that soldiers were dangerous, could act with impunity and might (indeed, would) shoot at random. As for that iconic picture of a priest holding his blood-splashed handkerchief in a flag of truce, while attempting to evacuate a wounded boy: that became a symbol of the Troubles.

Amid the shock in my community, a spike of approval poked through the gloom when Bernadette Devlin gave the British Home Secretary a wallop. The fiery young Member of Parliament for mid-Ulster – our constituency – was reacting to his shameless whitewash of Bloody Sunday events. Stop demonising us, that slap seemed to say. Stop denying our common humanity. And don't expect us to lie down for you to walk over us.

Bernadette Devlin, later McAliskey, was part of the civil rights movement and is depicted on a Bogside mural under the slogan 'You are now entering Free Derry' – where barricades had been erected to keep police and soldiers out. She was in the area when the paratroopers started shooting. Now, in London, she took exception to Reginald Maudling, who hadn't been present, telling the House of Commons on behalf of the government that soldiers fired in self-defence. Devlin tried to give her version of events but the Speaker wouldn't allow it. Incandescent, she called the Home Secretary a 'murdering hypocrite' and crossed Westminster's chamber floor to strike him on the face. She hit him a clatter, she told me years later, bunching her fist at the memory. It was an impulse – but not one she regretted.

In Derry, as in other cities, towns and villages across Ireland, people burned with a shared sense of injustice at the Bloody Sunday violence – and in Northern Ireland, with a fear that similar, state-supported carnage might be visited on us. A national day of mourning was held in the Irish Republic and the Irish government also withdrew its ambassador to Britain. A crowd besieged the British embassy in Dublin for days, the ambassador and staff had to be evacuated, and the embassy was set ablaze and destroyed on the day when eleven of Derry's dead were buried. The Irish government apologised for the attack and agreed to pay compensation.

Meanwhile, Lord Widgery, a former army brigadier, was appointed to investigate Bloody Sunday. He sat alone. His tribunal exonerated the armed forces, blaming the tragedy on the Northern Ireland Civil Rights Association for organising an illegal march. The Widgery report claimed there was a 'strong suspicion' that the victims had either fired weapons or handled bombs – a judgement which angered the nationalist community because there was no evidence to back it up, whereas independent eyewitness accounts indicated the opposite. Lord Widgery also accepted the soldiers' accounts that they had only returned fire. One paratrooper shot between four and six of the victims and claimed he had fired on a 'nail bomber.' His Lordship's sole criticism of the soldiers was that firing 'bordered on the reckless' at times.

The inquiry was counterproductive. It settled nothing. Bloody Sunday acted as a recruiting agent for the IRA and increased hostility towards the British Army, contributing to the duration of the conflict. No British soldier had been wounded or reported injuries as a result of Bloody Sunday. No nail bombs were recovered. Meanwhile, teachers took to wagging a finger at us when any classmate offered up an untruth. 'Don't be telling Widgeries,' we were warned.

It took almost forty years before the lie was recognised. Lord Saville was appointed by then Prime Minister Tony Blair to conduct an independent investigation, a marathon undertaking which finally concluded in 2010 that all who died were innocent. Soldiers had lied under oath. No warnings were given before they opened fire on unarmed civilians. David Cameron, as Prime Minister of Britain, made a formal state apology saying Bloody Sunday was 'both unjustified and unjustifiable. It was wrong.'

Almost half a century after Ballymurphy, a long-delayed inquest into the killings opened in late 2018 and is ongoing at the time of writing. It is possible that prosecutions may ensue. As scrutiny was focused on what happened in Ballymurphy, it was announced in 2019 by the Public Prosecution Service that one retired soldier would be charged with murder and attempted murder over events on Bloody Sunday. British military leaders repeatedly denounce such developments but these cases continue to rankle and cannot be buried forever. The record needs to be set straight – not alone for the sake of dead victims and their grieving families, but because official denial of facts is a stumbling block to reconciliation. It hinders Northern Ireland's healing process.

Bishop Daly always kept a photograph on his desk of that dying teenager. His name was Jackie Duddy, he was a textile worker. When he saw him fall, he crouched down to give him the Last Rites before attempting to have him moved for medical attention. By the time the priest led four men with Jackie in their arms past the soldiers, the boy was dead. He took his final breath as the cameras clicked and rolled and the paratroopers looked on. He had been shot in the back.

A generation has grown up for whom the Troubles are history – as remote as those grainy images of the first man walking on the moon, or newsreel of the concentration camps being liberated. These people can afford to take the peace process for granted. But not me. My memory stretches beyond that 1998 breakthrough, slip-sliding into years that cast a shadow across my childhood.

Don't misunderstand me. It was also a happy upbringing in Omagh. Yes, that Omagh. The place where the centre was blown to kingdom come, with the ink barely dry on the Good Friday Agreement, by dissident republicans bent on subverting the peace process. But the place, too, whose Catholic and Protestant communities crossed the invisible tribal divide to support one another in the aftershock of massacre.

The centre held, Mr Yeats.

Children adapt to anything. To the sight of army foot patrols passing by the bottom of their garden. To the blare of sirens interrupting their sleep. To roadblocks springing up without warning – identities checked, car boots searched.

'Those checkpoints spout like weeds,' grumbled my father, but he was mannerly with the military personnel controlling them. No point in looking for trouble. We were on a journey, maybe to the seaside in Donegal, the car flagged down, an armed boy in a helmet inserted his head through the driver's window and – improbably – called my father 'dad'.

'All right, dad, where you 'eaded?'

Lately, I've wondered if one of those soldiers wasn't Corporal Atkins.

The highly-visible presence of armed security forces were the trappings of our everyday life. Normality was under constant siege. Even if today was quiet, no guarantees about tomorrow were possible. Research suggests such an environment has most impact on children and young people. The message absorbed was that violence was random, some adults were dangerous and the world inherently was an unsafe place.

As a child, I was never told to find a policeman if I was lost. I knew no one who was given that advice.

Here's a memory from the Troubles. It's a Sunday morning and I'm taken on an outing by my uncle to call on friends of his in Lurgan, an hour or so away. The family we're visiting has a nine-year-old girl, our birthdays a few months apart, and we two are sent to the playground. Outdoors, she hints at something more impressive to show me. There's a place, she says, where money is lying on the ground, waiting – no, begging – to be lifted.

Naturally I follow where she leads. A few streets away, we begin to pick our way through shattered glass clumped across the pavement and road. Around us, the window of every building is demolished.

'What happened?'

'There was a riot last night.' She is blasé. Observing my astonishment, her tone shades into pity. 'Don't you have riots in Omagh?'

Ashamed on its behalf, I admit to Omagh's lack of riots.

She finds a stick and uses it to sift through the broken glass. 'Look, there's one!' She ducks down and a fifty pence piece is held aloft.

The seven-sided coins are strewn through the wreckage. In the rioters' hands they became weapons, hurled, pointed-side out, to break windows. I delve for some of this booty lying, literally, underfoot but fail to find any – handicapped by my lack of previous experience at scavenging. Meanwhile, my guide rummages up several more fifty pence coins and, in a spirit of comradeship, gives me one.

By now, older children are gathering to forage, and she advises that we've had the best of the pickings. I am overwhelmed by her worldliness. We'll be friends forever.

At home that evening I display my loot to my parents, expressing the hope that Omagh might improve its game in relation to rioting. Or failing that, could we move to Lurgan? Tension quivers in the air. My father and mother exchange glances. I am marched into the sitting room to deposit the coin in the Trócaire charity box and a lecture follows. Firstly, that metal disc represents ill-gotten gains and will not be spent in Mrs Quinn's sweetshop. Secondly, Lurgan is out of bounds – the new friendship is about to wither. Thirdly, I am to thank my lucky stars I live in a town where people have more respect for hard-earned money than to use it for smashing windows. Fourthly, it's high time I was in bed.

Years later, I discovered that the twig held by Britannia on the reverse of a fifty pence piece is an olive branch. An irrelevant factoid. Except if you've experienced that same coin's use for rioting.

In excess of 3,500 deaths occurred as a result of the conflict. Premature death, causal death, bloody death became quotidian. Nearly half of the total killings within Northern Ireland took place in Belfast. Nine in ten of the dead were men, with younger age groups most at risk. Some 257 were children and those under seventeen.

The 1970s were particularly bloody, with 480 people dying in 1972 alone, according to CAIN, the Conflict Archive on the Internet – the year when Bloody Sunday happened. Figures can be anonymous. But behind each number is a face.

The political incompetence and downright stupidity are what strike me most. How else to explain that avoidable, wasteful loss of civilians, soldiers and police officers alike? If civil rights had been extended when lobbying started – if British law had only been applied to Northern Ireland in exactly the same way as it was delivered in any English, Scottish or Welsh city – there would have been virtually no support among the population for violence. Instead, the situation was mishandled and grievances ratcheted up.

However, the Good Friday Agreement has transformed Northern Ireland. In recent times, bombs planted by dissident republicans have been a worrying development, and there was widespread horror in April 2019 at the death of a 29-year-old journalist who was killed by anti-Good Friday Agreement paramilitaries during unrest in Derry. But these people do not attract support among the community from which they spring. 'Not in our name', read the graffiti on Free Derry Corner immediately after that shooting.

Clearly, Brexit threatens Ireland's hard-won peace in a way Brexiteers neither envisaged, nor took seriously, when the implications of a visible border on the island of Ireland were pointed out to them. If one positive can be gleaned from the Brexit shambles, it is that people who call themselves Irish and people who call themselves British in this corner of the world know alike the value of the post-Troubles era. We are in no doubt about what we gained and what we stand to lose. Most of us have the sense to prize our peace accord and oppose anything which undermines it. The view is widespread that the Good Friday Agreement, a moment in time when hope and history rhymed, must be upheld.

Corporal Atkins sees me put on my coat and crosses the room for a final word. As we say goodbye, I ask him one remaining question. Have you been back? In peacetime, I mean?

He says no. There are days when he thinks he'd like to take a look but, on balance, maybe not. Too much water under the bridge. Sometimes it's best simply to keep looking ahead.

Gerard Donovan

A Novel Forms

1

I lived in a train depot for over fifteen years at the edge of
woods large enough to get lost in. Twenty metres away, at
the end of a gravel surface, trains passed eight times a day
to and from the city, four hours away. The trains were
loud enough to rattle some things and shake the rest.
Sometimes I'd wake at four in the morning, convinced the
thing had come off the tracks and was heading for the
bedroom. It was a shack by any definition of the word, but
one of the rooms was large: trees as far as the eye could
see. And the benefit of such a place was the living space
enhanced by that extra room: the door I could open and be
outside. The cabin was formerly a train sub-station, where
a century before people bought tickets and waited for the
sound of the engine.

I kept my own company, but in a place welcome to
others. I took in a pit bull terrier, Hobart, who was the
image of the dog in the paperback of Coetzee's *Disgrace*. I

lived a minute's walk from where a neighbour kept guinea fowl, roosters and hens, and two other adopted dogs, a Rottweiler-Dane mix and a wolf mix. Add Max the black cat, who was befriended by the Rottweiler. At midnight, they went for walks, Max with her white paws moving beneath the protection of her massive, also largely black companion. Trees ringed the enclosure, and over my roof with an elaborate, useless antenna, towered a 35-metre Norwegian spruce, and a history of storms that couldn't knock it down. I felt that I had a tenuous and secondary function there as a human. I was an observer, not participant. I brought my human rhythms, and in the years I spent there I learned other rhythms – intelligences that worked their way into my writing.

Previously I had written three books of poetry. About eight poems out of those three books were decent. Too many were polished vanities, revised hundreds of times until pointed and somehow pointless despite the scores of periodicals that gave them a home. Being published is just that. It doesn't have a great deal to do with writing. It's what happens to it afterwards.

Fiction was a relief from the inwardness of poetry, but I inherited an economy in my work from much reading in Poetics and my studies in a tradition that prizes economy and a completeness-in-itself of prose.

This was followed by a fellowship to the Johns Hopkins Writing Seminars and workshops with Grace Paley and Stephen Dixon. You might say that *Schopenhauer's Telescope* (2003), my first novel, was my first book of poetry.

The novel was written in a room in the cabin without heat in a very cold winter. As my two very cold protagonists fought for their lives, the vapour above my typing made me a witness to the scene I described. I was in that cold, and the wall in front of me (a blank wall is richest), conjured up the scenes that announced themselves as they came.

The farm had its own heartbeat: the rhythms of the animals that called it home reverberated in the background, a hum of counterpoint that took years to appreciate.

Even the slowest creatures had their stories: I'd find snapping turtles on their way to the pond, armoured for battle, an ancient species with the ability to sever my hand if I was foolish enough to reach too close. To this was added various birds of prey in the form of silent shadows gliding across the ground. The nearness of life and death around the cabin became the default setting. Primitive, uncompromising, unrelenting.

Guinea fowl go back to the age of dinosaurs. They sleep in the trees at night, which is why I suspect they've lasted so long, and they frequented the ferns, which reach further back in time. During the day they wandered, bursting into cackles and chirping. After a while, I didn't hear them. They joined the train as background. The bantam roosters and the running drama of hen-courting sent another level of sound across the stage. Imagine the cacophony, patterns and variations far from random, only arranged differently from the average human 'unit of meaning' in a sentence or in how we talk to one another.

And now imagine that my brain accepted those distracting rhythms and created a framework for them. The context was survival, not art. How much art is there in the art of survival? More than I could have imagined. I took this intrusion of subversive rhythms, proficient in the art of survival, and translated them into prose, the immediacy of language.

First published in 2006, and later in a dozen languages, the first true product of those woods was the novel *Julius Winsome*.

2

A passage from *A Writer's Notebook* by Somerset Maugham:

> One takes pains to be simple, clear and succinct. One aims at rhythms and balance ... [but] Tolstoi, Dickens, Balzac and Dostoievsky wrote their respective languages very indifferently. It proves that if you can tell stories, devise incidents, and if you have sincerity and passion, it doesn't matter a damn how you write.

In the end, I think that Maugham is talking about *voice*. The great destroyer of all rules in fiction. It's amazing to me how many definitions exist for voice in the pages of *how to* books. Most agree that a 'writer's voice' is unique but needs to be developed.

If I may put the issue in fundamental terms, there are two *voices*. We speak by virtue of having a physical voice – a synecdoche for the larynx and structures of the lungs, jaw and tongue. Voice in fiction is a hallmark that identifies a particular writer's mind at work. We view our speaking voice as a way to express thoughts, and our writing voice as a composer of thoughts. The potential for confusion is legion.

I see voice in fiction not as one defining feature but as a combination of factors: the words I choose; how I compose sentences in terms of cadence and ordering information; how I proceed from one event to another in a manner that spotlights story rather than writing; whether I employ description as functional or ornament; how the setting is employed as a character; and the manner in which I try to make my characters urgent.

The above could be re-classed in any number of terms, such as diction, style and verisimilitude – it all seems so clinical and so circular when we set about defining terms to define the features we find in fiction.

Instead, we might accept here that voice is a combination of elements, and that the *combination* is what's unique to a writer.

The art of survival has left its mark on my writing.

Plot: I see upheaval. I see reaction on the part of the character and identification on the part of the reader.

We don't begin a Shakespeare play, we stumble across it, we hear people speaking. We possess next to no information about any of these characters. No one is prepared; it's never the right time to do anything. But these people already *are* what they are going to do. They were this way before we met them. In time we'll see them wear through masks and abandon distortions of themselves until they come to terms with what they are. In the way we first met them, they were strangers to themselves.

That sense of witness and hurry is at odds with the dominant iambic pentameter of blank verse. A fault line of tension develops as the rhetorical pace – the urgency of the characters to deal with their situation – grinds against the metrical pace. This same principle works in *Julius Winsome*: the process of an explosion unwinding in restrained prose.

Take a scene from the novel, where the protagonist acts decisively, but I buried it in plain view: a short sentence in the middle of a long paragraph. Readers reported going back over the paragraph to confirm what had just happened, which magnified the event all the more. Here is an excerpt from that paragraph:

> He had probably decided to spend the morning here, waiting for the silence that brings deer in, a buck wandering at the edge of the field or bigger game down from the mountain. I brought the rifle up to my shoulder and fired those eighty yards, one bullet that slapped into the folds of his neck. He grabbed for it as if for an insect ...

Fulcrum: the fulcrum upends our notions about what will happen. It is that point in the novel where a momentous shift occurs, exposing a character's motivations and fears and challenging our perceptions. Julius' mental state allows for no transitions. The prose in the novel reflects that mental state, and the reader has no resources and no process to follow, only the mind of Julius.

If I don't sense a fulcrum in a novel – then I don't have a novel.

Parataxis: I did away with transitions, because I don't see any when I step outside every day. Transitions smooth the passage from one circumstance to another by mixing elements of both. But they can overshadow the effect of the previous and dilute the presence of the next. What I leave out of fiction is often as important as what I put in. In fact, what I omit is part of the writing.

I trust readers to match instantaneously the movement of scenes across space and time. Just go there. Let's not hold hands.

Given current reading habits and the march backwards to hieroglyphics in our digital communications, I'm convinced that soon we'll have a novel style I'll call *click-lit*, characterised by random references that haunt the reader to the novel's end. A kind of weekend syndrome, the sense that everyone is having a better time somewhere else.

But I'm speaking here of the classic version of parataxis. A rich, undeveloped vein is left to run between episodes. The reader writes into the novel where I have written nothing.

Logic: I stopped looking for reasons to justify an event, if the event was important enough to include in the first place. One day a guinea hen died and the others kicked dirt over the body and chirped in a circle for ten minutes, and moved away. If you live with creatures for fifteen years, you'll see what others don't. Explanation is a fatal infection if caught by fiction. I gave complete agency to anything that entered the pages and earned a lasting place in the story. I told myself to present the scene as I witnessed it – and to move on. I cannot force fiction to be true or real as I write. It's immediate, it's here and it's gone. The artifice of fiction is what stays and delays.

Tone: The undiscovered narrative of a novel. What bothers the writer.

Every night, especially during winter, the trees seethed with wind. Without being conscious of it, I incorporated that sound into the narrative style with which Julius recounts his five days of killing. This created in my mind the sense of the story being *whispered* into the ear. That seemed the best way for this mysterious man to relate his story. The tone and character bound together.

Before I left my cabin, I buried Hobart, my companion for almost my entire time there, and the star of the novel, in the place he belonged. I made a hole and covered him by scraping dirt with both hands backward into the grave, in the way a terrier does. He's facing the opening to the trail into the woods he loved so much.

And that is perhaps the greatest lesson I take with me. I had written my goodbye a decade before he died. When a subject comes of its own accord – and it's powerful and immediate – perhaps that other project can wait.

The time I spent writing the novel – six weeks – was followed by two months in revision. The dream of a particular story can and does go away. Tone and treatment are fragile and transient. You can lose those.

Notes made for later may not be enough to bring it all back. And such novels take an age to write, in my experience.

3

My first extended novel is indeed by far the longest I've written, at about 130,000 words. The story begins in Java in 1825 and ends in a small railway station in England in May of 1940. Along the way we visit Paris, Blackpool, Flanders, Berlin and Margate. This is a journey far from the compressed time and place of my first novel, which occupies a single day; my second, which takes no heed of time; and the third novel's five days, with a brief central flashback.

The idea was so compelling to me that I faced telling the story in, for me, ungovernable narrative territory. I had a few advantages: I could describe the plot in one sentence; the narrative arc in a short paragraph; the bulk of the novel takes place from 1905–1940; the important characters jump the boundaries of multiple chapters.

Three immediate possibilities presented themselves as arrangement strategies for the material:

– Create discreet stories or novellas and place them in a sequence of 'chapters' held together with just enough narrative glue to justify 'novel'. Similar locations, conversations, etc.

– Enter *click-lit* – simply juxtapose the unconnected (not disconnected, which implies a connection at some point). The reader establishes cohesion and meaning where I have not. Or the reader discovers what I do know but am unable to enunciate. Failing that, I roll a chapter into place and know that opinions as to why will follow.

– Use motifs and planned repetition as a unifying architecture (Hugh Kenner refers to it as 'subject rhyme' in connection with Pound's *Cantos*).

All three seemed to represent the triumph of artifice over storytelling.

In 2005 in Aspen I answered a question from a person in the audience – he turned out to be a respected science-fiction writer grappling with a range of subject matter that defied structure. I suggested that, as the creator of the world of that novel, he could establish a law of physics that allowed the material to exist as he wished it to.

In short, I was suggesting that the material comes first. Once assembled, it creates its own containment system. Let me suggest a formula: *Content creates gravity; gravity structures the content.*

In terms of the novel's organisation, any contest between the reader's perception and your intent as the novelist will produce a clear winner: perception. As it should.

Scientists have ample evidence that shows the brain will 'compose' one colour or another, depending on surrounding colours. Red can appear as grey – and this is not a trick 'grey.' The brain actually presents grey, and no amount of reason will have you see red, which will appear as such once the other shapes or colours are removed. What's on the page is secondary to the brain's assimilation of content and how it makes sense of it. And what the brain decides, is what you see.

In the same way, the sense of passing time is unique to a situation. A simple example: twenty minutes of standing in a queue and twenty listening to a Bach fugue are two very different twenty minutes. Time flexes with context. If I accept that time is an experience, and like colour, that it alters with context, I am in possession of useful knowledge as the writer of a long novel. A hundred pages to describe the events of a day. A page to cover five years.

Characters place each other in context and are thus defined by each other in a streaming fashion. On Page 90, the reader accepts the reality of an entirely different person from the one on Page 30, even if the character *has not changed*. But other characters have, and that's all it takes. Reason plays no part. We are captive to context.

We can parlay this thinking about context into the question of what a novel is, as opposed to a novella or short story.

How many short stories exist that easily might have been novellas or indeed novels? I think of Chekhov's 'The

Lady with the Dog'. This short story begins at the embankment in the seaside setting of Yalta and ends at a Moscow opera house. The embankment is a stage of sorts; it represents a neutral meeting place where secrets are new. At the opera, status is given a seat number, and popular secrets pour from the stage in practiced song. That's a great reversal and a good place to stop. Chekhov rings the bell.

But what if he had continued? Gurov, an adept hand at the one week provincial romance, is now out of his league – or is he? And is Anna everything she appeared to be? If Chekhov had written a novella, and we never knew of a shorter version, how many readers today would point out that the story should stop at the opera?

I view J.L. Carr's *A Month in the Country* as a novel, at about 32,000 very compact words. The author could have gently padded the writing to 50,000, and ended up creating a sense of unfinished business. The story remains etched in the mind long after the reading, and is the longer for it. Can certain material end at one of several plot points and still retain its essential nature, resonating in a time-delayed secretion?

Years later, my response to the audience member's question applied itself to my own particular case, writing a long novel.

I made each chapter as rich and sonorous in its own right as possible, and it formed its own complete story. I discovered that a memorable character will survive re-positioning. I'm always re-thinking the originating scene, placing it elsewhere and watching how other scenes reposition themselves with Machiavellian enterprise.

The same principle governs my sense for chapter length. Notions of beginnings and endings are really moments of joining and parting.

I swept up the dead weight of research detail. I took imagery from later chapters and brought them forward in flashes. The slow turn of a German Taube in 1914 in a chapter on the pumpkin seeds of Java almost a century before served to put one thread through two chapters.

I varied the syntax in chapters when new narrators recounted their stories, but the tone remained uniform throughout.

In the end, I trusted the narrative, or as Randall Jarrell puts it, 'pure narrative.' The less I thought about style, the more polished the work became, and the richer, the more tonally consistent across chapters. Despite the popular term, I don't see how it's possible to separate 'showing' and 'telling' into discreet camps. They blend, often in the same sentence. Like flashbacks, telling can be a fragment or a long account in summary. And showing can sound programmatic very quickly.

I suspect Maugham is right about a certain indifference helping to bring about excellence. Sometimes piling everything carelessly onto the page does work, because the storytelling gene still filters and selects in the background. When composing, as opposed to revising, perhaps putting the conscious filter away does result in more and better writing.

Another aspect to this issue. As you read this sentence, are you 'reading' the words mentally – so that you 'hear' them simultaneously? Most people are. Try eliminating that mental sound so that the eye and the brain communicate directly, in complete silence. It's difficult.

That's the power of the conscious filter.

I'd like to mention another aspect to the experience of composing a long novel: the effect on the writer. Characters inhabited my thinking for longer than would normally be the case. Writing isn't a desk job. I turn around and there they are, the entities I'd made, because they don't have anyone else to talk to. I wrote one fellow out of the novel – yes, I still remember Sebastian – just to be rid of him.

As the work coalesced, characters I believed indispensable disappeared and took entire sequences with them, sequences I hated to lose. But they had to go. Passages that shine as writing can damage the novel, and the longer they stay on the page during an extended process of composition, the more indispensable they appear. The reason for deleting passages – or whole sections – has little to do with quality and everything to do with relevance and resonance. And the fact remains that a 'jewel' of a passage will resist to the end. When it is gone, I often see the story emerge that this 'beautiful' writing had buried.

A novel hires and fires. Players audition, seem promising, fade. The minor steps forward and is major. Cinderellas appear and hunchbacks cower in the shadows. Much drama unfolds in the netherworld of creation.

Roddy Doyle

On Music and Writing

I used to like filling the room with music as I worked. It was company and a way to measure time. But now, today, I need music if what I do is going to be worth reading.

When I started writing I was a secondary school teacher. By the time I was writing my fourth novel, *Paddy Clarke Ha Ha Ha*, I was also a father. I often wrote about music but I never listened to it as I worked. I didn't have the time. I grabbed half an hour to write early in the morning before going to work, or twenty minutes late at night, while the baby slept. Actually, even without the baby, it wouldn't have occurred to me to play music while I wrote.

My first novel is called *The Commitments*. It's about a group of young men and women who form a band. The novel is short and full of music; take out the lyrics and it's much, much shorter. It's often assumed that I listened incessantly to black American music while I wrote *The Commitments*. I didn't. When I played music it was to choose a new song for my fictional band. I'd select the song and play it again and again while I transcribed the lyrics. I peeled the words away from the song, and stopped listening. I didn't want to listen while I worked. I had to concentrate; I was writing.

Five years later and three more novels, I was doing the same thing. The book I was writing, *Paddy Clarke Ha Ha Ha*, had its soundtrack, the songs of American country singer, Hank Williams. His words are in the book but I wasn't listening to his songs as I worked.

I was afraid to listen to music. I was afraid that I wouldn't concentrate, that I'd drift with the music. (It took me years to understand that drifting – day-dreaming, wasting time – is a big part of the writer's working day). When I listened to music I sat in front of the stereo, staring at it. Listening to music was like washing the dishes; it was something you did. I couldn't write and wash the dishes at the same time. I couldn't write and watch television at the same time. How could I write and listen to music?

Then I gave up teaching. On the first Friday of June, 1993, I walked out of the school for the last time. The following Monday I sat down to write – all day. *Paddy Clarke Ha Ha Ha* had just been published. I was about to start the story that would become *The Woman Who Walked Into Doors*. The computer screen in front of me was blank and the day seemed, suddenly, very long. I wrote 'Chapter One'. I changed it to 'Chapter 1', then 'Ch.1', then decided on 'One'. I looked at 'One'. I liked it. I made it bold. **One**. I was very happy with that. I looked at my watch. It was 9.15.

I was actually delighted to have all this time to work. *The Woman Who Walked Into Doors* is narrated by a woman who has been a victim of domestic violence for two decades. It wasn't something I could have written in spurts, an hour here, half an hour there. It took me a long time – a year – to find the voice of the narrator, Paula Spencer. I needed the full working day. I had no colleagues now to meet at lunch and coffee breaks. I was self-employed, alone; the day was very long. I can't remember when I decided that music in the room might help. It just seemed like a good idea. Both the room and the day would feel less empty.

But it didn't work. I couldn't work and listen. I kept swerving away from the words on the screen and listening to the music instead. Not literally. I'd keep my eyes on the screen – that bit was easy – but my head would be miles away. In the battle between creating big art – a three-hundred-page novel – and listening to little art – the three-minute song – little art was winning. I had to ban the three-minute song from my office.

I knew nothing about classical music; my ignorance was almost absolute. I could listen to classical music while I wrote, I decided. There would be no lyrics to nudge me away from my work. There'd be no drum-kits or electric guitars. So I bought some classical music CDs and I started my education.

It worked for a while, but not for long. This music seemed too familiar. I'd heard it before in supermarkets, in restaurants, in television commercials. Dvorak's *New World Symphony* had sold Hovis bread when I was a teenager. Another piece – I can't remember the name but I can hum it – had been used in an ad for wool. I grew bored very quickly. Luckily, neither Mozart's *Requiem* nor Pergolesi's *Stabat Mater* had been used to sell cars or ice-cream. So they both seemed fresh and wonderful. But back then, when I was 35, classical music just wasn't good enough. I preferred the silence.

Arvo Pärt rescued me. The biographical note on one of his CD covers included his date of birth, 1935. But there was no year given for his death. And it hit me: Arvo Pärt was still alive. That discovery led me to the 'Contemporary' section of the record shop's classical department. And I found Philip Glass, Steve Reich and the other minimalists; and Michael Nyman, and Henryk

Gorecki, and Gavin Bryars, and John Tavener and Frederic Rzewski and John Adams and other living composers. It wasn't the fact that they still inhaled and exhaled; it was the unpredictability of their work. I'd never step into a lift and hear Bryars' *Farewell to Philosophy* as the doors slid shut behind me. And it was the rhythm. It took me three years to write my novel, *A Star Called Henry*. If I hadn't started playing Philip Glass's *Music With Changing Parts* early in the third year, it would have taken much longer. I played that strange piece of music every afternoon for months. Its mad insistent rhythm became, for me, the rhythm of that book's last pages.

My novel, *Oh Play That Thing*, is full of the music of Louis Armstrong. I *did* listen to Armstrong as I worked, and to Duke Ellington, and Cab Calloway – all those three-minute songs. I tried to make sure that, somehow, the rhythm of the book was the rhythm of 1920s jazz. But, actually, I didn't often listen to jazz as I wrote. Steve Reich's *Different Trains* is the piece of music I will always associate with the writing of that novel. Its driving rhythm, the constant movement, the looped broken voices, they were all there as I wrote. It went beyond listening. In fact, I wasn't really listening at all. The music got into me. It infected me and put me on edge.

It's only in recent years that I've become actively aware that I need music to work. I need a new piece, or form, or composer, if I'm going to do more than simply fill pages. I've written eleven novels and it doesn't get easier. It's not the story; it's *how* to tell the story. It's about trying to achieve the feeling – and I think it is a feeling – that I'm not doing something I've done before, but that I'm attempting something new. Experience can be reassuring. I have my routine and my rules and they've kept me going for more than thirty years. I could say I know my limits. But I don't – and I don't want to. And that's where music comes in.

In the second chapter of his memoir, *Chronicles: Volume One*, Bob Dylan describes his arrival in New York. He's a very young man, known to no one. He's ambitious; he has a body of songs he wants to play. But he visits the Greenwich Village folk music clubs and hears music he hasn't heard before and, immediately, he decides that what he has isn't enough. '[T]hings had become too familiar,' he writes, 'and I might have to disorientate myself.'

That's what I'm trying to do when I start a new novel. I'm trying to rattle myself, or to knock myself off my own map. Music used to lend me its rhythm and energy; it was vital in the last hours of the working day. It still does that: the music I play in the late afternoon *is* vital. But now I ask more of it.

My last novel, *Smile*, was written with the help of an Australian ensemble called The Necks. I don't know how to classify their music – jazz, rock, post-rock? – and that's one of the reasons why I listen to them and why I played them loud as I wrote *Smile*. There's an unsettling quality to their sound, a predictability that isn't actually there, a rhythm that's misleading. There's something new every time I listen, a beat or a note, or the absence of a beat or a note, that jolts me. They are doing what I was hoping to do as I wrote.

The right music seems to put me into a place where I can't relax, where I won't take too much for granted as I sit and type. For *Smile*, it was The Necks – especially their pieces, *Drive By* and *Townsville*. For the novel I'm working on now, it's jazz. It's the wild, exhilarating music of Art Blakey, Charles Mingus, John Coltrane, Horace Silver.

But I don't want to lose the run of myself. I don't want to overstate the music's importance. It's only music. I'm not being possessed by Charles Mingus or Charlie Parker. I'm the writer. I'm in control. I'm choosing the words, rejecting the words, composing the sentences. On the good days the music stops and I don't notice.

But I still need to get up the stairs every morning and music, the prospect of music, makes that task much easier.

Catherine Dunne

GRAPPLING WITH THE 'SLIPPERY DOUBLE'

In *Frantumaglia*, Elena Ferrante observes:

> The characters you try to give life to are merely tools with which you circle around the elusive, unnamed, shapeless thing that belongs to you alone, and which nevertheless is a sort of key to all the doors, the real reason that you spend so much of your life sitting at a table tapping away, filling pages.

I'd be inclined to turn that idea around. In my experience, that 'elusive, unnamed [and] shapeless thing' that resides in my unconscious eventually resolves itself into the dreaming shapes of fictional characters, complete with all their attendant anxieties and complexities. They then take over my 'real' life.

I agree with Ferrante that the characters we create:

> never leave you, they have a space-time of their own in which they are alive and increasingly vivid, they are inside and outside you, they exist solidly in the streets, in the houses, in the places where the story must unfold.

The characters and the story: the story is the mechanism that, in its unfolding, reveals the nature of the characters. The plot is secondary. It is, in the words of Andrew Miller 'the chicken wire' that holds together the 'collection of anxieties' that is the novel.

Characters, on the other hand, according to Miller:

> are members of that shifting population of men, women and children who inhabit our inner worlds. Where they come from, whether they are curious versions of ourselves, figures of the collective unconscious, reconfigurings of those we did indeed once know but have now forgotten, or a mix of all such, no one, to my knowledge, has ever convincingly answered. It does not matter. No one writes for long without understanding that they are entering mystery and will never leave it.

Writing comes from within that space where the conscious and the unconscious collide. At some point, the writer makes a decision – a conscious act – to put words on paper. A decision to meet the silent challenge of the waiting screen, or the blank pages of a notebook. Often, the 'pre-writing' phase – the chaotic, unconscious phase – will have been completed by then: but not necessarily. Either way, the two – the 'slippery double' – have to be present, to overlap, if not to coexist.

For me, what we call 'space-time' or 'dream-time' often culminates in a single, visceral moment of illumination. That one moment of inspiration is then followed by months, sometimes years, of elusiveness. It evolves into a kind of absent presence that fuels my self-doubt: Why can't I recapture the energy of that first imagined moment? Its presence, however elusive, is one that excites my creativity. In the early days of its absence, nothing seems to work. The text is flat and stale. It doesn't 'speak' to me.

And then comes the realisation – one that visits over and over again: that single moment of insight, or illumination, or inspiration, is all a writer gets. It is mine as the result of a long process of unconscious gestation, of dreaming.

Now, I just have to get down to the writing. And the rewriting. And the rewriting all over again.

It is a process that constantly repeats itself. It's possible that the process differs from one piece of creative work to the next. But at its core is the elusiveness of the dream and the dream-people who take over every moment – waking as well as sleeping.

The mystery is that it *feels* different every time.

John Banville, in 'Fiction and the Dream', writes:

> A man wakes in the morning, feeling light-headed, even somewhat dazed. Standing in the curtained gloom ... he feels that somehow he is not his real, vital, fully conscious self. It is as if that other, alert version of him is still in bed, and that what has got up is a sort of shadow-self, tremulous, two-dimensional ... Is he 'coming down with something'? He does seem a little feverish. But no, he decides, what is afflicting him is no physical malady. There is, rather, something the matter with his mind. His brain feels heavy, and as if it were a size too large for his skull. Then, suddenly, in a rush, he remembers the dream. The writing of fiction is far more than the telling of stories. It is an ancient, an elemental, urge which springs, like the dream, from a desperate imperative to encode and preserve things that are buried in us deep beyond words.

Some time after I came across these lines, I read *Forest Dark* by Nicole Krauss. In the novel, Krauss explores, among many things, the art of writing fiction, and how it feels when that creative urge is blocked. She describes the sense she has one day of already being present in her house when she opens her front door, although clearly she can't be: she's only at the entrance. At the time, it felt like an eerie echo of Banville's words. She writes:

> I was myself, I felt utterly normal in my own skin, and yet at the same time I also had the sudden sense that I was no longer confined to my body, not to the hands, arms, and legs that I had been looking at all my life, and which I had observed

minute by minute for thirty-nine years, were not in fact my extremities after all, were not the furthest limit of myself, but that I existed beyond and separately from them. And not in an abstract sense, either. Not as a soul or a frequency. But full-bodied, exactly as I was there on the threshold of the kitchen, but, somehow – elsewhere – upstairs *again*.

It felt as though all the everyday, ordinary objects around her seemed different, 'touched by stillness', and that time seemed to have 'sped up' while she, the writer, had somehow 'fallen behind'.

Both writers express this feeling of duality: of the challenges of grappling with what Margaret Atwood calls 'the slippery double'. That is: the me who dreams, imagines, intuits, and the me who observes, dissects and crafts.

Many years ago, immersing myself in ideas for my second novel, I had that rare experience of an already fully-formed character appearing to me in a kind of waking dream. Not unlike what Banville and Krauss describe above, I suddenly saw myself, sitting at my kitchen table, the slow luxury of a Saturday newspaper open on the table before me. It was the first experience I'd had of that 'doubleness' of the self that seems to be an essential part of being a writer.

Everything around me became still – the 'me' that was sitting at the table, that is. The other 'me' was observing, experiencing this strange moment which felt deep and wide and familiar all at once. Each object in the room became more like itself – the teapot like some essential teapot, its presence hyper-real. In the same way, the table felt more solid, the air more charged, the normal domestic bits and pieces around me brighter, more luminous. Where light fell on them, they shimmered. And my heart was pounding, as it often does after a particularly disturbing dream.

I hadn't been frightened, not at all. But in that moment, the moment when I seemed to split from myself, something in my imagination had just given birth to a character I didn't even know I wanted to write about.

He came to me already complete. Even his name presented itself to me: Vinny Farrell. And along with his particular self came the fact that this man's obsession was to find a sense of self, to forge an identity far removed from the deprived, working-class background that he originally came from. Even the title of the novel made itself known to me with such force that I began to believe it had been lying in the interior reaches of my imagination, gestating quietly, waiting for the moment that would ignite it. *A Name for Himself* began a journey into a personal heart of darkness. And Farrell was my guide.

I know there are writers who become impatient at the notion of fictional characters 'taking over' and going where they will. And, of course, I accept that every writer has ultimate control over what we write – but there is still a very real sense in which the character that we begin to imagine has the power to unlock something unexpected within us. That, in their creation, the writer is led down an often startling, entirely unimagined path. In that way, we relinquish control and go where the most interior paths of the creative imagination take us. It's often challenging, difficult work. But it is, in my experience, never less than exhilarating.

Graham Swift observes that the act of writing 'constantly brings you up against yourself and surprises you with the discovery of what you have inside.' This is, as he says 'writing from within' – where else does writing come from? – but that is an entirely different thing from autobiography, or the endless recycling of a writer's life.

I've always been interested in delving into characters who bear no similarity to me: whose lives are different in every possible way. In some kind of inverse process, the more familiar the character, the more difficult he or she is to develop. The more experiences we have in common, the more problematic the invented character's authenticity becomes. Layers of nuance seem to come more easily from deep within the unconscious, from wherever the perception of difference is at its strongest.

And the more extreme the difference, the better. From a man searching for a sense of self whose obsessive love for his wife drives him to commit the ultimate crime, to a young teenager who commits suicide, to a child with a disability; it seems the more distant from my own experience, the deeper I have to dig, the more authentic the fictional character becomes.

In my ninth novel, *The Things We Know Now*, the main character, Daniel, appeared to me as a moving image – in both senses of that word. He was clearly distressed. A young teenager, cycling madly towards home, or perhaps away from it. Back then, I had no idea. I had to write his story in order to find out. I knew only that he was bent on some unnamed act of destruction. I didn't know what he was trying to tell me. I couldn't hear his words. But I saw him very clearly. And my heart went out to him.

After that initial sighting, Daniel wouldn't leave me alone. I saw him everywhere. Eventually, the contours of his nature began to take shape. A golden child, talented, loved and loving, but deeply, inescapably unhappy. That much was immediately clear. But why?

Around the time I was immersing myself in the emerging narrative of Daniel's young life, events in the parallel world – the one we call the 'real' one – were unfolding in a distressing manner. One by one, media reports of young teenagers committing suicide seemed to be everywhere. Bewildered parents, friends, teachers tried to grapple with the 'why' of this sudden and shocking epidemic.

As I wrote, from within the shadow world of the imagination, my character, imperceptibly at first, became transformed into a victim of the relentless cyber-bullying that was everwhere exercising its murderous grip on vulnerable young people.

I hadn't planned it that way. But clearly some writer's antenna had picked up something of what was going on in that other world. I did not write Daniel's story *after* I became aware of the epidemic of teenage suicide: I wrote it *before* I had become aware of it, and then continued to write during the tragedy of its unfolding. It was a contemporaneous activity, not one that came about after a prolonged period of reflection.

I believe that writers often have a sense of what's going on underneath the surface of things – if that doesn't sound too precious. Nadine Gordimer, in her introduction to *Selected Stories* says:

> Powers of observation heightened beyond the normal imply extraordinary disinvolvement: or rather the double process, excessive preoccupation and identification with the lives of others, and at the same time a monstrous detachment ... The tension between standing apart and being fully involved: that is what makes a writer.

And here again is that sense of Atwood's 'slippery double'. The writer, imagining, intuiting, absorbing 'the lives of others', and then sifting, crafting, editing those things we learn in order to produce the illusion of a real person, a character with flaws and strengths and prejudices. A person who does not exist: a person created by a silent agreement between writer and reader.

I think writers are primed to intuit stories. To create them out of silence, or misunderstanding. To be aware of undercurrents of emotion – like stepping into some unfamiliar place and knowing that something strange, or upsetting, or dangerous is about to happen there. A sixth sense? Perhaps not: maybe a dream-sense might be a better description. But it is, above all, a desire to bring something from the inchoate darkness of the dream world out into the light.

Margaret Atwood, in *Negotiating With the Dead* says:

> Possibly, then, writing has to do with darkness, and a desire or perhaps a compulsion to enter it, and, with luck, to illuminate it, and to bring something back out to the light.

For me, the novel *is* character. Plot matters, of course, as does structure and pacing and style and language and voice. But they are essential only in that they illuminate the inner workings, the motivations, the complexities and contradictions of the character into whose skin I have chosen to step, and to inhabit for a long time. Sometimes for years.

Perhaps an extreme example is in one of my latest creations: the character of Mitros in my most recent novel *The Way the Light Falls*.

Some years ago, I embarked on the ambitious project of immersing myself in Greek mythology. I wanted to breathe contemporary life into those myths that evoked in me that most magical of responses: the sudden moment of illumination, of recognition – almost as though something had made its way into an internal writerly stillness that had long been prepared for it, however unconsciously.

In the first novel of the planned trilogy, *The Years That Followed*, I reimagined the character of Clytemnestra, wife of Agamemnon, mother to Iphigenia and Orestes. Female characters rarely get a fair shake in Greek tales, and so I set myself the task of creating the voice of a modern Clytemnestra. She's generally regarded as scheming and vengeful in the tales others tell about her life. I tell the story of a woman raped, kidnapped and abused by her power-hungry husband. A husband who kills his own daughter in order to further his warmongering career. I think any of us might be equally scheming and vengeful, if the circumstances demanded.

In the second novel, *The Way the Light Falls*, I began with a fairly fluid idea of the structure. The main character, Phaedra, was already familiar to me, but in that stiff, on-the-page historical way that told me nothing about what sort of woman she was. I knew I wanted to work with her narrative: to tell Phaedra's story, from her point of view, in a way that would engage a modern audience. And I wanted to stay close to as many elements of the myth as possible.

And so, I needed to invent a family for Phaedra: a mother, a father. A sister, Ariadne, and a half-brother, the Minotaur. I wanted the family dynamic to be as complex as possible. As I looked at this ancient family, and the boy that was half-animal, half-human, something came to me, working its way up from the depths. It seemed to me that the sisters, Ariadne and Phaedra, had an astonishing presence in their family life: a sibling who reminded them of all that was elemental, and of all that was civilised, in one and the same body.

A fourth-century Etruscan wine goblet became further inspiration for my interpretation of Mitros's character. It shows Pasiphae, the mother of the Minotaur, holding her young son in her arms. She gazes at him, tenderly. This unexpected image stuck me forcibly as one of unconditional maternal love. It was not the accepted view of the monster Minotaur: the one who devoured human sacrifice from the centre of his Labyrinth. Because when I thought about it, the human sacrifice was not demanded by the Minotaur himself, but by King Minos, as punishment for the citizens of Athens; a bloody atonement for the death of his son.

And so, in the Minotaur, I had a vision of the character who became Mitros. A boy whose human form was equally challenged, a boy doted on by his parents, loved completely by his sisters. In this waking dream, I saw Mitros as a child with a serious disability. One who was non-verbal, unable to walk, to care for himself, to be independent.

Mitros became, immediately, the first beating heart of my narrative, just as he would become the beating heart of his family. As I wrote, his character took shape. The boy himself, his unexpected humour, his joy in simple things. The love he wrested from everyone around him. The boy who was 'saved', ultimately, by Art.

I have learned, over the past three decades or so, that I cannot 'will' a character into being. It's a process that cannot be forced. It is, above all, a state of being actively passive – not straining anxiously to capture something, but being alert instead to its shadowy presence.

I suppose above all, it is a question of trust, of allowing this elusive 'something' to reveal itself when we are both ready, and when it's no longer possible for us to be separate entities.

In the words of Andrew Miller: 'You have to have faith.'

WORKS CITED:

Atwood, Margaret, *Negotiating With the Dead: A Writer on Writing* (Cambridge University Press, 2002).

Banville, John, 'Fiction and the Dream', *John Banville Translation Project* (www.johnbanville.eu/essay/fiction-and-dream).

Ferrante, Elena, *Frantumaglia: A Writer's Journey* (Europa Editions, 2016).

Gordimer, Nadine, *Selected Stories* (Bloomsbury, 2000).

Krauss, Nicole, *Forest Dark* (Bloomsbury, 2017).

Miller, Andrew, 'How to write fiction', *The Guardian*, 16 October 2011.

Swift, Graham, *Making an Elephant: Writing from Within* (Random House, 2009).

Anne Enright

SHE DOES IT FOR COMFORT

'She does it for comfort.' This rather wondering sentence
was said about me by one friend to another, some decades
ago. They were trying to figure out why I wrote, the way
people wonder what the appeal of running is, in the
winter, for example, or when it is dark. Because many
people fantasise about such a thing – about finishing a
novel or running a marathon – we think how that might
improve our lives, or make it, oddly, worse. It is easy to
see the benefits of running, after you have stopped, but a
writer suffers at the desk for a result that is hard to define.
The pay is often poor. The book is always terrible. It does
not make you feel better. And back you go to do it again.

I took my pulse today, when I was in the middle of
writing a novel. It was lower than when I woke this
morning. What does this mean? That my heart, when I am
working, is more peaceful than when I am at rest.

In the long term – over two or three decades perhaps –
writing does make you feel better. You have to settle in to
it, of course. You have to get used to being alone. It helps if

you like words (but who doesn't?). I still do not know if to name a thing is to possess it or destroy it, but this game – of possession or destruction or of love – that happens in language is one I find deeply pleasurable, almost essential. It seems to me that once you find language you must keep finding it and you must use what you find to the limit of your ability, because the process of writing is the only thing that empties you out and sustains you, both at the same time.

Of course, there are structural concerns; shapes to be discovered, stories to be invented and told. I find writing hard work. I am often lost. Sometimes I am lost for years. I live in uncertainty. The act of production leaves me permanently undone. And yet there is a fugitive sweetness there, that I seek out over and again. Making things up is a lovely thing to do. And it is comforting. I need to write the way some people need to run, just because they have legs. I need it, above all, when the world impinges. I go to the keyboard the way other people go to bed. I wrap myself in work. I dream.

Wendy Erskine

INSPIRATION

Ted Hughes had his fox appearing out of the darkness, just as the Romantics took the Aeolian harp as an analogue for inspiration. An instrument which makes its sound when vibrated by the breeze, this harp suggests the poet/writer as receptor and inspiration as elusive, capricious. I favour the idea of the arcade game, *Penny Falls*, where coins are inserted through a slot perhaps to the sound of beeps and electronic rings of the kind not yet heard on Mount Parnassus. Mostly the new penny causes no movement but sometimes it sets up an unexpected chain which causes a cascade down the metal chute.

For each of the stories in the collection *Sweet Home* I can attempt to trace the notes that blew, the hot and stinking animal that appeared out of the clearing, the chain of coins that fell.

'To All Their Dues' is a story about the owner of a beauty salon, a small-time gangster and his wife. The imperative verb form can be both beseeching or commanding, contingent on situation. I thought about how power could shift in three different situations involving the same three different people, the weak becoming powerful, the powerful becoming weak. I recalled being in a café many years ago when the staff were intimidated by a local thug. His leather jacket looked butter soft. I thought of beauty salons and the obliging response to orders: close your eyes, turn over, bend your knee. And in all of the situations skin; being torn, soft, cut, hit, touched. 'Render therefore to all their dues', Romans 13:7, provided the title.

'Inakeen': a tale of a lonely woman who becomes fascinated with her niqab-wearing neighbours. Two niqabi women once walked past me on the Albertbridge Road in Belfast and a plastic bag caught on the foot of the taller one so she did an elaborate kick to get rid of it. I heard the other woman laugh. I remembered as well a camera course I'd once gone on, the lectures on apertures, the interest in how the light fell on young women's faces. I thought of looking; through a lens, through curtains. The sound of 'Black Sail' by Chastity Belt, the touch of an edge of a curtain, Google Translate, French classes, je m'appelle Wendy, bonjour, au revoir.

'Observation': a teenage girl observes the dynamic between her friend, her friend's mother, and her friend's mother's boyfriend. I noticed people like the friend's mother at the gym as they considered the calibration of the kettle bells. I observed where their straps cut their tattoos in half, the bas-relief of deltoids as they pull down the metal bar. From the top deck of a bus, I saw two girls eating noodles in the bus shelter. One of them looked up to see me watching her. I imagine their sleepovers, lying on a blow-up mattress on the floor, the thinness of the walls of the rooms.

'Locksmiths': Re-grouting a bathroom floor, I scraped out dirt and old cement from between the tiles with a knife. I thought of the skips I pass, filled with rubble and the things that were once the constituent parts of a home – old lamps, tables, sofas. My reading at the time: *God Help the Child* by Toni Morrison, where one woman waits outside prison for another. The skips I pass daily outside houses, the legacy of Le Corbusier in the nearby estate and the things that make up a home – trays, rugs, stains, cups – coalesce with a half-remembered newspaper story about locksmiths in Pamplona who refuse to change the locks of the houses of evictees. And so came a story about a mother being released from jail and her daughter who does not want to share a house with her. D.W. Harding's phrase: 'regulated hatred.'

'Sweet Home': The Chekhov story 'New Villa' is about an engineer and his family who buy a house in the country. They treat the locals with kindness, but these people in turn have little respect for the new arrivals. They prefer masters who act like it. Move it to Belfast, and what, substitute a female architect for the male engineer? A community centre for the engineer's bridge? Keep the disdain versus the generous impetus? In the pristine new community centre the occupants have Blu Tacked A4 pages to the windows. The disruption of design intentions.

'Last Supper': this is a story about a small café that is collaboratively run by a church and a mental health charity. I was thinking of a 3-D piece by the Dutch artist Maurice van Tellingen of a birdhouse in a bleak garden. It's a sanctuary, albeit a sad one. I thought as well of Hemingway's 'A Clean, Well-Lighted Place.' Outside there is apocalypse waiting to happen because the café cannot keep going in the face of dwindling customers and employee misbehaviour. Things fall apart and 'The Second Coming' is transposed to the most mundane of settings, with scones and paninis. There is time for one last supper however. They put down a white paper tablecloth, the manager in the middle as they eat Battenberg cake and drink non-alcoholic cava.

'Arab States: Mind and Narrative': a story where a woman, in an attempt to recapture an aspect of her youth, travels from Belfast to Newcastle upon Tyne to hear an author talk about his book. This writer is someone she briefly knew at university. A row of shops near Wansbeck Road Metro Station. A night in a hotel room, untethered from the paraphernalia of home. In my mind, *Death in Venice*, Aschenbach's dyed hair and painted face, converges with adverts for anti-ageing and illuminating creams.

'Lady and Dog': a middle-aged Protestant schoolteacher develops an unlikely romantic interest in a young Gaelic football player who comes to give lessons to the children in her class. 'The Lady with the Dog' by Chekhov presented itself. In this story there would also be a man, a woman, a dog and an affair but they would be connected differently. A box of pencils and a mechanical pencil sharpener where the shavings fall into the plastic container suggested the repeated, precise movements of the teacher. I remembered someone who said that they would not, on ideological grounds, eat the green sweet in any packet of Fruit Pastilles. Celtic signifiers, sweets and mugs, the enormity of the unsaid.

'77 Pop Facts you did not know about Gil Courtney' is an account, told in a list of 'pop facts', of the life of a reclusive musician who spends the last of his days in the house where he was born. Here, over thirty years of reading music books and magazines generated names and places, failures and missed opportunities, successes and thrills: *Smash Hits*, No 1, *Record Mirror*, *Flexipop*, *Hellfire* by Nick Tosches, reading accounts of Eric Burdon's mother, Lester Bangs, Greil Marcus, Ian Hunter, *Diary of a Rock and Roll Star*; reading about Arthur Russell, Nicky Hopkins, Gene Clark, Alex Chilton. I thought about visiting Keats's grave in the Protestant Cemetery in Rome and reading the lines on his grave 'Here lies one whose name was writ in water'.

'The Soul has no Skin' takes its title from a few lines from Bukowski:

> the soul has no skin: the soul only has insides that want to sing, finally, can't you hear it, brothers? Softly, can't you hear it brothers? A hot piece of ass and a new Cadillac ain't going to solve a god-damned thing.

It is a story about a young man with a chronic skin condition who works in a shop in Belfast. Despite a stoical attitude, he has difficulty forgetting past events. I thought about the people I see at bus stops early in the morning, quietly waiting in their liveried work clothes. But, most of all, I thought of my favourite scene from any film. It's from *Crazy Love* by Dominique Deruddere, based on various Bukowski stories. Harry Voss goes to the bathroom to cover his terrible skin with toilet roll so he can dance with the beautiful girl as 'Love Hurts' plays.

That's how my pennies fell, more or less.

Mia Gallagher

ANSWERING ANNIE

When we write, we go looking for Trouble.
– Ted Deppe (from talk 'Making Trouble for Yourself,
Making Trouble for Others'), Dingle, 2018

Writing as Pain, Writing as Trouble? Mmm.
I'd love to hear someone talk about Writing as Joy.
– Annie Deppe (in conversation, paraphrased from memory), Dingle, 2018

The questions jam my brain. I flail about, my ideas hopping like mosquitos. First I draw a spider-map, and from that decide to write freely for an hour. Nothing much comes, beyond some words around the challenges that the representation of multi-dimensional action, unfolding in and through the body, places on the linear, cerebral process that is writing. At the end of this, I do another mind-map. The word 'impossible' appears twice. On my next session, I plump down at the PC, with the intention of discussing the conditions that support my writing. I have Andrew O'Hagan's distinction between auditory and visual writers in my mind and I'm thinking I'll explore my own auditoryness – specifically, my need for silence at key stages of the writing process – but very quickly I begin to write about getting hung-up, at final proofs stage, on visual layout and commas. Then I find myself writing about longhand and typing and I realise how different my attitude is to 'mistakes' I make in each mode, and this leads me into an experiment where I try to type the way I write – not correcting, just keeping going – and this throws up more unexpected information, like how, in anticipating errors, I hold my breath when I type, something I don't do when I write, and how I never learnt to type with my little finger properly, so there's always a jolt before I reach for 'q' or a quote mark, and how, when I make a 'mistake', instead of pausing the way I do in longhand before fluidly moving on, leaving the error uncorrected to write the next word, I keep jabbing at the keys, creating an arpeggio of wrongness, and I conclude with the realisation that, contrary to my argument, I am, at times, a writer most definitely trapped by the visual.

On my next session, I start fresh, trying to reclaim the aural, except half a paragraph in I'm writing about longhand again, trying to describe the experience, how it feels, how I think doing it, and then I'm onto flow, but now anxiety is setting in because I've written about longhand recently for another essay and I'm worried I'll just repeat myself. By this point, I may have already made the third mind-map – containing the words 'revenge', 'retribution', Ted Deppe's name and the phrase 'R. in the garden' – though I don't know anymore because I haven't dated it. Maybe this is why I start pushing the piece into a new direction, about R., a young person I know. This material feels promising, but before I know it, my hour is up, so I stop. Next day, overwhelmed by the different directions I've gone in, I decide to make a stab at po-mo; I'll write up the process of creating this piece as a quasi-scientific experiment. I go at it with gusto; a day later, when I read the text, I realise it's flat and pretentious.

The results are in. So far, I've failed because I'm avoiding the hardest question.

What is the purpose of writing?

When I'm not writing, I've no idea. By this, I mean I don't know why *I*, more than anyone else, should write. I grew up believing it's important to contribute to society, to use my skills to make a material, positive difference. When I'm not engaged in artistic work, it's easy to feel that what I do doesn't amount to much; it's just feeding the machine of capitalist-consumerism or my own lonely ego. It's then I wonder if I should do something more worthwhile, like teaching young people, or return to working in an addiction treatment centre. At the same time, I'm aware a small wizened bit of me wants the world to throw up its hands in horror and go 'Oh No, You Must Write'. Yet I know the whole tortured dialogue is bullshit, because the moment I start into the next project the agonising will stop. Here's my shame: I write, in the first instance, because I feel worse when I don't.

I recently spoke in Dingle at a residential week run by Bay Path University as part of their MFA in Creative Writing. My topic was 'Sitting with the Pain'. In preparation for the talk, I'd emailed a group of writers from WORD (a collective that meets quarterly at the Irish Writers Centre), asking them what stages of the writing process were painful for them, and how they dealt with it. The answers were funny, honest and articulate. They spoke about RSI, conflict during the publication process, and the trauma of filling in funding applications. A lot of the writers talked of doubt – losing faith in your ability to say anything, thinking what you're writing is shit, or that you're no good as a writer. Others described process issues: not being able to start a project, getting stuck in the middle, trying to finish, having to let work go. Many spoke about the pain of *not* writing. All the answers resonated with me, the last one in particular.

John Cleese once said when asked to advise would-be actors: *Don't do it if you want to, do it if you need to.* This is great advice, but it took me a long time to realise that writing for me is a question of need, and for the act of writing itself above the need to say something through it. I can't recall ever *wanting* to be a writer. When I was a kid, I just wrote. I wasn't aware of feeling bad when I didn't, but then I was always playing at something. Reading, dress-up, drawing, ball games, wandering, running, chasing. I loved making stuff up, acting it out or giving life to the inanimate. With my cousin Karen, I'd often assume the role of *auteur*, directing siblings and neighbours in the creation of long, meandering plays. In my early to mid-teens, I continued to play; I wrote terrible poetry, made paintings of David Bowie from his album covers, turned my essay assignments from English class into short stories and joined the Dublin Youth Theatre. The year I left school, I started making paintings influenced by Jugendstil and J.G. Ballard and devised a theatre piece with friends from the DYT; that summer, after visiting Amalfi, I wrote a short story about a swimming pool attendant. The stage, it seemed, was set for something. Then in November, at 17, I went to Germany to au pair.

I au paired for six months, but I always say 'a year' when I talk about that time because it had such a formative impact on me. On my first day there, I collected the youngest of my charges, M., from playschool. When we returned, his mother asked me to play with him in his room for an hour before his siblings came home. At the start, it was fun in a nostalgic kind of way, muddling around with his wooden farmyard animals and miniature shop full of tiny wooden things, giving them voices and names, watching him invest in the imagined universe unfurling in front of him.

It was like acting the role of a child, a role I'd only recently divested myself from (or so I thought), and I liked acting, and M. was a good audience. '*Nochmal*,' he'd shout. 'Again!' After a while, I started thinking ahead to lunch. Because once his siblings were back and we'd eaten, then surely I'd do what I normally did when I babysat in Ireland – read or catch up on my German grammar, keeping an eye on the kids as they played their own games, only getting involved the odd time, only if they asked.

I can't remember checking the time during that hour, but I remember feeling very dazed, almost out-of-it, by the time lunch was called. Once I'd done the dishes, I sat down at the table and took out my book. The kids were messing around in the drawing-room, visible through the dividing doors. Their mother came in. She frowned. '*Bitte*,' she said, '*spiel mit den Kindern.*' *Please, play with the children. Huh?* I thought, and there I was, swept upstairs with the kids, down on hands and knees, making stuff up again, out of it again, till 6 o'clock sounded and it was time for *Sesamstrasse* and *Abendbrot*.

My terms of employment were basic: bed, board and pocket money in exchange for looking after the children and light housework. No time off had been specified beyond the evenings. Not having any daytime activities planned or friends to meet, I ended up playing with those kids every weekday from 11.30am to 6pm and all day on the weekends, holidays included.

I think I went a little mad that year. Time is different when you're younger, minutes can feel like days, but those hours I spent playing with the German children stretched into something else altogether. Trapped, bored stupid, I felt myself shrink against the infinite cliff-face of each afternoon, reduce to the size of the children. At the same time I felt too big, squashed like Alice into a house that refused to fit me. What do you do when the things you love to do become things you have to do, when play becomes work? I think it's significant that I didn't write much that year, though I did a lot of drawing and painting in those few hours in the evening that I could call my own.

I painted landscapes, cityscapes and trees. The paintings were usually a response to a visual cue I'd see on my walks or out a window – a forest glade, the purple hue of a twilight. I'd see a shape and colour in my mind and when I sat down to paint, would start making marks; either with pastel or acrylic. Sometimes a figure or other form would come first, then a background; other times abstract shapes would emerge, making the background, and I'd incorporate a figure on top. Behind the visual impetus, there was always something else, something wordless, that I wanted to communicate. A physical-emotional feeling. A tone I hoped would sound through the work.

Adam Wyeth, one of the writers I surveyed for 'Sitting with the Pain', talks about creativity as 'serious play'. 'As Hemingway said, [says his email] writing is easy, you just sit by the typewriter and bleed. Bleeding sounds like pain here, but bleeding itself isn't actually painful?' My dominant memory of making those paintings is feeling a sense of calmness. Was I bleeding painting them? It seemed more like an act of capture – though letting a tone sound is a release, of sorts, isn't it? While that calm feeling, isn't that a bit like the effect of the blood-letting done by doctors of old, to balance their patients' humours?

And now I realise I'm wrong in saying I didn't write much in Germany. In fact I wrote lots. Letters, long ones, every day, to family, friends, anyone who'd reached out to me. With some correspondents I only mentioned the good stuff; with others I shared the bad, particularly my difficulties with the kids. I'm interested in why I so readily overlooked my letters as 'writing'. What need didn't they meet? What purpose didn't they serve? Those texts were serious, but there was no sign of play in them, and writing them didn't feel like letting go of anything.

In 2011, interviewed by Robert Crum, Michael Ondaatje spoke about a phrase he had once read: 'people who lose their childhood eventually have to retrieve it'. I enjoyed most of my childhood, but I hated the last six months of it before I turned eighteen. There were positives: I learnt German, I met some great people, I saw wonderful places. But the experience of au pairing was to change the foundations of my relationship with myself, and not just because of the boredom. I was living in what was tantamount to an abusive situation – the children verbally or physically attacked me every day – but instead of leaving, I made myself stay. As the weeks passed, my trust in myself frayed. In its place accumulated a profound unease, a sense of bad faith that oozed into my life for years afterwards, affecting my experiences of intimacy, family, work and play.

It seems to me that my entire adult life as an artist has been about reclaiming that lost part of my childhood: learning to seize back those six months, those endless hours in the playroom, re-own my imagination, play the way I want to, need to, not the way someone else has made me. I play now, seriously and with a vengeance. I play because if I don't, I feel bad. And if I feel bad, I'm not good for anything.

Five and a half years after returning from Germany, I wrote a story, 'Departure', which felt different to anything I'd written before – apart, perhaps, from that very early story about the swimming pool attendant. I've discussed 'Departure' in other essays because it was such a watershed; it was personal and revealing and I felt reluctant to show it to anyone when I'd finished it. In terms of this piece, I can see I definitely bled into it, though the bleeding itself wasn't painful. But nor did it seem like play; more like channelling. I became a conduit for a voice, a stream of images and, most of all, a feeling: shame, that core of bad faith in myself. In the years after Germany, I'd previously tried approaching this unease through writing. But I'd always found myself skittering away, into heightened genre, or abstract ideas influenced by my time in college. In painting, I'd got closer, making dark, stylised pieces of hairless humanoids eviscerating themselves or huddled for protection under the roots of a dying tree. I'm a little embarrassed writing about them now. Oh God, I want to say, aren't they so adolescent? I'm not sure if they were a successful release of blood, but I knew making them was a conscious attempt to get a handle on my unhappiness, to communicate it – though I'm not sure to whom. As in Germany, I'd start with an image: something I'd seen in real life, or from a deeper, unconscious place. This was always linked to an emotional feeling, or to a set of conflicting feelings. Then I'd begin mark-making. The act of painting felt serious, but playful too: I was working with oil and I remember the flash of satisfaction when I'd discover a new way of creating dimension or light with the materials. When the pieces emerged, there was a tone sounding in them; bloody, yes, at times painful, but they also felt strangely organised, far more resolved than what was going on inside. Later a friend told me that in order to really communicate, to convey meaning through paint, I needed to know the language better.

By the time I wrote 'Departure', I was ready to go back to words, my other language, one I knew I had a better grasp on. Writing that story, I knew there was a wound there, but the act itself wasn't wounding. It flowed. I've happened on flow in other work since, sometimes when writing about troubled fictional situations, or digging into my own pain, sometimes just writing. Like this passage in my second novel, *Beautiful Pictures of the Lost Homeland*:

She steps into the shimmery mirage of wobbling air. The lane breathes out and the sounds of the neighbourhood fade, leaving her quarantined in a hidden dimension of silence. Under the sun's glare, the images around her sharpen: hotch-potch limestone render, a patchwork of doors leading to other people's back gardens; scruffy dandelion heads and parched green weeds in tiny triangles of dirt. Halfway down the lane gleams the disintegrating carcass of the stolen Cortina the robbers dumped there at the start of summer. Something percolates up through her awareness; something is not right. The broken and whole bits of the car are bouncing back white splinters of sun that hurt her eyes. The tyres are flat and droopy, as if melting into the ground. The crack in the back windscreen, extrapolated into a frosty, glittering spiderweb, stares at her. From its crazed glass eye comes the sound of music.

It is a tinny sound, faint but recognisable. The sound of a transistor radio playing pop, the type of music Joanie Flynn listens to, the type that makes your feet want to tap and your bottom and shoulders shake. Curious, cautious, Georgie draws closer. A flicker of movement behind the windscreen. She stops. The lane breathes in. Georgie finds herself looking into a pair of cool, heavy-lidded eyes reflected in the rearview mirror.

A couple of the images had appeared in earlier drafts, but the passage as a whole came later. I remember writing it with a sense of integration, aware of being neurologically invested in multiple modes simultaneously. Feeling, emotionally and kinaesthetically, the attitude, body and action of the character in their world. At the same time seeing what they see, hearing what they hear, smell, taste and touch. I think – though I'm not sure – that the emotion/kinesis comes first, then the images, then the other senses. As I begin recording, I realise I'm thinking in words, seeing/hearing the scene unfold, getting it down, dancing with it. There are, I see now, so many parallels between this and painting. Shape, colour, feeling; a tone sounding through the work. Is this the bleeding that's play?

Last July I had an intense conversation with Ireland's new Fiction Laureate, Sebastian Barry. He's doing a series of podcasts over the next three years, interviewing Irish writers about the point of writing. He's releasing the podcasts on a phased schedule, so I won't say too much about our chat here, apart from the fact that I was surprised by how easy it was for me to talk about purpose when I spoke about reading, rather than writing.

Reading is a gift that I'm privileged to have. I'm educated, unlike many women past and present; I live in a society that allows relative freedom of access to texts of all kinds; and I don't have dyslexia or other conditions that make reading difficult. I love it. When I read a book that *gets* me, I'm gone. I'm not out there anymore, in the untenable present. I'm in there, with them, the characters. With a special book, I carry its people and world around with me for days, and I try not to watch telly or read something else straight after I've finished in case it contaminates the experience.

During my time in Germany, reading aloud to the children was the one bit of play with them I had no problem with. In spite of my bad mispronunciations, it seemed to calm the kids, providing a respite from the hours of insults, running away and violence that constituted their usual MO with me. Like my paintings, it calmed me too, allowing me a way out of our enforced collaborative playtime, the children's capricious game-rules. It was no longer on me to entertain, serve as jester, come up with ideas, or try to control their behaviour. I could let the book do that. Reading kept us away from the dangerous cliff-edge of boredom; by allowing us access into the writers' worlds, it also gave us a space we could share as equals – our differences temporarily surrendered to the power of story. Crucially, reading let me get away from myself; the powerless, inept, eejity Irish *Kindermädchen* I became every time we played Shop or Farm or Cowboy & Jesus.

It's a wonderful feeling, to be undivided, even just for a moment.

When I painted, a key part of the process was showing the work to others. I wanted them to see something: the images, but also the tone bleeding out through them. Maybe I wanted them to see me, what was going on under the surface. With writing too, the act is not just for myself, but also for readers. I want readers to see, hear and feel the characters and the world I've created. I want them to 'get' whatever tone I am trying to imbue the text with, even if I, and they, don't know what they're getting. I want them to immerse themselves in the act of reading, find undivision inside the text, forget themselves, like I do when I read. However, I don't think I'm writing to be seen, in the same way I wanted to be seen through my paintings. I want my readers, maybe, to see what's going on under their own surface.

Adam Wyeth said something else in his email which stuck with me: 'There are several ways in which we bleed, from giving blood to the menstrual cycle, and then, of course, there's blood sacrifice, an offering to the gods.' Maybe it's hubristic to claim that writing has a fundamentally spiritual purpose. I could argue that storytelling has roots in shamanistic practice, or draw parallels between what I do and the catharsis of the first Athenian theatre festivals where the city's population came out to the amphitheatres, and by participating in stories enacted by masked actors, attempted to feel, share, and transmute their collective pain. But this feels very big, and my blood sacrifice – if that's what it is – is a small thing. I can't see it saving lions or halting the forward momentum of the plastic sea. My booksales to date have a modest reach and, unlike the Athenians, we live in a fragmented cultural multiverse, so I'm not sure how collective a catharsis my work might trigger. Even though there'll be individuals who get that feeling of immersion reading my work, there'll probably always be someone who doesn't. But I still need to do it. I still do it. And part of that doing is wanting others to read it.

In the past, if someone asked why I didn't have kids, I used to joke that my experience as an au pair put me off it. But the truth is, I've never had a *grá* for motherhood; if I'd wanted children of my own, I think I'd have gone for it. I'm happy with my choice, though it's meant I've needed to actively create opportunities to meet younger people on this planet, through teaching or hanging out with my friends' children. Like C. and A. from Cork – gifted and sensitive, one about to finish secondary school, the other about to enter it – or D. and L., from Dún Laoghaire, adult now, both skilled writers in their own right, making fresh stories in Dublin and Berlin. Eighteen-year-old B. in London too, with his wicked sense of humour, and G. in Ringsend, who I often catch observing our adult goings-on with an amused glint in his ten-year-old eyes. Or the other C., living near Blessington Street Basin, who sings and paints and recently decided I should be her godmother (oh, pride!), and her sister S., nimble and mischievous tiny dancer. I love being with these young people, listening to them, witnessing their creative exploits. I've even loved playing with them.

And so I'm back to the start of this essay, with R., who appeared in my second spider-map. At the time of writing, R. is ten, 41 years my junior. She's also a fellow-Taurean and, like me, the daughter of a writer-actor named Miriam. About eight years ago, I spent a weekend in R.'s house in County Clare. We played adventure games on her kitchen floor, pretending to be cats and using her toys as other characters. At one point, I realised where I was: on the ground, at child-level, the place where I'd played with the German kids. In writing now, I try to re-engage with what I felt in that moment of recognition. My psyche gingerly reaches in, a tongue poking a gap where a tooth used to be, the place inside where the past lives. What do I expect? Pain? A rush of blood? What do I feel? Nothing. Just a sense of okayness. The game with R. was, in fact, great fun. A few months after that visit I found myself facing a major setback. I'd finished my second novel, but no publisher wanted to pick it up. It was around then that I made a decision to write not because I'd anything to say, or the world wanted me to, but because I had to.

Are these moments connected? I'm not sure, but it feels like there's something interesting at work there.

Now the years spin forward, and it's August 2018, a week into trying to write this essay. R. and I are sitting in her back garden in Ranelagh, four streets away from where I grew up. Miriam, her mum, is out at a screening of *The Meg*; R. didn't want to go because the trailer creeped her out, so I'm babysitting.

The grass is dry and rough. It's been the hottest summer since 1976. One of R.'s cats, crazy Frankie, is curled up against a very low wall, his haunches in shade while his head still gets the rays. R. and I are lying on a woollen blanket on top of which is a cotton spread, yellow, patterned with flowers. R. has just read me the start of her latest novel-in-progress. It's compelling, I say, when she asks what I think. What does that mean? She'll ask me later. Well, I'll say, starting to explain the word 'compel' – No, she'll say, I know what the word means. I want to know what *makes* it compelling.

This is a great question: the type it took me years as an adult to learn to ask when I wanted feedback. But Miriam, who approaches parenting with the rigorous commitment of an artist, taught R. baby sign language when she was an infant so they could communicate before R. learnt to verbalise words. So it's not surprising that R. has learnt, much younger than many kids, how to ask for things, and that when she asks, she'll be understood.

Well, I say again ... then I begin to articulate what's compelling about R.'s work. The fact that it's happening in the present tense, through the form of a letter conversation between two girls, Thea and Brey. The tense, I say, makes me feel that it's very urgent. Something might happen to Thea any moment – it might happen NOW. I'm gripped by R.'s use of the second person. It makes me feel like I'm Brey when Thea's speaking, and Thea when Brey is, and this makes me feel I'm *in* the story, not just listening to it. I tell R. that I also admire her choice to have Brey ask Thea questions; it's a great way of getting the story out. Thea HAS to answer Brey, and Brey HAS to wait for the answers, and that's compulsion.

My anxiety about the purpose of my creative work stems from lots of things: upbringing, education, the year in Germany, my own mosquito-hopping curiosity. It took me ages to trust my adult voice, the things I wanted – *needed* – to say. My song, as Sebastian Barry might put it. The only way I can find purpose in any individual act of writing is to discover what interests me, latch onto that, and follow its course. The only way I can do that is by asking enough questions, until I come to the hardest one. Then, having faith that the difficulty itself is a key to something, stop; allow myself feel, see, hear, taste and smell, and start putting down the words that arise in response to those sensations. Sometimes there's flow, sometimes the words come one at a time, trickling slowly onto the page. Sometimes they make a shape that might, if I'm lucky, carry something like blood in it.

As the hot evening lowered over that Ranelagh garden so like the one my childhood self played in, R. drew a picture of me. Then it was my turn. I've long given up on the idea that I can paint my bad faith, let it bleed onto a canvas or piece of watercolour paper. My pictures in words seem to release more effectively whatever my creativity requires out. Over the years I've destroyed and got rid of a few of my paintings – the dystopian ones I did in college and the one my friend said showed how I wasn't a painter – but I've kept all the others, including the little twilit skylines and Alpine forestscapes that I made in Germany. Maybe I've held onto them because of the calmness that emanates from them, the calmness I remember experiencing as I made them. You'd never know that painter was going a little mad. If there's blood in those marks, it's hard to see. Or maybe I've kept them because they offer a touchstone; a continuum that's endured from child me to adult me.

Although I've left painting behind, I still love drawing. It's so unloaded. All I have to do is look, see and make a mark. Not worry about purpose, or meaning, or readers, or the right word, or being misunderstood, or judged, or my own bad head. Everytime I draw, I think Christ, I should do more.

Hey, I said to R., curious, still thinking at the back of my mind about conditions and aural and visual writers and what a great essay that would make. 'You know when you're drawing, R., or you're writing, what sort of feelings do you have?' 'What d'you mean?' said R. 'Well,' I said, 'I'm just wondering if, you know, there's a different feeling between one or the other.' 'Hmm,' said R. She thought. 'No,' she said eventually. 'It's the same. Bliss.'

Anne Haverty

THE SENTENCE

Life

Life and writing, writing and life ... Symbiotic, mutually dependent, each intermittently awful and intermittently joyful. Bound together while at the same time being inimical to each other. To a writer they can look like enemies; or competitors, like jealous children competing for her allegiance.

It's not only a question of time to write, though time to write is nearly everything to a writer. It's a question of psychic occupation.

Death

For this writer – for all writers? – there is a certain shame in that the living of life by people who are not writers can look to her like a waste of time. Like a lesser means of passing the time. There is also envy. She envies their ability to look forward simply and wholeheartedly to the next football match or holiday or party. Oh, she can look forward to a holiday or a party. But what she really looks forward to is the next bout of writing. This looking forward is suffused with terror. She envies those who do not write their freedom from this terror.

The terror may be a refuge from the terror of death. This could be a reason for writing. A reason allied to the need to attempt to interpret the intractable, the heart and the soul, allow them to speak out of their secrecy and solitude.

And yet she is involved in life, in her own life and in life itself, because it's beautiful and seductive as much as it's awful. And anyway you can't write if you don't live. (Whether you have to 'have a life' to write is another question). But there is always that problem, the struggle between the self in the world and the secret writing self. The self in the world may not want it; but what her writing self secretly wants is to be Philip Larkin's 'shit in the shuttered chateau', disengaged and free. Free for what? This is a daily problem the writer faces. You could call it the daily torment.

The Chateau

My chateau is a small room with two windows, one looking north, the other west; the brightest and coldest place in the house. But I don't use it. It has for various reasons been closed since my beloved, the poet and writer Anthony Cronin, died two and a bit years ago. I mean to return there. But for the moment I can't. For the moment I move, carrying my writing apparatus, notebooks, pen, laptop, from couch to kitchen table to the other table, depending on how and where the light outside is coming in. Always feeling, is this possible, is this finishable, is it any good. And why this idea that it should be 'good'? When 'bad' writing is often what people prefer to read? But whatever I feel about it, I never feel it's a waste of time, or a means of passing the time.

Where does this sensation that only writing is not a waste of time come from? If my job was essential to maintaining life, a doctor keeping people alive, say, or a farmer cultivating their food, would I also regard time away from the job as a waste? I will never know. I know only that good writing which is food for the soul -- yes, whatever that is -- is no less necessary for our welfare and happiness than medicine or milk. Necessary for the reader's soul and the writer's soul, necessary for humanity. Even if humanity often fails to recognise it.

Truth

Writers don't answer questions, they ask them. This is why Politics is perilous to writing. Politics provides answers, excluding other answers and other questions. But politics with a small p, the politics of the interpersonal, of how we relate to one another, what we do to each other and what we mean to each other, what our relation to the world is and what the world's is to us – this is the matrix of art. It won't be quantifiable in stats and figures but it can be as important and as transformative in the body politic as Politics seeks to be.

Art is inherently political, a suggestion of how our lives could be different or better if he or she didn't do or say this, or they weren't like that.

To the question of truth though the writer must own the answer. Without truth – whatever that is, yes, though like the soul we know it when we see it – we fall into loneliness and despair. Writing is one of the few means left to us to display the truth. Truth sounds serious, it sounds grim. But it can be joyous and playful. Good writing is playful, even when it's profound. My latest novel, *Fidelity*, is the first novel I've written that may be lacking in playfulness in that it isn't funny. Is this a development in me or a failing? Did I write it in more sombre a mood than I like to write? Have I given in to the new grimness and humourlessness of the culture?

Taking the Dog for a Walk

Writing well can feel like labour. To the mind it can feel like being doomed to hard labour for life. And to the body too which longs to be on the move, would rather be washing the dishes or taking the dog for a walk. But walking the dog is a time when the best line can turn up. An illumination, an insight. A sentence with a cadence, a tone, a distillation that you know is invincible. The trick is to remember it. And not to be disappointed by its banality when you see it written down. A line that comes when you're walking the dog, or walking yourself from the shop or the meeting, or have just woken up – some poems have come to me entire on waking up – is a joy and a solace. You hurry home with it as you hurry home to your beloved.

Love

Writing is akin to love. The preoccupation with it that excludes other interests and concerns. The wish for consummation. The disappointments, the illusions and disillusions. As reading is akin to love. Between the good writer and the good reader there is an emotional and intellectual and instinctual exchange. One mind speaks to another, a heart feels for another.

Writing and reading can serve as a substitute for love, if they have to. The writer's relation with the reader, the ideal reader, could be compared to the relationship with the beloved. Even if, looking around you in the tram going to and from the city you ruefully, realistically, think, no one here would be interested in reading my poem or my novel. The ideal reader is one who savours the fall of your sentences. Who 'gets' you, gets your way of seeing the world, gets your jokes and what you mean to say.

And in the tram there are more people than there were a year ago who are reading real books and not looking at screens. I haven't seen anyone reading a book of mine yet. But it gives me hope. It gives me hope that the reading of books and the writing of books will go on despite all the signs that they won't.

Neil Hegarty

PUT IT IN WRITING

Some years ago, I happened to reread Derek Mahon's poem 'A Disused Shed in County Wexford'. I was directed towards it, in fact, by a friend who is a poet: *You should read this again*, she said – and so I did. We had been talking about the ways in which a writer can think about their work, about the means by which they can nourish the life they have chosen, and give it a sustained sense of focus. I was at that time in the midst of a substantial non-fiction project: *The Story of Ireland*, a history of Ireland written to accompany the BBC-RTÉ television series of the same title – and so I was naturally absorbed in our common, and individual, and conflicting stories, pulling them apart, and meshing them together again. And I was working too on fiction, snatching time here and there, as it presented itself.

I read Mahon's poem, in which 'a thousand mushrooms crowd to a keyhole': and meaning and focus were for me renewed. As the launch in Dublin of *The Story of Ireland*, I quoted one of the lines in the poem: this work is much anthologised and appreciated, and I knew that my listeners would recognise the words – and it was true, I heard the breath, and the murmur in the room as I invoked the image of the mushrooms growing in the dark in the abandoned shed, straining for the thin single beam of light shining through the keyhole, for the possibility of illumination and redemption and change:

> They are begging us, you see, in their wordless way,
> To do something, to speak on their behalf
> Or at least not to close the door again.

I remember feeling the constriction in my throat as I spoke, and the welling of emotion that accompanied the words. I also remember the sense that this emotion had caught me unawares – but I think now that I ought not to have felt surprised, because it is a powerful thing to have one's *credo* thus encapsulated, and even more powerful to speak that *credo* aloud. For, while it is a commonplace that writers 'tell stories', the ubiquity of this remark can disguise the duty and obligation we have to catch at lives and histories that are silenced and lost, one by one, generation by generation – and revivify and honour them in writing.

A colonised society understands this duty and obligation: understands it intellectually, instinctively, emotionally – and understands too its moral force. Colonisation brings with it a great silencing: silence being *both* a powerful weapon and shield against the effects of colonisation, a potent means of withholding consent – *and* a form of poison when permitted to become internalised. We know all about silence in Ireland, as a result both of colonial history, and the effects of overweening church power and authority – and it is only now, in our contemporary society, that we are shaking off that particular curse. And it remains the task of the writer to catch at the stories that haven't been told, that have been silenced.

When my novel *Inch Levels* began to form in my head, I set out to explore a silence. The story pivots on a secret, on a story that dare not be told, that has its roots in a real-life episode sixty years previously, in the neutral wartime Ireland of 1943. In the spring of that year, a sea mine detonated on a west Donegal beach, and killed nineteen men and boys – a devastating loss of life in a remote townland already decimated by emigration. There was no secret about this disaster – how could there be? – but neither was it much discussed, either at the time or in the decades that followed. Wartime history, wartime neutrality, deaths in a conflict that officially was not Ireland's conflict – these factors conspired to close down history, to have it fall away. As I wrote in the afterword to the novel, this episode of history became 'secluded'.

When I enquired of acquaintances in that district of Donegal, seeking to pick their brains and their local knowledge, I found my questions slapped away in exasperation. *Those fellas*, said one, speaking of these long-dead men and boys, *they shouldn't have been down on that beach in the first place*. I was taken aback – but I took the energy and the understanding of the remark, and distilled it into the novel I was writing, and let it do its work. And so, when *Inch Levels* was published, I felt I had honoured that episode in history, as best I could.

And I understand silence, and its spacious hinterlands. I grew up in Northern Ireland, and this fact inculcates an acute sensitivity to the presence of stories and histories not told, or redacted, or rejected, or dismissed. When we drove across the border from Derry into Donegal and back again – heading for the beach, heading home again – we would fall silent as the car approached the border checkpoint, with its teenaged British soldiers, dangerously nervy, dangerously armed. 'Don't speak to the Brits,' as Colette Bryce has it in her poem, 'just pretend they don't exist': and so we drove and flowed from one freedom towards the other, maintaining silence, and aware of its heft, and its power to speak volumes. And when we do speak in

Northern Ireland, as Anna Burns recognises in *Milkman*, it tends to be in code, deploying heavily ritualised and ceremonial language – and whatever we say, as Heaney observed, we say nothing.

The result – of training, of context – is an awareness of the character of language, as well as its obverse of silence. Language is a tool and a weapon, to be turned to any end: to nullify experience – or to transfuse it, and give it renewed meaning and life, and to create a space, textual and social, where none existed before. It is inherently personal, and social, and political. It must be all of these.

Lately, I have completed a new novel, *The Jewel*, to be published in 2019. Sections of the narrative are set in Ireland, but most of the story takes place elsewhere – in England, in Germany. The characters in this story each look for a place they can call home, with varied results. They negotiate crossings, and borders, and silences, and they work as best they can with the ability of words both to summon truth and to conceal it. In this case, the writing of *The Jewel* has allowed me to create new textual and social spaces, to make sense of certain ideas, to create a play of light and shadow – and then to hand that space over, complete with its shadows, for others to inhabit and use as they see fit.

I put it in writing, and pass it on.

Sophia Hillan

'WHAT IS THE PURPOSE OF WRITING FOR YOU?'

'I rhyme/ To see myself, to set the darkness echoing.'

It was, of course, Seamus Heaney who wrote those memorable closing words to his poem 'Personal Helicon'. Though I neither rhyme, nor aspire to, the words resonate with me, not least because shortly after the time of its publication in *Death of a Naturalist*, I had the good fortune to be his student in the English Department of Queen's University Belfast during the momentous years of 1968–1972. At that time, in that place, it seemed to many of us impossible to do anything but react or respond, whether directly or obliquely, in words. Some, like my contemporaries Medbh McGuckian and Paul Muldoon, made their mark early and were deservedly heard and lauded: others, like myself, felt unable to articulate what we thought until the upheavals of our lives had somehow settled into what passed for normality. I don't mean to suggest that my purpose was to write about what is euphemistically described as our 'Troubles': it was rather to find out how to write within its ever-present context.

Critics of Jane Austen are inclined to accuse her of ignoring the Napoleonic War, while I maintain that she had no need to write of it directly: fear of invasion, or of the death of loved ones in that war was simply a fact of life for her readers; and I think that Anna Burns, in *Milkman*, has most tellingly and intelligently addressed our similar awareness of the dread that dared not speak its name.

Living in a permanent state of cautious awareness, I found myself unable to write seriously until the end of another decade, until I was necessarily distant — if only by a hundred miles — from the place where I had grown up. Suddenly in a different Irish town; suddenly, though on the same island, among people and politics other than my own, it seemed that something of the darkness that had fallen on my place and my time cleared a little. I finally began, as Kavanagh had urged, to look beyond the provincial to the universal and, perhaps, to return to Seamus Heaney's striking metaphor, 'to set the darkness echoing'.

I believe my original intention was to discover through the medium of fiction, and specifically the short story, for its unique ability to penetrate quickly and sharply to the heart of an issue, what it was I valued and wanted to restore in myself and beyond. At first, I concentrated on what I knew best, which was the world I had experienced as a child. My earliest short story, recently republished by Arlen House as 'The Broom Tree House' in my collection, *The Cocktail Hour*, won a prize in 1979 in a BBC competition run by one of our Northern pioneers, Sam Hanna Bell, who had twenty years before championed the controversial work of playwright Sam Thompson and taken on the blank intransigence of the then Unionist controllers of the arts. My next, 'The Cliff Path', won a prize at Listowel in 1980 from Bell's Dublin-based counterpart, the great Irish editor, David Marcus, and made the final shortlist the following year for a Hennessy

Award. I felt after these validations that I had found where I wanted to be and to go: and the impression was confirmed in 1980 when I was introduced to a writer whose work I had long admired: Seamus Heaney's early mentor, Michael McLaverty. To me, as to so many other young writers, he became a generous and kindly encourager. Nonetheless, I was completely taken by surprise when he offered me the privilege of consulting his papers, including manuscripts, journals and letters, not only from the then younger greats such as McGahern, Friel and Heaney, but also from the passing generation he had known, including writers like Mary Lavin, Sean O'Faolain and Peadar O'Donnell.

It was an extraordinary and unlooked-for gift, but it had an unintended consequence: it led me to question whether my job as a writer was to be that of commentator or practitioner. Somehow it came about that for a long number of years, completing and publishing my Ph.D on McLaverty, then working first as Fellow and afterwards Assistant Director of Queen's University's Institute of Irish Studies, I thought of myself as a researcher and a teacher and, if a writer, an academic writer. Did it bother me that I wasn't writing fiction? It did. Did I feel I should still have been writing fiction? Yes. I remember a conversation on the subject in the mid-1980s with Jennifer Johnston, who told me: 'If it's in you, you won't be able to stop it.' I took some comfort from that: yet, from the early 1980s until the very late 1990s, I wrote only two short stories and made no serious attempt to publish them. I almost came to the conclusion that that particular train had long pulled out of the station: and I thought that in teaching and writing about interdisciplinary Irish Studies – which naturally embraced any field of study concerning the island of Ireland – I could address the questions to which I wanted answers.

Then, one day in the late 1990s, everything changed again. I noticed in the *London Review of Books* that the Royal Society of Literature was holding its first short story competition, its inaugural V.S. Pritchett Memorial Award. I might have stopped writing fiction, but I had never stopped reading it, and Pritchett was a particular favourite. I was always intrigued by his idea of the short story as a space where people were 'strangers to one another'. Reading that notice in the *LRB*, something shifted, sharply, in my mind: and I began to wonder if I could still do it. The idea grew, and with it a brand-new story, 'The Cocktail Hour', which to my surprise and delight came runner-up in that first RSL competition to a story by playwright John Arden, and was first published in David Marcus's original *Faber Book of Best New Irish Short Stories*. That recognition, after so long a writerly silence, compelled me to realise that Jennifer Johnston had, of course, been correct: I couldn't stop it. The realisation seemed to release whatever had been blocked. Encouraged yet again by David Marcus, who wrote and asked me in 2001 where the novel he had wanted me to write in the early 1980s had got to, I sat down and began it. Since then, I have had work commissioned and broadcast by BBC's Radio 4 and published two novels: the first, promised so long ago to David Marcus, was published in 2014 as *The Friday Tree* by the publishing house he had co-founded, Poolbeg Press, as was in 2016 a second, *The Way We Danced* – though not before one other unexpected turn in the road.

In 2006, finding by chance a footnote in an edition of Jane Austen's letters mentioning that one of her nieces had married an Irish nobleman named Lord George Hill, I found myself inexorably drawn once more towards research, uncovering the apparently forgotten, and previously-unexplored fact that Lord George had married not one but two of Jane Austen's nieces, that a third niece later came to live in Ireland with her widowed sister, and that all three lived out their lives and lay buried in almost forgotten graves in Donegal. There followed five years of the most delightful research in archives and libraries throughout Ireland and England, and in 2011 my book on the subject, *May, Lou and Cass: Jane Austen's Nieces in Ireland*, was published by Belfast's Blackstaff Press. And then, last year in 2018, by what seemed delightful chance, another thoughtful and tireless editor who had not forgotten that I was also a writer of fiction, Alan Hayes of Arlen House, not only asked me to contribute to his anthology *Reading the Future: New Writing from Ireland*, but also most generously worked with me towards the book I had from the beginning always hoped to see: a short story collection, *The Cocktail Hour*.

Can I be sure that I won't segue into the area of non-fiction again? I can't be certain, given that the family of Jane Austen in Ireland has generously given me access to additional unpublished and consequently irresistible material, and that an album of the family's previously unseen photographs, into which I have been privileged by the finder to have a tantalising glimpse, has now been discovered. I no longer worry, however, that moving in and out of the area of research and recoverable fact will take away from the writing of fiction: I found that my almost twenty-year foray in that direction so enhanced and enriched my understanding of the questions that troubled me, that when I did come back to fiction first in 1999, and again last year, I returned renewed, and ready to begin again. After all, wasn't that what Seamus Heaney used to say to those who asked him the secret to writing: that it lay in 'getting started, keeping going, getting started again'? Every day, remembering that, I start again.

Rosemary Jenkinson

The Extremities of Writing

Writing is everything to me. It's my husband, my children, my religion and my lover. Next to it, living is merely a hobby.

Those words might sound overintense but the nature of writing is that it takes over your life. I don't fit my writing into my life; I fit my life into my writing. When I look back to being a child, I had this built-in bookcase in my bedroom and I used to keep climbing it to the top. How could there be a more apt metaphor for a writer's dreams?

As a teenager I liked to say inappropriate things to shock people, and still do to a certain extent. Writing needs spice and confrontation, and theatre in particular is the best place for saying the unsayable, so what was a verbal liability earlier in my life has become a written asset. Funnily enough, the most flattered I ever felt as a writer was when the playwright, Philip Ridley, called one of my plays 'vile'.

Writing affects my mind deeply. Friends sometimes say to me, 'Do you remember that time we ...?' and they can't believe I've no recollection of it at all. The thing is I have so many fictional stories in my head, half my memories get superseded.

I think as a writer you feel that you can never quite capture the right words. There is no such thing as perfection, but you always want to try and wrestle your writing into submission. I remember once being really upset that I'd lost a set of rewrites on a play. There was nothing else for it but another rewrite. A few days later I found the original rewrites and ... guess what? The second rewrites were word for word the same as the first. It just goes to show that, in a certain time and location, you can't aspire to write any better than you do.

Brevity of form makes it easier to be experimental within a short story than a novel. The one guiding force I try to adhere to is 'story over style'. Although I do stand back and look at my work critically, I deliberately try not to overthink. To analyse is to paralyse. Analysis is for academics, not fiction writers. Why would you ever take a scientific approach to writing when art is greater than science? Science is a set of rules waiting to be discovered; art is a set of rules waiting to be broken.

Most of us writers would die for our art. The doctor once told me I needed an immediate operation with an overnight stay, the day before I was due to have a reading of my play at the Abbey Theatre. So what did I do? I chose the play over the op, undergoing makeshift treatment with terrible consequences, leaving me with infections over the following months and needing a bigger operation in the end. I'm not alone – I've known a writer who postponed cancer treatment just to attend a writing workshop!

Dorothy Parker said: 'I hate writing, I love having written.' Personally, the part of writing I most love is having been published. The act of writing to me is futile unless the end goal is publication. Without it, I'd much rather go out and dance in the daisies than sit writing in a shaded room.

Writers talk about the holiness of their art and it's true there are times we've had to sacrifice ourselves at the altar of literature. As John Banville notes, a writer is 'priest-like', devoting his/her life to 'etherial faith'. However, thanks to the revelatory scandals in Ireland, it transpires that some priests did have a considerable amount of sex which to me somewhat dilutes the metaphor.

Being a female writer has always been a hurdle. Even the words critics use for bold writing like 'ballsy' exclude women. What's wrong with 'breasty'? I remember a time when I was tired of short story rejections, so I sent a story off under the more gender-neutral name, Jo Eliot (yes, it was consciously like George Eliot). The story was picked up and the comments about it were hugely positive. I did think about adopting Jo Eliot as my pseudonym but there was the vain, ignoble part of me that kept asking, 'Why change your identity when it means you can't flaunt your success in front of all the teachers and publishers who never supported you?'

All of us writers are mythomanes. I love the image of myself as a latter-day Brendan Behan. My father likes a drink every day and he once said to me when I was complaining about a hangover, 'Sure you're no daughter of mine unless you can drink five pints.' It was certainly something to live up to. When I die, I'd like a pinch of my ashes sprinkled into a big vat of mulled wine for a post-funeral party. The wine can be passed around and consumed by the guests, so that it can be said of me, 'Drunk in life, drunk in death'.

My mother had an enormous influence on my life. She'd longed to be an artist (painting, not writing) but told me that having a family had taken up too much of her time. Her words definitely deterred me from marrying or having children, so I do think I was the repository of my mother's dreams. However, I don't believe that a writer's life without children is in any way barren or sterile. I've given birth over the years to so many characters I'm almost the Prometheus of my own bedroom. Sometimes, a voice from plays or short stories cries out to me in the night like a teething child.

Poverty, or the fear of it, is the big drawback to writing. It's more than ironic that the one symbol which doesn't work on my keyboard is the pound sign. But I want to keep experimenting with my work and, after all, it's far better to be a poor living writer than a rich dead one. I still live in a rented house but the most important thing is that I'm writing nearly every day. While I may not have my dream house, I will always have what is infinitely and gloriously better ... my inner house of dreams.

Claire Kilroy

LOCKED OUT OF MY HEAD

When I was a teenager, getting locked out of your head meant getting drunk. When I had a baby, I got locked out of my head on a more literal level. Such was the clamour, the level of constant panicky demands, I could no longer think. I barely had time to speak in full sentences, let alone write them.

It turns out I have a mind that needs writing. It needs to make sentences. Sentences iron life out on the page. I understand this now that I've had to live for several years without the freedom to write. I had to give up writing when I became a mother because childcare is so expensive in Ireland. Without the thinking and wondering and mental straining that goes with battling away at a novel, I have developed some form of cognitive disruption. I don't always understand the symbols when I look at the clock or, if I'm pulling out onto an empty road, I can't remember which side I have to drive on and, oh God, all the stuff I have lost, the amount of stuff that I have left behind on buses, on benches, on tables and chairs. So I now regard writing as something I must get back to. Either that, or remain locked out of my head for the rest of my life, which is not as much fun as it sounds.

The trick now is to get locked back into my head. I published four novels before I had a baby, one every three years. My baby was born in 2012. I haven't published since. Best case scenario, we're looking at 2021 for my fifth novel. Next year will be better for my writing life as the school day will go up to five hours and forty minutes, 183 days a year. The primary requirement for me for writing is to be alone. I have always written. Since learning to write, it has been a compulsion. I wrote my first story when I was maybe seven. It was about a child entering a haunted house, that is, it was about mystery and fear. Writing is how I get by in a world that I find confusing and alluring in equal measure. By structuring the world into sentences which reflect that confusion and allure, I feel – in my own head at least – that I am keeping my head above water, that I am living. When I'm not writing, when there is no response to the world on the page, I feel I am just treading water.

I used to keep a diary. Technically, I still do, but the entries have gone from being daily to maybe one every six weeks. The only entry for last June was 'I'm enjoying the bit I'm working on – getting lots out of it. She's walking on the beach.' It made me sad because now it's November and I'm still on the same section. It's eight pages long, but I couldn't write all summer because I was teaching and my son was off school, then we moved house and, now that my son is back at school, I find it almost comical, the unavoidable obstacles that crop up on an almost daily basis to keep me from the page – my son is sick, one of my parents is sick, the dog is sick, I'm sick, the school is shut, I've to write a piece like this instead of returning to my narrator where I left her five months ago still walking on the beach in the middle of the night with her teething baby as she chases a wraith. The section is called 'Death of a Girl'.

There is no such thing as a wasted emotion, a friend once told me, and the difficult emotions are the ones that fuel the endeavour, the ones that are messy and painful and inconclusive. My novels look quite structured on the page but they all delve into chaos. Although I don't have the mind for it, I am drawn to physics. Physics uses precise scientific language to describe the world in terms of phenomena that I can't quite get my head around. I like to employ the terminology of physics. I've done it in all the novels but particularly in *Tenderwire*, a novel about a violin, because music and physics are both mathematical and operate on wavelengths that are difficult to adequately explain. A definition I am particularly drawn to, and which I will misquote here, is that chaos is what existed before matter. I regard myself as descending into chaos when I write, and trying to fashion matter out of it. I am frightened of chaos (the blank page, the messy emotions) but feel I have to descend into it, otherwise I am giving in. Without writing, I am not living. Without that mental calibration, I am going to pull out on the wrong side of the road and crash the car.

Caitriona Lally

MUDDLING THROUGH

There is a constant effort to secure writing time in my life, and, no doubt, in virtually every writer's life. Last year, when I was pregnant with my first child, some mothers would gaze wryly at my bump and, along with the Oh-you've-it-all-ahead-of-you style platitudes, tell me I'd have no time to read a book, never mind write one when the baby came. The notion of being trapped in a book-less world for the next decade frightened me so I fought that prediction tooth and nail. Yes, I've had to prioritise writing over sleeping, over physical fitness, over TV binge-watching, but it was worth it to keep a semblance of my former self in a time when that seemed under threat.

I wrote my first book several years ago, having never published a short story before. It was something I'd wanted to do, to be able to tell myself I'd done, like running a marathon. I was giddy writing it; I found pure pleasure in taking on the persona of a very eccentric character and describing her world. My debut novel, *Eggshells*, is about a socially-isolated woman called Vivian who walks the streets of Dublin searching for meaning and belonging, taking notes of street signs with letters missing and placenames that might hold a deeper significance and help her find a way home. Vivian returns home after each of her walks and plots her routes on a map, tracing them onto greaseproof paper. Researching the novel involved lots of walking and notetaking and map drawing. I had more free time then. I had no children, and I had recently been laid off from my job when I walked Vivian's walks and took notes of street signs and placenames that would interest her. After a year of job hunting I found work and was working full-time when I finally wrote my notes up as a novel but hours were easy got, snatched before work and after work and days off and weekends.

A few years on, I tried to finish my second novel while I was pregnant, but life conspired against me: daily vomiting, an early-morning cleaning job in a university, doing all the feature writing and media work necessary to promote my book in America, getting work done at home and trying to paint every wall in the house before the baby came. Writing couldn't compete with those practical concerns. Then came the baby and maternity leave from work in which I found myself writing notes and snippets and various bits and pieces that I couldn't even begin to collect as a cohesive whole, but which made me feel part of the writing world again.

After maternity leave I went back to my job as a cleaner in a beautiful old building in the university. I was quite happy to have colleagues again, people to chat with about the weather and other ordinary things. Also, the physical nature of the work appeals to me – there is great satisfaction to be had in making a dirty surface clean again and getting paid for it. When I write, I never know when I'm finished, when I should stop tweaking and honing my words, but when I clean, the endpoint is clear.

However, a 4.45am wake-up after getting up multiple times a night to comfort a sleepless baby was not conducive to the major restructuring my novel required at this point; snatched hours here and there with a very tired brain were just not enough. And then, I struck literary gold in the form of a burst appendix. I had surgery and a cert for a month off work (a physically-demanding job is best avoided after abdominal surgery). I couldn't lift the baby so full-time childcare was required. And this meant ... a month of full days which I could fill as I pleased. I felt rough, physically rundown, bad about taking a month off work so soon after I was back from maternity leave, bad about not being able to lift a baby who only wanted to be lifted, and so I made a very conscious decision to turn a tough time into a productive time.

That month broke the back of the second novel. I worked and worked and worked on the novel and by the end of the month, got it to a workable state. Still nowhere near finished, but I knew what needed to be done now. Since then I've been chipping away at it, distracted by various life events and holidays and other nice things, but for the most part, I make time for writing. I'm finished my cleaning job by 9.30am. Three mornings a week, I have some hours to write before I collect my child from crèche, and those two and a half hours have to be used productively, otherwise what's the point? I used to fritter away writing time on emails and find myself down internet labyrinths; now I write without wifi and try to make it count. I write in libraries or cafes because writing at home is too fraught with domestic duties; I struggle to ignore the piles of clothes to be washed, the rooms to be Hoovered, the meals to be cooked. I prefer the background noise of strangers chatting and coffee machines hissing to the silence of an empty home.

My writing routine doesn't always work. There are days when I can't see solutions to problems in the novel, days when I wonder if it's any good or if there is any point, days when I'm barely able to focus on the screen for tiredness, but for the most part I think of the large sum from my paycheque spent buying crèche hours so I can write, and that's enough to spur me on. But, before I sound like I have this thing sorted and figured out and boxed up nicely with a bow on top, life is set to change again. I'm expecting my second child, which, all going well, will mean another round of sleepless nights and even greater efforts to find writing time. Financially, I will be working for minus sums of money if I pay for childcare for two children a few mornings a week, so I hope I can maintain the confidence required to make writing a priority. My current routine will be shaken up before it settles back into the next wave of juggling and muddling through. Whatever happens with work and childcare though, the writing will find its own hours; if the words are there, they will push through.

Paul Lynch

STRANGE WORK

Strange work is the writing of a novel. A book begins in the mind as an itch and the writer discovers a compulsion to scratch. An image arrives and resonates, sometimes for years. The writer thinks, why this image and not another you might like?

Who is this shadowy person that haunts your waking mind? You walk to the shop to buy eggs and a character suddenly quivers like a plucked string. You discover it is a teenage girl. Why is she here? What does she want to say? It's not as if you want to write another novel set in the nineteenth century. And yet she is beckoning from 1845. Why this year and not another? (Something forbidding began that year and it would be best to have nothing to do with it).

The writer is the priest of the deepest self, the self that remains unknowable. You are called to exorcise this feeling and discover its secret meaning. This might be thought of as the beginning of theme.

But how to begin? A novelist before an unwritten book is a speaker without a language yet to exist. The beginning is a baton pass from the unconscious, the part of the mind older than language. The tongue-tied writer awaits wearing a blindfold. A hand reaches into the dark and something shapeless is placed in your grip. Whatever it is, you've got to run with it along terrain that quickly assumes the topography of a mountain.

You stare toward the icy summit and see palls of cloud. The base of the mountain is covered with snow and there is no path. There is no Sherpa, no map for this. (The maps exist for the day-trippers who wander the hills of the national parks where signage shows the gravelled path, the toilets, the café and safe exit).

You plunge into the snow and discover you are wearing sandalled slippers. A blizzard tosses east into west. You find yourself in biting hedgerow with thorns that grow out your fingernails as you type.

If you are a writer with experience, you might wonder what supplies you have against hazard. You examine your backpack and see it is empty but for matches. This might be all you need – a small flame in the dark to see step by step. (The writer wonders, if you knew the way in the light would you go there?). Fortitude and toughness, you discover, do not come in an Acme pack.

There are times when you step with self-assurance and tumble down a ravine. The snow falls in drifts, and days pass caught on your back and soon you grow stiff. Then you think of Xenophon in the *Anabasis* with his flagging, frost-bitten army on Armenia's wintered slopes. Under whacking snowfall they give up for dead until Xenophon without a cloak climbs up and starts chopping down a tree. You light a small fire and begin again.

The writer should ask – why am I doing this? You remind yourself that serious fiction is a form of knowledge. That the writer seeks to understand the truths that define the human condition. Isn't it so that finitude and suffering are our lot? That victories are short and love is borrowed? That the unwanted likes to knock upon our door? That sometimes the knocker takes the form of chance, and sometimes what darkens our door is malevolence? We stare at life and are bewildered. You have the right to ask, who are we in relation to all this? How do we define our loss or overcoming?

Literary style is a way of knowing how the world is met in its unfolding. Style is also an unknowing and should alert the reader to the mysterious. Czesław Miłosz had a constant regret that 'human experience defies description'. So you write and seek to express life's infinite, unconquerable strangeness.

'Keep right on to the end of the road,' went the Harry Lauder song. What you practice grows stronger.

Bernard MacLaverty

RANDOM JOTTINGS[1]

I was born and brought up in Belfast and my memories begin in Atlantic Avenue. It was a terraced redbrick house which backed onto the Holy Family chapel yard. My father invited my maternal grandmother and grandfather and my Great Aunt Mary (who was a primary school teacher) to live with us. It was a deeply religious household. There were a few books which were kept in a glass-fronted case the way the good china was – and they were used just about as often. I read very few of them but it is funny how I know the names of the authors and can recall the colouring and typography of the spines. They all seemed to have the cricketer's love of double initials – D.K. Broster, H.V. Morton, A.J. Cronin. There was a set of novels by Canon Sheehan and a complete set of Dickens my Great Aunt Mary got by saving Cornflakes tokens supposedly.

When I was young I liked playing farms – setting out the toy animals, ducks on a round mirror pond, and the farmer and his wife, maybe one day face to face, the next day with their backs to each other. Making up a world, moving people in it.

At Holy Family Primary School I had an interesting teacher, Gerry Tracey, during my Eleven Plus year (Qualifying Examination). I was ten. There were about fifty pupils in the class. He was the first one to encourage me to write. He set a composition – 'A Rainy Day' – and I was given a Bull's Eye and a sixpence for my effort – my first money for writing. My mother kept the pages in a posh box (previously containing a canteen of cutlery) with other important mortgage documents. Embarrassing efforts – 'the rain pommelled noisily against the window'; 'Boiling potatoes knocking on the lid to be let out'. At secondary school the teachers were not interested in metaphors. As long as one paragraph connected to the next with the strength of Lego they were happy. But I think I go on writing because it is the same kind of play activity.

I began to attempt to write in my final year at grammar school. I didn't set out to write bad poetry, it's just the way it came out. I liked everything about words – their sound, the multiple meanings, their rhythms when strung together. I even liked reading *Roget's Thesaurus*. Twenty different ways to say the same thing. But one word may improve the rhythm, another may be closer to the meaning I wanted. A thesaurus contains a box of jewels and you can scrabble among them and pick out a sapphire or the emerald, whichever is closest to what you require. Sometimes a list of synonyms can seem like a poem by Gerard Manley Hopkins:

> HOW to kéep – is there ány any, is there none such, nowhere
>   known some, bow or brooch
> or braid or brace, láce, latch or catch or key to keep
> Back beauty, keep it, beauty, beauty, beauty, … from
>   vanishing away?

Or there is the enjoyment of reading twenty different ways to say 'drunk'. Or the enjoyment of coming across the word 'wig' in Brewer's *Dictionary of Phrase & Fable*. When the object was in use the words for it seemed to multiply:

> In the middle of the eighteenth century we meet with 30 or 40 different names for wigs; as the artichoke, bag, barrister's, bishop's, brush, bush [buzz], buckle, busby, chain, chancellor's, corded wolf's paw, Count Saxe's mode, the crutch, the cut bob, the detached buckle, the Dalmahoy (a bob wig worn by tradesmen), the drop, the Dutch, the full, the half natural, the Jansenist bob, the judge's, the ladder, the long bob, the Louis, the periwig, the pigeon's wing, the rhinoceros, the rose, the scratch, the she-dragon, the small back, the spinach seed, the staircase, the Welsh and the wild boar's back.

In the mid-sixties I was invited to join 'the Group' by Queen's University lecturer Philip Hobsbaum, which was a valuable experience for many of the aspiring writers around the university at that time – especially for the poets. Seventeen years after leaving school I published a book of short stories, *Secrets*. Because of the mayhem and murder that was going on in Belfast I moved with my wife and family in 1975 to Edinburgh where I had just been offered a teaching job.

Scotland has been good to me – awarding me prizes, giving me insights, enriching me with friendships. It's hard to say what effect it's had on my writing but I can only hope it has improved it. In Ireland the politics were parochial – orange and green. Moving to Scotland widened the struggle to the more universal – capitalist, socialist debate. To have had such varied prose mentors as George Mackay Brown, James Kelman, Alasdair Gray, was enriching – as was listening to the poetry of Norman MacCaig, Iain Crichton Smith, Kathleen Jamie, Don Paterson and Robin Robertson. Of course there are many missing from these two lists.

I mostly write in the study I have at home. But it wasn't always so. In the early days it was the kitchen or a bedroom, the latter for the peace and quiet. In winter it could get really cold, so I went for 'Eiderdown Writing'. When outside of the study I usually have a notebook in my pocket for ideas and words that may occur on my current projects – I could be writing three or four stories or projects. As time advances and memory deteriorates this technique becomes all the more necessary. I try not to be seen writing in public but the chances are that nobody will see me because everybody else is glued to a screen of some sort.

As to the question, *What is the nature of writing/literature?* My answer is:

to be as big and as good and as beautiful as religion, without being false.

Writing is a bit like breastfeeding. The baby's act of feeding stimulates the milk to arrive just as the act of writing stimulates words to come onto the page. These words create pictures and feelings in both the writer and the reader. So a writer who plans excessively but avoids sitting down to write will be losing the stimulation. It's probably the same with the act of painting. The strokes you make lead to other strokes, mistakes lead to new marks which in turn modify the original concept and inevitably improve it.

In the beginning it took a long time before I finished anything. Like at this very moment, I was always writing fragments of things. And copying other famous writers' ways of writing. Then one day I wrote a story which was in my own voice about a place I knew and people I knew. That got me started.

The only way to begin is to begin.

It is a paradox that some of the things I have written have grown out of the inability to think of anything to write. One day I sat down at the keyboard and could think of absolutely nothing – my screen saver from Wittgenstein came on – *In art it is hard to say anything, that is as good as saying nothing.* It paraded time after time across the screen, dissuading me from touching the keys. What could be worse than this? To be a deaf composer, or a blind painter, or an architect without a sense of space? The idea of a blind painter stayed with me and began to grow. He would have to be old and have diabetes, induced blindness. He would get someone else to put the paint on the canvas for him – but this is a very intimate action – so he has to be a homosexual painter and his much younger lover is his amanuensis. At that time Ireland could not have coped with such a man so he moved, long ago, to live in Portugal. It became a short story called 'The Drapery Man' which begins with the younger man walking up a hot pavement in Portugal with a string bag full of tennis balls whose fur he will use to apply paint to a canvas, including the decoration of their negative S, according to the old man's instructions.[2] So out of nothing comes something.

I now devote all of my life to being a part-time writer.

My whole being is invested in writing to the best of my ability. I find that when I am writing something it is the thing uppermost in my mind. All day. Every day.

NOTES

1 I pinch my title from a section in *The Irish News* which came into our house daily in Belfast when I was a boy.
2 On every tennis ball there is fur. There are also lines. At some angles they look like an S. If the ball was dipped in red paint and pressed to a canvas it would leave a round, red mark and in that mark would be a negative line shaped like an S. The old artist gives his amanuensis instructions as to where and how to press the paint-sodden tennis ball against the painting's surface.

Patrick McCabe

WILD POLKAS ON THE MOON

When you first encounter the lyrics of the Charlie Feathers 1950s country song hit 'I Forgot To Remember To Forget'*, you might reasonably expect the pending narrative to be characterised by a certain wayward, if not wilfully obstinate, tendency towards ellipsis.

And which is arguably also the case with this particular composition, putatively entitled *A High Lonesome Frolic* – suggesting, perhaps, an amber-tinted, warm-hearted, by-the-fireside narrative peregrination through the winding, noirish intersections of the Irish/American rural mind, its concomitant hint of communal wantonness and deep, glacial solitude among the 'hills 'n hollers' notwithstanding.

Yes, a lyrical investigation of an imagination which, among other things, has been described as an ongoing cultural conspiracy against reality in favour of romance.

A thesis which, in my own case, may well be considered commendably accurate, given the number of disparate, particularly musical references identifiable in my humble oeuvre over the course of some years – advocating sentiments familiar from, among others, Jim Reeves, John McCormack, Commander Cody & The Lost Planet Airmen, Townes Van Zandt – and, a perennial favourite, the Carter family.

And which might, conceivably, certainly the latter – seem a little strange for someone who was actually born in the mid-1950s, and having, culturally, come of age in the early 1970s.

But, as V.S. Naipaul, among others, has pointed out, it would be a mistake to underestimate the capacity for flight which is in the DNA of the remote mountain or rural mind, of which my own might be considered a common-or-garden example – especially in these dying days when, more than ever, it is a caged bird yearning to soar, as the twenty-first century comes pouring over the hill.

That is, of course, if you happen to believe in a concept so quaint and convenient as that of 'Time'.

With which Bob Dylan, amongst others, not least the film-maker David Lynch, plays fast and loose – as he does with the fluidity and interchangeability of 'dimensions'.

And who also, in my view, with his astonishing recall, precision and fiercely enduring lack of pretension, may well be one of the finest commentators alive on the subject of art and its creation. For there can be few finer works in any language on the complications of creation than his masterwork, *Chronicles*, with his insights proceeding from his knowledge of the 'heartland' of his birthplace of Hibbing, Minnesota – both meta- and physical.

Back when I was a boy, what used to be called *Come-all-ye* songs were routinely derided – as if both the matter of which they spoke and the treatment of it were of negligible currency – cheap tales about hillbillies leading circumscribed lives, far from the country club and all its attendant respectabilities.

But, if I was misfortunate enough to be forced to accept such glum appraisals of a bowed people routinely devaluing their own life currency, I was also blessed to be around when a certain person had this to say:

> I sang a lot of come-all-ye songs. There's plenty of them. There's way too many to be counted. 'Come along boys and listen to my tale' – I sang that.

The author of *Chronicles* made those remarks only recently – as he did this: 'Yeah, many's the time I performed that mini-Shakespearean mystery play, which is what those songs are.'

Why, and how – Mr Dylan has the answer there too, as has Johnny Cash.

'There's nothing secret about it,' Maestro Zimmermann contends, 'You just do it subliminally and subconsciously.'

'Get rhythm,' Cash urges, 'get rhythm when you get the blues.'

Then, with luck, they'll start making their way up to you, the soundings.

Those signals from the wavering, protean depths sitting there right in front of your eyes – in a country bar, in a main street on market day.

In the heart of that elusive, ever-shifting but indomitably yet fixed enduring heartland country of the soul which, at once, is dark and, simultaneously, magnesium-bright.

Where you can hear the wild voices of the crowd at a cockfight melding into an eerie music as above it comes the shrill of the cocks crowing at a false dawn.

Throatpiercing in the night, there can be apprehended a vast and continental space, one that is chillingly existential, as lonely as America and yet at once as warm and homely as to break, like Hank Williams might have it, the heart of a child.

Quiet and still as the breath of a bird.

In a world – be it Wales or Scotland or Ireland or Indiana, which is rough and surly, not to say pitiless and will have no problem whatsoever drowning either man or woman and swallowing your ship like an infinitesimal grain of dust.

'The Heartland' of the McPeakes and Jim Reeves, of Slim Whitman, The Cramps and George Jones, is an endless flat plain that suddenly soars.

With tall grass blowing in the wind – as the whip-poor-will screeches and even the very prairie grass seems to wail. 'Let us combine,' it conceivably might suggest, in the words of Brian Boyd while contemplating the method of Vladimir Nabokov, 'the diamond-pattern of art and the muscles of memory in one strong and supple movement.'

As the funeral party of the Celtic long-dead shoulder a pine casket between the peaks under a pearl-white moon, soon to be bloodied.

What has all of this got to do with writing, I hear you ask – and, if it's the rarified world of the elegant artificer of the mid-to-late nineteenth century you seek, scratching away in some Georgian pile, secure in the knowledge of the safety net of independent means, then I accept I would have to admit, precious little.

A world, it has recently been suggested, to which we may well be in the process of returning, what with the over-representation of privileged, overgroomed thespians trading blithe ironies on popular talk shows revealing the intricacies of their character's 'journey' – often as not, it transpires, that of Cyclops from the *X-Men* franchise or perhaps Doc Octopus, archvillain of the *Spiderman* Marvel marquee movie 'brand.'

It is no revelation that the world, in recent decades, has become more commodified than ever – in the arena of the arts, arguably, perhaps most of all. With little patience now evident for what I would regard as genuine 'dissent' – which, in previous decades and, indeed, epochs, always provided some measure of comfort to the aspirant artificer. Whether in the form of samizdat manifestoes or poetry 'happenings' in the Royal Albert Hall.

Scratchers and scribblers and paintpot pokers who – then, as now, once again – didn't have a penny, beavering away in the course of pursuing their rarefied calling in some hovel up a lane – as Philip Larkin has observed, with 'fires in a bucket.'

I am often asked why I persist in writing the books I do – why I insist wearily in analysing this patently 'old-fashioned' world – that, alternately, of the small town and the mountain, largely covering the period of the early 1900s until now.

With the answer, distressingly, being tediously obvious and scarcely worth uttering. 'This whole world is an ozone-blue shiver,' Nabokov writes. 'And we are in the middle of it.'

Because, with luck, by describing it in words – for anyone who might be interested enough to listen – and that there's your audience – somehow you might simultaneously comprehend it and even find a way out of it. By mimicking it, maybe, in all of its burlesque complexity.

It has been observed of Nikolai Gogol that, in his work, he never drew portraits – he used looking glasses and as a writer lived in his own looking-glass world, refracting the material through a mirror of his own making.

The author of *Lolita* composed the foregoing, and I have to say that ever since first becoming acquainted with another work adopting a similar approach, namely (*The Fabulous Adventures of*) *Baron Munchausen* in the old school third class *Mellifont Reader*, this philosophy has spoken out loud and clear to me – clarifying from an early age the importance of the writer seeking and locating one's own essential nature – one's personality, really – and finding the most comfortable means of expressing that worldview.

Whether that turns out to be akin to that of Paddy Kavanagh laying waste the Irish 'Renaissance' – or, as he described it in his own memorable, combative phrase: 'the thoroughgoing, English-bred lie' or any one of the following, which became favourites:

Hemingway's Spain.

Elizabeth Bowen's Ireland.

Eudora Welty's American South.

Roddy Doyle's Dublin.

Shane McGowan's London.

Dylan Thomas's Wales

'Dylan' Dylan's Midwest.

Watch them as on every single page they entwine, both soul and style – indivisible, inextricable.

As Donleavy might have it, 'in all their sins and graces.'

But I really must insist that it was Gogol who opened the door widest of all for me – yes, this particular Ukrainian genius, artificer with the upside-down glasses, always demonstrating that, in this fantastic world, the difference between the cosmic and the comic depends on but one sibilant.

Writing, for me, after that – and, most assuredly, when I first came to grips with Lord Snooty and Captain Hurricane, along with the deliriously-gaudy panels of Classics Illustrated – *Off on a Comet, The Count of Monte Cristo* – was always a 'calling' – and I figured from the start that, in all likelihood, it would be a lonesome one. How did I know that? Just read the biographies – the library was full of them. See under Oscar, Behan, the late, great Jean Rhys, Carson McCullers, Tennessee Williams – with the latter being a writer who is 'all', Elia Kazan has observed, 'In the same way the lion is just that – all lion.'

Lots of qualities have been ascribed to the folks who scratch on the mountain: pig-iron proud, child-men where the primitive stuff of humanity lies very close to the surface. Prone to accepting what pleases him and rejecting what he does not, and in general preferring the extravagant, the flashing, the brightly-coloured, perpetually suspended in the great haze of memory – poised, as it were, between the earth and sky – dwarfed underneath a colossal immensity, quoting Brendan Behan at a capricious God. 'Up hell and down with heaven!'

Delusional, perhaps – but they have pride and honour, nonetheless – this tribal infantry of the hillside's ancient heartland.

As they strive for that endless, elusive note that defines who they are and where they belong – high and lonesome, for sure – and which, one day – up yonder, when that bugle calls in heaven – they know that they will reach it. Lots of things have been said about writers down the years – not least among them, why do they do it.

Once, in an analysis of the songs of Bob Dylan, Greil Marcus, the *Rolling Stone* journalist, spoke of the 'old weird America.'

Well, I have always felt that, from birth to death this world is quite unknowable – as is the little lump of rock I was born onto, called Ireland.

As for readers and one's responsibility to them – I defer to Degas, who said that he painted his pictures for 'three' – three people, that is.

For me, these days, that's about right.

I don't consider I have a duty of any kind – except that of a general morality. But I do have a need. And so, tediously, the response to the question: Why? must be the one routinely advanced by authors – one has to.

You want to be set free of it – willingly co-operating with the whirlpools of the subconscious, until that moment, hopefully, comes when an emotional experience often as not maddeningly uncrystallised, somehow fuses with one from the present – when you can sense some kind of a thing taking shape.

Something like John McGahern reported concerning the writing of one of his stories, when the play of light on a fantail of woodchips in a wood in Leitrim somehow combined with an unfocussed memory from childhood – hastening past, unanticipatedly, to give him – well, essentially, whatever his story was.

With the most important thing being that he hadn't been expecting it – as you so often don't. And why you are always in a state of what might best be described as 'lying in wait for yourself.'

Like some poor sad red-nose slurring in a dingy bar: 'Tomorrow's the day I'm going to take the plunge – this will be the last drink I'll ever have.'

The very last time I'll ever hold a pen.

Because I'm sick of leaving family gatherings to make up non-existent dialogue, scratch out 'characters' spouting gibberish across a room – or, just as likely, on an oil rig on Jupiter or the moon.

Yes, exasperated sitting there all alone, growing pale in 'the writer's room.'

Of trawling the murky, uncooperative depths of half-dreams searching for – well what, exactly?

So this is the last word, in my life, I'll ever- …

I'm nauseated by this search for the right word in rote order business. It makes me sick – go get me a drink.

Sure, at times, you might make some money.

You might.

But then it dries up.

'Not quite there, I'm afraid,' they will say to you then – regarding you with some small measure of what looks suspiciously like pity.

Because The Muse comes and goes.

So that's why, this time, I'm giving it all up for good – and will never again be seen to type: 'The End.'

Or, indeed: 'The Beginning,' for that matter.

Aye, or unzip an iPad, either – with the only tablets on view in the artist's study thenceforth being the tried-and-trusted old reliables, the hallucinogenics – complemented by a substantial quantity of Benzedrine and Nembuttal, so significant in the preparation of Mr Burroughs' various masterpieces – *The Naked Lunch*, most notably – along with *On the Road* by Kerouac, and indeed maybe *Howl* by his friend and fellow arts agitator Allen Ginsberg.

Except that, if you believe that, the only book you need to read, I'm afraid, is *Go & Get Your Head Examined* – as I've long since learned that all you ever succeed in getting out of such indulgences, creatively, are snake-like squiggles such as your grandchildren might possibly contrive with the assistance of a crayon on a bedroom wall.

With the Doors of Perception – while interesting, up to a point, proving in the end little more than a form of literary experimentation and diversion – a little comedic dalliance. What was it Philip Larkin used to say about Picasso? That he got fed up with looking at two eyes on the same side of a nose, and preferred to write about things the way they actually seem to a normal person.

Was he right?

That's a long debate, but I sure do find his impertinence invigorating. With his wry and weary demolitions of sixties narcissism being essential to someone who, in their youth, perhaps permitted it a little too much latitude.

Depending on shock and greedy, incremental irrationality, it is fated not to last, he claimed – and in which to, some degree, he was accurate. But it also must be remembered that he was among the first to laud the young Dylan.

So, for whatever reason, as they say, or used to: DRUGS OUT.

No tablets then, most emphatically – no tap-tap-tap on an iPad or Android.

Not even so much as clicketty-click on an old half-remembered eighties Olivetti.

Because this is the day, at long last – goodbye words!

So long exegesis, deconstruction and ennui – and goodbye one two three four five star reviews – because, at last – hee hee! – it's all over, I'm signing myself into rehab tomorrow!

Even if you know that, properly, you never will – not until the very last handful of clay goes down – or whumph! goes the flaring Swan vesta on top of the gliding pine casket.

Underneath the impassive lamp of the world – whether it be pearled or crimson.

And, idiot that you are, even after that – pursuing to the very limits of your capacity that briefest of elusive moments when you might somehow hold that old, weird, Celtic heart captive, in your own particular snare of words, for better or worse described as *Ulysses* meets *Oor Wullie*.

Or, should you prefer, The Carter Family still hard at it out there somewhere in space, sawing wild polkas up beyond the blue – a galaxy distant from the caprice of fashion and the admirable solidity of the well-made tale – located, paradoxically, somewhere between *Blue Velvet* and *Mr Bleaney* – David Lynch watched and tempered by a sepulchral Philip Larkin.

High upon the moon, where the mystery of fiction properly belongs.

Molly McCloskey

THE IDEAL AND THE REAL

The ideal conditions for me to write have been emotional equilibrium and a quiet, private place to work. They say happiness writes white – meaning if one is too satisfied with life, too comfortable, then the tensions that give rise to writing just don't exist – and I think that may be true, but life is such that periods of blissful calm are rare and fleeting, so I've found that being too happy to work hasn't been much of a problem.

The other end of the spectrum has been more of a challenge, and I'm always amazed at people who can produce work when they are in very bad states. For me, a little grit – the kind that comes with everyday living – but not so much that it's debilitating. I think I have to feel relatively safe in my inner life in order to take risks in my work, as well as to be able to just sit alone in a room all day with my own thoughts, which is what a writer's work day largely consists of. Sometimes I wish this weren't the case, because when we're at our most raw, our most off-balance – when we're mourning a loss, for instance, and the grief is overwhelming – we have access to psychological and emotional states that are kind of sealed off to us when things are running smoothly. Depression can be solipsistic, whereas deep grief can engender empathy and porousness to the lives and suffering of others, and to the world's woes generally. To be able to write from within that state, and to depict – with real immediacy – your characters experiencing it, can be powerful. But it's difficult to do, and you can't possibly wish deep grief upon yourself – or at least I wouldn't; the trade-off wouldn't be worth it. So the thing is to conjure those extreme states while you yourself are feeling grounded enough to actually sit down alone at your desk for the day and write.

In a way, I almost resist the moment when I get some distance on my distress, that first moment of: *Oh, that's an interesting thought – I should write that down*. It's the return to the working life, which is great, of course, but after 25 years of that sort of translation of inner and outer experience, there's also the feeling of: *Oh, here we go again*. Perhaps that's the upside of being swamped by grief – one is fully *in* life, in a way that, as a writer, one often isn't. Writers tend to be at a remove, noting, notating, reshaping, narrativising. To have a break from that remove – even if the reason for the break is painful – is somehow reassuring. One isn't just a notetaker; one is part of the human race, the stream of life, after all.

At the same time, the unconscious plays a fascinating role, which is why I don't think we should over-direct things as writers. Often I've begun writing something, not sure what the narrative line is and just jotting down fragments, and found that the fragments begin to link up with each other. There are connections between the things I'm thinking about and taking note of that I'm not (yet) consciously aware of – but there are reasons I'm alighting on those particular details or anecdotes or people, and those reasons will become clear if I trust in the process. It's associative, and the connections that begin to appear often surprise me. The role of the unconscious is also why I tell my students *never* to insert symbols in their work – the unconscious has its own way of generating symbols, and consciously creating them will be excessive and result in some heavy-handed prose.

Mike McCormack

WRITE FROM THE BEGINNING

I'm old school so I come to my trade with pen and paper. I always have and I consider it to be one of the pleasures of writing – just a pen and paper and you are ready to rock. I love that bare bones approach, the slow pace of ink leaving its mark on the paper, that incremental progress of the pen crossing the page … There is something about the whole process of handwriting that creates an intimacy between the writer and the idea, they enter into a common purpose, a common agreement. Right from childhood I thought there was something magic about this whole process and I am even more sure now, all these years later. So, pen and paper, the beginning and the end of what I do.

I wrote my first book – a collection of short stories – in two separate places. The first half of the book was written in a small bedsit over a very busy pub in lower Salthill, just outside Galway city. That room was about ten feet long by four feet wide and at night the voices and thumping music of the musicians below would rise through the floorboards into my room. I have often wondered if that noise and the rhythm that underwrote it ever got into my prose. At the time I was supposed to be researching a MA in Philosophy. But gradually, over the space of about two years my fictional ideas overtook my philosophical ones. That was a strange process, stealthy and totally unbidden. I remember one day looking out the window from my desk and realising that I was a much better fiction writer than a philosopher. I am tempted to say it was a sunny morn and that a shaft of light fell across my desk – my vocation had announced itself!

The second half of my first book was written in the sitting room of a small flat in Prospect Hill, the highest part of Galway city. There were five of us in that flat and we would sit around in that sitting room – about ten feet by ten – all of us smoking – how we could ever see each other I do not know – and talking and listening to My Bloody Valentine, The Smiths, Cocteau Twins and so on. And I would write my stories long hand on a piece of eighteen-inch square melamine. Thirty years later I still have that sheet of melamine and I still use is as a writing desk.

At the time I worked as a floor sweep in a city shopping centre. I had a large, open section of the central floor to mop and polish. I used a mopping machine to do the first clean and then went over it by hand to take any soap stains out of the tiles. It was great work, long and rhythmic and I could get physically lost in it for four hours every evening. Up and down the floor, up and down the floor, swishing a mop for hours … I can remember working on my first ideas as a writer with a mop in my hands and I remember sorting out so many writing problems when my mind was lost to that work.

Now I have an office of my own with a proper desk in our house outside of Galway city. It is a small room, but it is lined with books and it is quiet and I do not smoke any more. Nor do I have to mop any floors either. From my window I look out on the looped turn of our cul-de-sac and watch the neighbour's children racing circuits on their bikes. And sometimes I wonder back to those days of writing in those cramped and smoky rooms and wonder how I got anything done at all.

As a writer you like to think that your instincts are pure, that your motives in picking up a pen have something to do with the good, the true and the beautiful. But I can categorically say that my own first twitches as a writer lay closer to envy and admiration than any wish to illumine or explore the great themes. I remember being at home in Louisburgh, County Mayo and during one particularly wet week I read Asimov's *I Robot*, Flann O Brien's *The Third Policeman* and Ernest Haycox's *The Wild Bunch*. Each of those books in their separate ways transported me to different worlds and different circumstances. The green fields and damp hills of west Mayo melted away outside my window and I was in outer space or the wild west, or I was orbiting in eternal circles between this world and the next. I marvelled at the power of this enchantment, how extraordinarily vivid it was and how simply it was affected by a succession of words on a page that was once blank. How was that possible? Who could do such a thing? Certainly not a farm-boy from west Mayo, that's for sure! It would take me years to break free of this mental stricture and write my first pieces.

I spend most of my time rewriting. Probably eighty-five percent of my time at the desk is rewriting and reshaping the raw uncultured stuff I have fired off blindly and with so little sense of direction or purpose. Sometimes there is a genuine sense of adventure in unspooling this raw stuff but most of this good feeling is tempered by the realisation that many dogged hours lie ahead in which it will have to be reshaped, chiselled, polished, sanded and varnished into the finished article. My fervent prayer then is that the finished piece will show nothing of the trudging labour that has gone into it – that it should come across as something delivered from on high straight to the page without any lumpish intervention on my part. It should sing and fly to the songs and rhythms of a more elevated plane.

There is no end to this prayer. None that I have found so far.

Barry McCrea

ISLAND VIEWS

I have come back to Ireland after more than twenty years abroad to finish a trilogy of novels provisionally called *Thorn Island*. The island in the title refers to many things, one of which is the legendary Hy-Brasil, the isle of the ever-young, which in Irish folklore is thought to occasionally appear at sunset off the Atlantic coast of Ireland; those who see it can make out a glass castle on the island, filled with young, beautiful, happy people making merry.

My trilogy is set in a Dublin suburb from 1982 to the present and follows the lives of ordinary people, but its structural foundation comes from one of the ancient myths associated with this island, the story of Oisín in the Land of Youth. In this legend, the young warrior Oisín is tempted away from Ireland by Niamh, a fairheaded woman who carries him across the ocean on her white horse to Hy-Brasil. Oisín lives in great happiness among the eternally young inhabitants of the island for three years, but grows homesick. He borrows Niamh's horse and gallops back across the waves for a visit home. In Ireland, he can find no sign of his former family and companions; his father's great fort is a pile of rocks and brambles; the country is populated by an unrecognisable people, weak and short in stature, nothing like the warrior giants he left behind. Oisín realizes he has been away on Niamh's island not for three years, but for three hundred. His stirrup snaps, he falls off his horse, and the moment his foot touches the soil of Ireland his young body withers to that of a very elderly man.

The three-volume novel I am writing, set in the present or recent past, might be called an 'Irish suburban epic'. The legend of Oisín is present in the background, giving form to the plot, and shaping its imagery, metaphors and rhythm. Only my own long time living overseas, and having this legend to hand, has allowed my writer's inner eye to transform the cul-de-sacs and laneways and newsagents of my childhood into a mythic expanse of longing and adventure.

Paradoxically, the past is much more vivid and alive to someone who emigrates than it is to someone who stays at home. The separation preserves it. That is why emigrants often have such difficulty growing up, why emigrants often retain certain features of immaturity which are shed by those who stay at home. If you stay living where you grew up, if you live as an adult in the place you were a child, the faces of the past are a regular, unremarkable feature of your daily existence, because they are always liable to return to you – in the queue for the supermarket checkout, at a rugby match, at the next table in a restaurant – slightly altered each time: hair a little thinner, jowls a little looser, voice just slightly more gravelled, a new flash of pride or disappointment in the eyes. For those like myself who leave the place we grew up in and have our adult lives somewhere else, among strangers, the faces of the past do not return sporadically, they are not part of our experience of daily life. Those left behind are frozen in the mind of the emigrant as they were at the moment of departure: a bully, a rake, a boastful idiot, like those ashen denizens of Pompeii condemned to embody for eternity whatever they had been doing at the moment that Vesuvius erupted – the lover, the eater of oysters, the owner of a dog – as though it were the whole of their identity. Just as the lived reality of antiquity is far more tangible in Pompeii, where life was stopped in its tracks, than it is in Rome or Athens, where building went on, where generations and factions and nationalities continued to succeed each other, so too for the emigrant that the past retains a purity and immediacy which it loses for those who stay.

This accounts, *inter alia*, for some of the differences between Joyce's *Ulysses* – the epic of an emigrant – and Proust's *Recherche*, that of someone who stayed at home. There is only one day in *Ulysses*: if you failed to buy a round on 16 June 1904, in *Ulysses* you are condemned to be the symbol of a miser, no matter how generous you might have been the next day. The inhabitants of Dublin must bear the heavy weight of allegorical and symbolic meaning: the Invalid, the Poet, the Drunkard, the Faithless Spouse. In exile, temporary characteristics are frozen as innate qualities, and the *routine* of everyday life, as we see so clearly in *Ulysses*, becomes sacralised and solidified as *ritual*. A life like Proust's, however, lived in or around one fixed place, offers space for reversals, returns and development, and unlike *Ulysses*, few characters in the *Recherche* turn out as they first seem. No one ends the novel as they began. The rich become poor, the cowardly become brave, the heartless adulterer becomes a devoted and caring husband, the most avid heterosexual turns out to have been secretly gay. Proust's own quotidian world always held out the possibilities of long-lost individuals showing up again, living proof of the passage of time and the constant work of change.

For those who stay where they grew up, who mingle and remingle with the faces and places of their youth, the past is completely contaminated by the present, no longer attainable in its pure, original form, a mess of different, overlapping times, an indecipherable palimpsest like the Roman Forum. For the emigrant, on the other hand, the past retains all its remoteness from the present, all its weirdness and immediacy; it loses none of its fresh cruelty. When I hear the name Ranelagh, the place where I went to secondary school, for example, I see before my eyes a Ranelagh of the early 1990s, full of chippers and video arcades, the air crowded with homophobic slurs, long-skirted girls in Doc Martens weeping in phone boxes as their Eircom cards run out of credit. For my classmates who had stayed living in Dublin, that old, anxious, adolescent Ranelagh has gone, gradually diluted into oblivion by all the other Ranelaghs they have seen and been in since then – a place where their wives frequent a *fabulous* tapas place, where there is a great 'grooming' salon for men, where their friends once bid on a house – to be visible any more. For people who stay living where they grew up, the past is constantly returning, its salty waves mingling with the freshwater flow of the present, so that their reality, 'the present', is a brackish mixture of the two.

For the emigrant, the past becomes falsely identified with a geographical place (so to think of 'going home to Ireland' really means to travel back in time). The past is not something hidden beneath the surface of everyday life (as it was for Proust, as it is for people who stay living close to where they grew up). For the emigrant, the past becomes a distant, unreachable island untouched by time, where the inhabitants are eternally young, a place which can be glimpsed only occasionally, and from a great distance, in irregular, vivid flashes from across the ocean, distorted by waves and foam and Atlantic spray.

Rosaleen McDonagh

ACTIVE PROTAGONIST

How do writing and politics/rhetorics relate in our era?
Writing in the epoch of fake news, one is very mindful
when writing issue-based themes not to drift into fiction.
Fiction is my favourite genre so writing politics can be
complex. The complexity comes from a lived experience of
racism, ableism and sexism. It's often a matter of playing
with fiction to work out facts.

What should your writing do to the ideal reader? To society?
Ideally, my writing should engage people. Minority
categories of people such as Irish Travellers/Roma and
people with disabilities should find themselves as active
protagonists in my work. In mainstream literature
minority categories of people are often prescribed a role of
victim or passive recipients of the writer's view of tragedy
and deviance. My characters are not heroes. They are not
inspirational nor are they extraordinary.

What is an ideal sentence to you and why? Are there any metaphors which are central to your perception/work?

An ideal sentence is usually the sentence that you have struggled to shape and make. It should encapsulate the essence of the motivation of a piece of writing. Metaphors and allegories have become the tools of convention in writing. They're usually in place to help the writer keep the reader focussed. In my own work metaphors are easily too tame, too conventional and it's difficult to work with a metaphor that encompasses obvious themes such as otherness. Metaphors are primarily for readers. The writer's intention is to make readers use their own imagination. However, as said, the task of thinking, developing and writing new metaphors can be quite difficult. For example, a Syrian refugee in Ireland living in a direct provision centre lives an otherness which may work better without metaphors. Or if s/he/they chose to use metaphors it would read as 're-othering the other'. Expressing an idea can be done via soft, lyrical, poetic images. The intellectual method should hold an idea whereby the metaphor compounds the idea into a vivid image.

Layering your writing adds intrigue and texture. There is more than one tension at play in a particular piece. If the writer has given previous indicators or pointers, the reader will follow a main theme without being intimidated by multi-plots or voices.

In which conditions does your writing come into being/flourish? Does mood play a role?

Ideas for a piece of writing come from various circumstances and contexts. The trick is to develop those ideas into strong compositions written in a light, easy and accessible way. If the idea has potency, then that brings passion to the writing.

Which conditions are detrimental to the right concentration?

Noise is a negative distraction. You need an equilibrium of mood; when the pendulum swings too high or too low, the writer cannot focus on the task of writing. Love or infatuation has a tendency to delay or ruin my writing.

Does writing need a room (physical, mental, emotional) of its own?

Writing needs many things. A space in your head, room in your heart and a commitment that is sustainable regardless of the immediate environment. The task of writing is about honour. To a writer honouring the time and effort that goes into anything and reworking a piece of writing is essential.

What place does writing have in your life? How does it interact/interfere with life, or does life interfere with writing?

Writing is a priority in my life. It's my greatest love and my precious gift. Having a significant speech impediment means talking or being understood is impossible. Writing even if it's only a message on your telephone is a wonderful relief of expression. My Traveller ethnicity meant historically that writing in any form was closed off to our community. We were the objects and never the subjects of our own narratives. As a professional writer, deadlines are a source of motivation. When things are going well, basically each aspect of writing is a favourite: planning, preparing, welcoming the idea and the gestation period where you are holding the elements of the idea in your head but have not decided how you would write it. This part of the process is exciting. The whole process of writing cleans the page, cleanses the mind and nourishes the soul.

Is the literary translation of life into stories/poetry/drama somehow an unceasing commitment? Could you give an example of how that works?

As a younger person finding myself in a book or in a piece of literature was difficult. Now, as a professional writer, I take great pride in the task of insuring that my characters, be they good or bad, be they disabled or from minority ethnic communities, will always have prominent roles in my work. At times this is difficult as there is no blueprint to work from. Nonetheless, working with other writers and working out ideas is always fruitful and fun. Colum McCann's novel *Zoli* grabbed the heart out of me. Her journey as a Roma poet based on the Polish poet Papusza saved me from despair. Her lazy eye was a metaphor and a marker of difference. He crafted a piece of work that captured the experience of being othered by your own. It was powerful and Colum has generously encouraged my writing onto another level. Each time my mind or my heart is aching with frustration, returning to this piece of fiction gives me calmness, a moment to reflect and a sense of purpose and warmth about the art of writing.

Does the unconscious come into play, and if so, how? Could you give an example of how something gestated over a certain time? Do the best passages come (un)intentionally?

Yes, the unconscious comes into play. As writers we are never off. Ideas come to me often in the most mundane ways; dreaming or cooking the dinner, having a conversation with a friend. Reading someone else's work can be incredibly inspirational. Technology means it's much easier to write anywhere and everywhere. The impetus is all in the impulse. Immediacy is the currency. This is the pull of globalisation. Access to information and technology is available with the press of a button. Due to its readiness the writing tends to be fast. There is very little room for reflection. Time to think. Time to read. Time to digest and a moment to recognise that maybe what you've written could be better. Although its idiom is used in more scientific vocabulary or genres, the word 'refraction' positions writing as something which is fluid and transparent. This can only happen when adequate time is given to a piece of written work.

What exactly can a wo/man's specific ways of perceiving bring to writing?

The lens is very important both to the writer and to the reader. Critical theory has influenced how we write but also how we read. My input is always to look for a narrative that is paying homage to integrity and authenticity. Identity matters. Gender matters. Disability matters. All these elements of our individual narratives make us open not only to being receptive in acknowledging the 'other realities' but they also help us to be confident, respecting and valuing our own journey in writing. Critical theory picked up in my academic learning spills into my reading of fiction. Take Alice Munro's collection of short stories entitled *Dear Life*; it has a piece called 'Corrie'. This character is a female with polio. The character Adah Ellen Price in Barbara Kingsolver's novel *The Poisonwood Bible* similarly has a character with cerebral palsy. Both writers pushed back against the grain and created strong, mischievous female characters with impairments who were morally ambiguous. They were neither pure nor perfect. Finding these two characters in novels was so unexpected and satisfying that time and time again these characters and how they're written gave me great joy.

What is your favourite genre and why?

James Baldwin, in *Notes of a Native Son* (1955) says 'I consider that I have many responsibilities.' Baldwin is my muse. The polemics of writing are not for everyone. Nor is the burden of resistance, representation and responsibility. When searching for stimulating reading, identity, oppression and poverty are the themes that draw me in. They keep drawing me in because my narrative is matched. There's a connection, a spark, a knowing where the imagination is bridged by a sense of realism. His essays are also a great source of enjoyment for me. Fiction is my way of communicating. It borrows from reality. It attempts to imply great hurt, injury and places of great love. Toni Morrison says 'all good art is political.' A romance novel can be very political.

Do you read critical theory? Could you specify which?
Critical theory is very important for my political, cultural and social consciousness. Feminist critical theory opens the lens of the position of women and how they are placed in society. Critical theory, disability theory and critical race theory are my inroads to reading. These elements of learning and reading filter down into my fictional writing. As I said, my Traveller ethnicity meant historically that writing in all its forms was closed off to our community. Due to systemic and endemic racism, Travellers were mostly the objects of other people's fiction.

What is the purpose of writing for you?
The purpose of writing for me has no purpose. My imagination is allowed to run wild when writing. Words, and the job of putting them together, fill me with energy, curiosity and contrariness. It's difficult, full of frustration with magnificent rejections. However, when not writing my head feels sore. My heart is empty and my body is sick. Life is aimless and lonely. Writing fills the hours of each day. It's stealing voices. Talking, walking, climbing, dancing, sitting with pain, responding to all these aspects of life come to me when writing. Loving a person nearly as much as loving writing or reading is beyond my capacity.

If you were to describe the act of writing in one scene, would that be a curse, a relief, bliss, a struggle, all of these?

No character, no journey, no novel, even on the last page is finished. Why else do we as humans have memory, humour, all sorts of emotions that remind us of how hard it was to write. Writing – is all in the challenge.

Bernie McGill

MEETING MRS THATCHER

A number of years ago, my mother introduced me and my sister to Margaret Thatcher. It was a surprise to hear that the former Prime Minister was paying a visit to a hospital ward in Coleraine, but it wasn't the most unexpected event that had taken place in those few days. My mother had suffered a stroke, had witnessed monkeys swing down through skylights, overalled mechanics emerge from under the bed. When she suddenly nudged me, hard, with her elbow, and nodded towards the door of her hospital room and announced, with awe, the arrival of the former PM, my sister and I exchanged worried looks.

'Mum ...' I began, but Mother was having none of it.

'Say hello!' she hissed at me, and in a louder, more formal voice, in the direction of the illusory Mrs Thatcher announced, 'This is my daughter.'

'Mum ...' I tried again but no, in my mother's eyes to ignore the visitor was the height of bad manners.

'Say hello to the woman!' she insisted. 'She's standing there, waiting.'

'Hello, Mrs Thatcher,' I said, without enthusiasm, looking towards the door.

'Shake her hand!' continued our mother, with another poke in the ribs, so I took a step towards the door, and reached out my hand to where I imagined the hand of the fanciful Mrs Thatcher to be.

'Pleased to meet you,' I said, which was a lie. Then, thinking she would be mollified, I returned to the bedside but Mother's face was a picture.

'The oul' witch!' she said, still staring at the door. 'She turned on her heel and walked out.'

And so I was snubbed by an imaginary Margaret Thatcher, which was somehow worse than being snubbed by the actual person, since I'd made a fool of myself by offering to shake her non-existent hand.

Our mother, as I've said, was very ill at the time, as, so it happens, was Mrs Thatcher herself, and I must confess that it crossed my mind that in some liminal space between this world and the next, that the two were, indeed, communing with each other. Mother had in the past displayed a grudging admiration for the woman, not because she agreed in any way with her political views (the politician was held responsible, in our house and in many others, for taking the free milk away from primary school children in the 1970s) but because she was a woman and a mother and had managed to be elected into the highest political position in the UK. I don't know what part of my mother's brain had conjured her up, or why, but there's no question in my mind that Mrs Thatcher was as real to her in that moment in time as was I or my sister. The brain is a very strange engine indeed.

I ought really to have embraced my mother's propensity for conjuring up people who weren't really there. After all, I spend much of my working life doing precisely that. I pass hours on end with apparitions, talking to them, asking them questions:

Why would you go there, knowing what you know?
Why would you do that?
Why would you care?

I'm a slow writer. I take my time getting to know my fictional characters, examining their motives, interrogating their behaviour. With me, a character often comes into being through the voice. I 'hear' them before I 'see' them, before I really know who they are. The voice seems particularly resonant to me. I'm poor at recognising people's faces, but I can often place a person when they begin to speak. I prefer the radio to the television. I always read my work aloud and encourage students and workshoppers to do the same – writing sounds differently to the ear than to the way it looks to the eye on the page. The imagined world seems to exist for me in a much more three-dimensional way through the aural rather than through the visual. It's the reason, I think, why so many of my stories are written in the first person. My characters are often story makers, narrators, tellers of their own tales.

Last year, I attended an event at the recently opened Seamus Heaney HomePlace[1] in Bellaghy at which author Jennifer Johnston was interviewed by writer and journalist Martina Devlin. Jennifer Johnston was talking about her creative process. She spoke about a day when she was writing in her study when a man wearing a hat walked in and sat down on the couch. She didn't know the man; he didn't speak to her, she said, he just sat there, as if expecting something. As it turns out, he was a character waiting for a story. The writer related this incident in a tongue-in-cheek tone, but it sent me back to a piece of theatre that has fascinated me for years: Pirandello's *Six Characters in Search of an Author*.[2] In his introduction to the play, Pirandello writes about how he found himself confronted one day at his door with an entire family of characters who set about telling him the whole sad series of events of their lives, often speaking over each other, cutting each other off, just as they eventually do in the play. He decided he wasn't interested in their story, that he'd heaped enough trouble on his readers already; he tried to put the characters out of his mind, but the characters persisted:

> They would pick on certain moments of my day to appear before me in the solitude of my study, one by one, or two at a time. They would try to entice me, suggesting various scenes I might write or describe and how to get the best out of them ...

There is something particularly appealing to me about this idea of a writer being hounded by her or his fictional characters, insisting, by their quiet presence or by their strident entreaty, that their stories be told. In the end, of course, Pirandello gave in, not to a story or to a novel but to what seemed to him to be the natural home for these creatures: 'why not let them go where dramatic characters usually go to live: put them on stage. And see what happens.'

See what happens. That sounds familiar. I know writers who like to outline chapters, who use laminated sheets and Post-It notes to plot, rolls of wallpaper, elaborate timelines, who have very clear structures in their head before they begin to write. I do write timelines, but I don't begin with a plan. I begin with a voice in a given place at a particular point in time and I do my best to be led by that, to listen to the story of what happens. These fictional characters respond to their environment with an experience and an attitude and a history that is not mine. Sometimes they're angry, sometimes they're contemplative, sometimes elated. I spend a lot of time 'listening' to learn what it is they know, what it is they've been through, and one of the things I've learned is that they don't always tell the truth, at least not straight away. I find that I like to be surprised in my writing as well as in my reading. Of course, there's a lot more to it than listening. A reader cannot access a story that exists inside my own head. Both the novels I've written have been historical works. There's hours upon hours of reading involved, of researching, notetaking, photographing, thinking, making connections, but at some point there has to be actual writing, and rewriting, and rewriting again. The lack of a plan makes life more difficult the more words you write. I wouldn't really recommend it as a method. It's a messy business and a slow process but to write freely seems to be the only way I can work. To do otherwise feels to me like the act of sewing myself into my own straitjacket. I'd feel, I think, like I was suffocating. It turns out that I don't like being told what to write, even when I'm the one doing the telling. Here's Jennifer Johnston again, writing in *The Irish Times* in June 2017:

> I have never been much good at writing to order. My head seems to object. It stops working. It doesn't seem to enjoy being bullied, not even gently. I get no pictures in my head. No music. No words burst out through my fingertips, leaving their marks on the paper. They can't be bothered looking for secrets. Or indeed, dreams.[3]

Secrets and dreams: the essential matter, surely, of which fiction writing is made.

There is an admission in Pirandello's introduction to *Six Characters in Search of an Author* as to the true origins of his meddlesome, roving characters. 'Each one of them,' he says, 'shows himself to be tormented by the same fierce sources of suffering that have racked my own spirit for years.' And there's the crux of it. However they may appear to us, fictional characters are not conjured out of thin air; they are conjured out of our own imagination, our own experiences, our own knowledge, our own desires and fears, our own, if you will, secrets and dreams. We may not know in a conscious way where they come from or why they have appeared, but they are our own creations and we have a responsibility to make them as believable as possible. *Six Characters in Search of an Author* is a tragi-comic classic in which the six members of one family, intent on having their harrowing story told, arrive in a theatre to interrupt the rehearsal of a Pirandello play, and browbeat the unsuspecting cast and production team into portraying their ready-made narrative. At one point, the Producer tries to comfort the distraught Mother by telling her that the trauma she has experienced is over, that there's no need for her to keep reliving it. 'No,' she says:

> it's happening now! It's happening all the time! My agony isn't made up! I am living my agony constantly, every moment; I am alive and it is alive and it keeps coming back, again and again, as fresh as the first time.

It seems to me that this is one of the best representations of traumatic memory that I have read. When sufferers of dementia become distressed at painful memories, it is not because they are 'remembering' but because they are reliving those moments afresh every time. And although the altered state of mind in which we found our Mother all those years ago was brought on by a cataclysmic physical event, this brings me back to her. You can't convince a person who says that their feet feel like ice that their limbs are warm to the touch; you can't convince a person who smells burning wood that there is no danger of fire; you can't convince a person who sees Margaret Thatcher that Margaret Thatcher is not there. We experience the world through our senses, so for that experience to be questioned, because we're repeatedly told that we're mistaken, that we cannot trust what we hear, smell, see, feel, taste, in essence that we cannot trust our own selves, must be absolutely shattering.

We are fortunate, most of us, to know when we are participating in an illusion. To read a book, to watch a play in the theatre, to enter the world of a piece of art, to listen to a piece of music is a willing act of immersion, of escape, and even then, when we are fully aware of the fantasy, it can be a wrench to leave that world behind. But to suspect that you are not able to trust your experience of reality, to have that experience constantly challenged and undermined by the people around you, I think that must be one of the most terrifying and disorientating experiences to undergo. My mother did recover from her brain trauma. My sister said that as she drove her from hospital weeks later, she grew more lucid with every mile travelled closer to home, but physically she was much depleted. She passed away four years ago at home, surrounded by her family. In her final few days, she was unable to speak but her eyes remained lucid, articulate, intelligent; they 'spoke' to us to the very end. On one occasion, when we were trying to persuade her to swallow a spoonful of a bitter-tasting liquid antibiotic, and Mother's eyes were loud with refusal, I voiced to my sister what I thought she would say if she had the words to do so: that as far as she was concerned, we could stick the spoon where the sun doesn't shine. Our mother's eyes positively danced in agreement as surely as if she'd uttered the words herself and my sister and I fell about laughing. There isn't a single day that has passed since then that I don't miss her real voice speaking. But for that final act of ventriloquism, for that last flash of humour, for that manifestation of her unquenchable personality, of her own true and undeniable self, I will always be grateful.

NOTES

1 http://www.seamusheaneyhome.com
2 *Pirandello: Collected Plays, Volume Two* (London, John Calder, 1988), in which *Six Characters in Search of an Author* is translated by Felicity Firth.
3 'Jennifer Johnston: the letter I kept in my wallet for 30 years', *The Irish Times*, 30 June 2017. https://www.irishtimes.com/culture/books/jennifer-johnston-the-letter-i-kept-in-my-wallet-for-30-years-1.3137996

Claire McGowan

A Floor of One's Own

As a child, I dreamed of being a writer. I read every profile of an author I could find in *The Irish Times* books section. I idolised Jo March, Emily Moon, Jo Bettany from the Chalet School series, all fictional writers who have so far enjoyed more success than me. I imagined I would have a study with a vast wooden desk, and the built-in shelves would be lined with my copies of my books, and I'd shut myself away in there and produce great masterpieces. Nowadays, since I moved into my new house last year, I finally have my own study, and the shelves (flat-pack rather than built-in) actually are lined with books I've written. The desk is vintage, the top scarred, the drawers deep. The walls are hung with pictures and inspiring postcards – places I've been and found interesting, quotes or messages, pictures of artists' studios, even some paintings done by friends and family. I have an aroma burner, a space heater, a small couch – in short, everything I need to get on with writing.

Except creativity doesn't always come when called, and I often don't want to work in my lovely office. Many afternoons I find myself with my chin propped in my hands, bored, listening to the toddler across the street howling in anger, watching the leaves fall from the Japanese maple tree outside. Now that I can write full time, something I've never done before this year, the lure of doing the washing is often stronger than that of my office. I'd sometimes rather cook the dinner or sort the socks than be in there.

For years, even after I had a book deal, I wouldn't give my writing any proper space or time. I wrote at the kitchen table, in a chair that gave me chronic back pain. I wrote on my commute, sometimes sitting on the floor of a packed train. I did a lot of work in bed (a childhood dream realised, but which also gave me chronic back pain – writing should come with a prescription for chiropracty). I wrote when I was exhausted or sick, or when I had no idea what the story was. It was just placing one word after another, with a deep and blind faith in the process. I never plotted or planned. I didn't know how my books came together, I just believed that they would, if I kept on typing. I worked on a cheap Netbook, held together by duct tape and hope. I worked with a laptop cable that had been partially chewed through by a dog. More than once these cheap computers died on me, taking reams of words with them. Sometimes I worked on my iPad, with a Bluetooth keyboard. It was glitchy and took ages to connect, and Pages messed up the formatting of my novels, creating hours more work. I told people I'd never get a Mac – too expensive.

It was a strange state of being – before I was published, I knew that being a writer was all I wanted, and yet I wouldn't invest any money or time in it. I would take night classes in anything else – Spanish, philosophy, meditation – but not writing. Almost like I couldn't give myself permission to even try. The fear of failing made me paralysed. I remember the day I first told someone 'I'm a writer', and immediately, ashamed, had to qualify it by saying I wasn't published yet. I just wrote in secret. Even after publication, I still wouldn't spend on a decent computer or desk or chair, as if afraid to admit that I was doing this professionally. It's only now, seven years into a writing career, that I've started to unravel why this is, and invest some actual money in what I do for a living. So, I now have a nice office and a proper chair, laptop and keyboard. I get massages and do yoga and take writing classes. I read books about the craft of writing and try to learn as much as I can. All of this helps me take myself seriously, even if none of it is strictly necessary.

Since I've been teaching writing – about six years now, including running an MA at City University in London – I've become almost as interested in the emotional side of the work as the craft. Some writers are born geniuses, with an innate feel for technique, but they hold themselves back because of various blocks and hang-ups. Fear of failure. Fear of success. Fear of exposure. Literary snobbery. The quest for perfection. Bitterness. A belief that nothing worthwhile can be done unless you quit your job, write for eight hours a day. I'm fascinated by the many barriers we put up to achieving our own goals. In some ways, writing a novel is the simplest thing in the world. You just get a computer, or a pen and paper, and you start. No need for training or equipment. And yet it can feel like the hardest thing, forcing us to confront our own limitations right there on the blank page.

After writing some fifteen books (eleven published so far), I've settled into a well-worn routine, where I know not to panic if it seems like things aren't working, and I recognise the different stages of pulling a book together. I've learned over the years that you do whatever works to get the story out, whether that's writing on the floor of trains or in beautiful silent libraries. Writing retreats have done wonders for me – heading off for a few days of seclusion, though it takes a while to adjust. Complete concentration and flow is harder to find these days than it was when I wrote my first book, eight years ago. Back then, I didn't know how to get email on my phone, and I had a three-hour commute, every minute of which I managed to wring dry for writing. I wrote my first book this way, and I'm convinced my concentration span has now been vastly reduced by social media and smartphones. In the Facebook groups I frequent, writers bandy back and forth various ways to deal with this issue of focus – leaving the phone in another room, Internet-blocking software, punishments and rewards. I've sometimes written 17,000 words in three days on a writing retreat, with no chores to do or meals to cook. It's amazing how much time you can fill up just with living, and also how much you can get done in a short space of time when you have to.

I've also learned to take it in stages. The initial writing can be done piecemeal, throwing down a thousand words whenever time presents itself. The quality doesn't matter so much as the regularity, growing the narrative an inch every day. During this time I let myself enjoy the writing without worrying if it's any good. The story comes as a surprise to me, since I haven't planned it. I write in stages – the enjoyable first 20–30k, which inevitably slips out easily. The hard grind between 40 and 60k, where nothing makes sense and the story feels like it will wobble over and collapse. The relief of 60 to 80 or 90k, when the story limps to a close, and you know it's just a case of filling in the gaps. For me the hard work is done in editing, when I have someone else's notes to brace myself against. It's when I fix the jumbled timeline and work out who the characters really are and why they're doing these ridiculous things. For this I need large blocks of unbroken time, and peace and quiet, and vast quantities of tea and biscuits. That's when the real book gets written.

So, to sum up my perfect state for writing – I would be somewhere with a large desk, so I can spread out all the scribbled notes I write to myself. There would be peace and quiet, but enough background noise to soothe my agitated conscious mind. In her wonderful book *Writing Down the Bones*, which someone gave me at eighteen and which I've lived by ever since, Natalie Goldberg recommends writing in cafes and launderettes. A good compromise is to use white noise, like the excellent website *mynoise.net* – it has an 'Irish coastal experience' which I find very soothing. I would have access to gallons of tea, a fancy leaf kind. Maybe the Marco Polo from Mariage Frères in Paris (hideously expensive). I would have biscuits that magically would not contain any calories (writing involves a lot of sitting down). A good chair and a mouse and ergonomic keyboard (to try to stave off Writer's Shoulder), a space heater (I get so cold just sitting typing, even on hot days) and ideally a writing friend on-hand to talk through plot knots with. What I'm saying is my ideal writing place is a fancy country spa hotel, with a friend. But the work can also be done in hammocks, on buses, in waiting rooms, anywhere time can be snatched. We're lucky that we can get in business as writers with so little outlay, and that even five minutes is enough to keep the story bubbling away, if that's all we have. So even if we might rely on rituals and routines to get our work done, these are tools rather than restrictions.

Lisa McInerney

HALF-ANSWERED QUESTIONS ON FICTION

Where does it come from?

It starts with a dialogue: one voice talking to another. The voices, then the light falling on the bodies they come from and the space around those bodies. I may be walking alone, or on the bus, eyes relaxed at the passing scenery, or at home engaged in some repetitive task. The voices might be mid-conversation, or teasing each other with nonsense. They might barely be talking at all, rather skirting around one another, saying much in not saying anything. There's always reading between the lines before I can get the lines down. This could go on for only minutes before I start typing, but some of these dialogues between one character and another haven't reached a conclusion since I first heard them years ago.

> *'... and what is the use of a book,' thought Alice,*
> *'without pictures or conversations?'*

I don't know if this is a strange way of working, if it seems affected, or if it will be my way of working forever; it is simply how stories come to me now.

What does it mean?

I learn nothing about myself when I write, and I don't feel I'm missing out until I have to think about what writing does to me or means to me or means coming from me. Apparently it's imperative that a writer be prone to bouts of intense self-reflection, otherwise how will she know what the drag to writing is, or what she hopes to do with herself? If she cannot explain why she focuses on a particular theme, or uses so many semicolons, or whether she's trying to say this or that about society, she will be of very little use to the world of writing, meaning the people or entities that rely on her work: readers, critics, journalists, bloggers, book festival audiences, university lecturers, booksellers, people who like to make lists, people who like to make inspirational memes, essayists, hipsters, philosophers ... Perhaps one day she'll even disappoint a historian or two.

The act becomes an idea only in dissection.

Why do I do this?

When a character comes to me – I believe characters are less created than they are excavated – I try to find aspects of his life that I can't easily understand, so as to make sure of some distance between us, something that I have to work to appreciate. I don't necessarily think this is something all writers should do, but it helps me feel less lazy. (I imagine that the supposed criticism 'they're secretly lazy' is the great horror for all Irish writers, because the importance of hard and physical labour is knotted into us very early on, and held as a great measure of our worth. Sitting on your arse all day making up stories; what kind of carry-on is that?). If I'm only writing about things I already like to do or already believe in, am I creating at all, or am I just waxing lyrical? What's the purpose of writing about people, if not to try to understand them better?

The distance I create between myself and my characters is artificial, because it's at this point I am most evidently thinking of myself as the writer and the characters as constructs and their quirks as negotiable. The more distance I tell myself I need, the more unreal the characters become, but, conversely, the better the writing is. This can feel very wounding.

But apart from this, my characters are very familiar to me because they're people I feel the need to represent in fiction, people similar to those I know and love in real life, who are often passed over in literature. I'm asked about this a lot: *Do you feel it's important to write about people who aren't often found in literary fiction?* I do and I don't. I write about people on the periphery, from the working or welfare or criminal class, because these are the people I'm drawn to. I don't write characters like this in order to tip the scales or because I think of myself as some sort of unelected representative for my community. On the other hand, I'm drawn to these characters because I can't find the right representations already in fiction. I write what I want to read. A lot of us like to write about people who are very, very like us, and not only because it's easier.

When I talk about writing, which I don't always do successfully (it is such a strange demand to make of people whose vocation is so solitary and so deeply personal), I tell listeners that writers should feel responsibility for their stories. *If you don't write this, no one will.* Therefore on some level I must see myself as a representative.

I carry characters around in my head for months or years or even decades. I am in the middle of writing my third novel in which the protagonist is a Corkonian *feen* named Ryan Cusack. I know Ryan better than I know myself, which is fine; I'd rather know him better than I know myself because I'm not writing about myself and frankly, I'm very boring. In order for me to feel less lazy, I needed to find things out about him that were unfamiliar to me. The first is plain and simple: he's male. Which is not to say that there's any real difficulty in writing a character with a different gender, at least no more than there should be when writing a character of the same gender. The same rules apply: take this character's physical presence, see how the world might react to them and then let that inform every sentence, every line of dialogue. Because I tell myself I need more distance I come up with other anomalies. Ryan is musical; I admire people who are musical but I cannot play an instrument myself and did not study music at school. Ryan is bilingual. I have English and only a smattering of Gaeilge. Ryan is handsome and ostensibly confident in how he presents himself. I'm confidently forgettable.

His story comes to me as I ask myself endless questions about him. These range from the important (his political leanings, his willingness to share his feelings, if he's a good liar) to the stupidly inconsequential (is he afraid of spiders?). I put him in a scenario and I see then how he reacts. I follow him around, taking notes.

As to what worth his story has to readers, or what good I think he'll do in the long run – these are the questions, aren't they? Why do I feel the need to tell this story; what is compelling me to freeze it on a page? I say it's a compulsion because I believe it's a compulsion; the only thing that makes me more miserable than writing is not writing.

Who do I do this for?

I don't do it just for myself; why would a writer risk putting their work out into the world if it's so deeply personal as to make the question of a projected readership irrelevant? Despite all of the writing about writers, writers write for readers.

For a long time I puzzled over writers writing about writers. Why are so many characters in novels and short stories writers? There aren't many of us, not in comparison to builders, civil servants, stay-at-home parents, teachers. Even if the writer character is a hobbyist, his kind is still over-represented in fiction; there must be many more readers, runners, hikers, cinephiles and gamers. And writers are not especially interesting people. We spend all day typing, staring into space or talking to ourselves. Occasionally, we go out in public to try to talk about a thing that only makes sense once it's written down.

But maybe writers write about writers so as to make writers more appealing to readers; maybe writing about a writer is a sort of yearning love letter to the reader. Maybe there's an overlap in my fiction. Ryan is a musician because I understand what it means to perform art. Isn't all art performance art? Does that mean, then, that what I do is inextricable from ego? Do I, despite any proclamations of humility, think I have something important to say?

But I learn nothing about myself when I write, and I don't bloody know what the drag to writing is, or what I hope to do with myself. I don't feel I'm casting any great light on Ireland, or helping readers better understand themselves or their society. What purpose is there in writing, then? Is it just a madness that gives of itself? Or worse, a madness that wants an audience? Am I just singling out voices from the chorus in my head?

It starts with a dialogue: one voice talking to another. No one asked for the transcript; I choose to share it. What is fiction, but an indulgent translation of a person who exists only in my head?

Belinda McKeon

ROUTINE

Another of these opportunities, to frame the writing self, to create it, put it out there for others to see.

What will I do this time? Will I write a piece about process, or will I write a piece about shame?

I will write a piece about shame.

Writing – not so much the act itself, but the act of getting to the page – is an immense struggle for me, and I am ashamed of this. I am ashamed that I haven't written enough, that I haven't made myself write enough, that I haven't allowed myself to write enough – I don't know which one it is, or it may be a combination of all three and then some other things thrown in. When I'm being interviewed for book publicity, or writing things like this about my writing habits which is often part of what writers have to do as part of book publicity – when I'm doing these things, I sometimes lie, and talk about a routine, a discipline, and a philosophy of practice and of creativity honed over years. I'll talk about writing first thing in the morning, turning off the Internet, trying to get down a few thousand words a day, keeping a notebook, keeping a journal.

Other times, if I'm not in the mood to dredge up that version, if I don't have the energy to, I'll tell the truth. I'll talk about procrastination and failure and doubt and dread. I've never mentioned depression yet in an interview (is this an interview?), but anyone who can read between the lines will probably see it clearly. At first writing was a way out of it, when I was very young, but by now writing has long since been in a co-dependent relationship with it. They gaslight one another daily, and I can't tell them apart a lot of the time.

I think a lot about the things I didn't write. They exist as ghost pieces, ghost stories and plays – not a ghost novel, not yet, I don't torment myself quite that deeply just yet – but shorter pieces, the kinds of things I imagine that I could have done, made, written, several times over, if I had just, I don't know ... insert motivational phrase here. Set my mind to it? The phrase brings up an image of setting a dog on a pack of sheep that need to be rounded up and driven into a pen – ugh, that metaphor, no, that pun, where did that come from; well, there is an answer to your question about the unconscious and how it pushes things through the surface unexpectedly – except that when you set a dog on anything, you're not asking it to bring the thing to you, but to frighten it from you.

The ghost pieces are the things that by now could have been written, should have been written, if I had turned out to be the kind of writer I really did think, at twenty, twenty-five, thirty-nine (I am ever, underneath it all, hopeful; there's the rub) that I would turn out to be. *What would that feel like, being that kind of writer*, my shrink asks me when I go on about this, and I stop for a moment and let my mind fill up again with the fantasy of it: the prolific, productive, clear-headed writer version of me; idea-drunk, process-sober; nipping brightly between genres and projects as though between huge, spacious Airbnbs on a never-ending grand tour; starting things; finishing them. I think it'd feel amazing, I say to my shrink, and she goes quiet, which always feels vaguely recriminatory, and I look at my watch, to see how many minutes, this time, until *but we do have to stop.*

'I don't understand,' a student said to me once, after I'd explained to the group how hard I had to push myself not to avoid the act of writing, even though it was the thing I always wanted most to do with my day. I was a guest speaker, or giving a guest seminar, to the group; they were not kids, but people who'd had lives, and who were taking this course, now, paying a lot of money, now, so that they could write the novel they had always wanted to write, or always seen themselves as writing. This student, this writer, was someone who worked for the same newspaper for which I'd written for years; he was a sub-editor, and he was completely baffled by what I was saying, about not being able to write. 'I just don't understand how, if you want to write, how you just don't *write*,' he said. 'I mean, nobody's stopping you.' And whether there was scorn in his tone or whether I was just projecting it there, and projecting it onto his face, I have not forgotten it, nearly ten years later, and I can remember the precise angle at which he was sitting in relation to me in that room, the precise angle at which his response came barreling at me, and the way the heat, the shame-heat, hit on my cheeks first, and then on my collarbone, and down to my fingers, my fingers which did not write enough then, and do not write enough now.

I have no wisdom to offer on this, by the way. There is no resolution, no epiphany up ahead here. I live in hope, every day, that I will snap out of this bullshit and write as much as I want to write, because when I do it, it makes me feel – what? Alive? I don't know. Excited. A bit excited, sometimes a lot excited, at the business of being alive. To make something is an astonishing, vertiginous thrill; to see it coming into view, to have that moment when you know it is not just the dross of your thoughts, but something other than you, something beyond you, and that you are going to be the channel, the long, sparking tram line, along which it shoots into itself, into its form.

That's all. What's the line? *That's all, I don't think of you that often.*

Yeah, but he did.

Danielle McLaughlin

THE OTHER WOMAN

It was a summer afternoon and I was dragging groceries across the car park of the nearest Centra – which is not, in fact, near at all – when a man called to me. He was a man I had known since my teenage years, but we'd lost contact. I'd moved away and though I was back a number of years, I hadn't met him since my return.

'I saw your photo in the paper,' he said, 'but the name was different. It wasn't you.'

And so it began. The un-ravelling.

Danielle is my real name in the sense that it is the name that appears on my birth certificate. But ever since I was a tiny baby, my parents have always called me by a different name. They still do. I have no recollection of anybody in my family ever referring to me as Danielle, not even once. And neither is McLaughlin, the name I choose to write under, my real surname; it is my husband's. In my rural County Cork parish where identity is explained by reference to one's parents – 'You know her,' someone might say, 'X's daughter' – Danielle McLaughlin meant nothing to anybody; using it, it was as if I had returned and not returned at the same time. If anyone had paused to wonder who Danielle McLaughlin might be, it would most likely have been decided that she was a blow-in, one of those exotic creatures who had moved here during the boom to live foreign, colourful, possibly debauched lives – at the very least lives more interesting than our own – in one of the many one-off new builds that dotted the fields.

Until I began to write, though I'd conceived of her, I'd barely used Danielle McLaughlin at all. If she was to serve as a keeper of distances, it was important that she would not become overly familiar – not with me, not with anybody. Part of the beauty of a new name was that it was an alias of sorts; a disembodied thing that I could pluck from the wardrobe when occasion required it, or, to be more precise, when occasion both required and allowed it, because there were always places where the name wouldn't work; places populated by people who knew my other name and insisted on using it. I was nervous of those places, a nervousness akin to what I imagine one might experience when one's spouse and one's illicit lover end up in the same room. And so, while Danielle McLaughlin did undertake certain things, mostly things that took place at a geographical remove, it was the Other Woman – the one whose name I am not going to tell you – who continued to do everything else. And then the writing happened.

From day one, Danielle McLaughlin wrote all the stories and the Other Woman wrote none. For a while, there was an understanding of sorts and each kept off the other's patch; they compartmentalised well. Then things began to change, mostly because McLaughlin, it turned out, had no understanding of the concept of give and take; she played fast and loose with Other Woman's time and obligations. She became, to borrow a Department of Speculation term, an Art Monster, and yes, from this point on, life would often be explained by reference to books, or things that happened in books.

Lines were crossed. Danielle McLaughlin no longer just wrote stories; she also phoned plumbers and took delivery of washing machines. She texted drama teachers and booked dental appointments and signed her name at the end of medical forms. She insinuated herself into every aspect of Other Woman's life, reading her emails and tut-tutting over clichés and clunky prose; reading the books on Other Woman's bookshelves in a way that they had not been read before, a way that was almost aggressive.

Once, she sought out medical records from Other Woman's attendances with a childhood psychiatrist. In doing this she was not motivated in any way by a concern for Other Woman. Truth was, she didn't give a shit about Other Woman, had no loyalty to her whatsoever, and gave no thought as to what might become of her. What she had was a vision for a particular piece of writing, structured loosely around medical language. There would be graphics, graphics that involved, among other things, photographed extracts of very private medical notes, yellowed and typewritten (it was, after all, a very long time since Other Woman was a child). And when – oh, the dismay! – the much-anticipated records turned out not to be available, she considered, if only for the briefest of moments, forging them. They must, after all, have existed once. How much of a lie could it be to 'reconstitute' them?

In the face of such a sustained assault, Other Woman disappeared almost entirely. She was not dead exactly. Dead was altogether too straightforward a word for what had become of her. Instead, picture her, if you will, bound and gagged in a small dark shed, a wad of rough cloth stuffed in her mouth. There are cockroaches in this shed and colonies of greenish flat-headed mushrooms. A fur of mouldy damp coats the walls. It is a shed far from anywhere, a mossed stone structure with a galvanised roof, deep in the bowels of a disused quarry, not visible from any road. In the back, atop a tangle of scrap metal, is the corpse of some dead animal, possibly several dead animals. Naturally.

But why tolerate the continued existence of Other Woman at all? Given the extent to which she has been side-lined, why not kill her off entirely, under the pretence, if needs be, of putting her out of her misery? This is where things become complicated. Other Woman is tiresome, certainly, something of a pedant perhaps, but she is occasionally useful. She has memories, for example, and if nothing else, she is a ready body of material to be harvested. An objective observer might venture that Danielle McLaughlin is in fact *afraid* to kill off Other Woman. That she is cognisant of the fact that at some indeterminate point in the future, a day might come when she will be very glad of her. On that day, she might just climb into the shed with her. In the meantime, there is the fact that Other Woman has proved stubborn; she insists on hanging in there, making her presence felt in a litany of half-choked guttural complaints. Recently, during a period of gales and upheaval, the lock on the shed door worked loose and Other Woman, briefly at large, proceeded to wreak havoc by signing her name – yes, her own name – to several writerly things that were none of her damn business. I'm still here, she seemed to be saying, I haven't gone away, you know.

Alan McMonagle

THE MISADVENTURES OF A DITHERING WRITER IN THIRTEEN AND A HALF FRAGMENTS

1

I flit anxiously and eagerly from genre to genre. I always have a few stories on the go. Some of them are like eels – they slip away if I do not make a fast grab. Some are like bold children – they pay absolutely no attention to anything I tell them to do. One or two arrive unannounced from the farthest recesses of my imagination and insist on writing themselves with little or no input from myself. A couple of plays require open heart surgery. Several poems are threatening to rise up en masse and bite off my fingers, feet and other unmentionables if I do not give them immediate attention. I have four novels to write and so I am tentatively trying to negotiate with the devil for more time. These nights said devil shows up at the foot of my bed brandishing a chess board. I feel like the knight in the Ingmar Bergman film *The Seventh Seal*. Heaven help me.

I don't know if my writing is in any way distinctive. I am an aural learner as opposed to say the more common visual learning that attends so much writing. I hear things before I see them. Often I mishear things. This can provide delightful moments. Last week, I misheard something. The actual statement was, *There are suspicious organisms in the water.* I heard it as, *There are suspicious orgasms in the water.* I like to use humour. I find it pleasingly challenging to make the reader smirk. Plus, I feel humour helps brings the unfunny moments into relief. Mark Twain said the secret source of humour is not in joy but in sorrow. And I think it was Chekhov who said happy people write sad stories and unhappy people write funny stories. I'm not sure what that says about me or my writing and I probably don't want to know. Any time the vaguest notion permits me to consider that I am in any way different I feel the devil at my shoulder, sniggering.

3

My reasons for writing are partly intrinsic, partly spiritual, partly fanatical. Intrinsic because if I do not write I will go mad. Spiritual because I like to hang around with people who do not exist. Fanatical because I love moving as quickly as possible from the everyday world into the world of the imagination. Stretching reality; bending it, distorting it, somehow twisting it out of shape. Watching what characters make of this tilt in their lives – this is what I like to do.

4

I began writing as a boy. Little stories, plays, poems. I remember churning out a radio play that featured, in its opening moments, the discovery in a hotel bedroom of the slain corpse of the neighbourhood gossip. Along with a lunchtime radio show I used to tune in to, my early offering was heavily influenced by an unlikely combination of

Agatha Christie and an anthology of Greek myths and legends devoured innumerable times in my local library. I named my sleuth Hercules Poirot. He was a cast-iron genius. By the age of twelve I declared myself a similar kind of genius and announced my retirement. I stopped writing and, for a long time, was reluctant to resume. Don't ask me why. I drifted. I procrastinated. I avoided. To misquote Don DeLillo, what we are reluctant to touch often seems to contain the fabric of our salvation. I believe very much in the redemptive powers of the imagination. And, having abandoned it for so long, when I returned to writing as an adult I was so grateful and so relieved upon realising that the realm of the imagination had not abandoned me. Let yourself be led by the child that you were. This is a tendency I adhered to upon my resumption and, indeed, return to when it all threatens to get away from me.

5

I am, at various times, a reluctant, plodding, instinctive, spontaneous writer. At times I feel that, if I stay awake for long enough, I can reach the very end of a considerable narrative arc. At other times I feel that uncapping a pen is a bridge too far. I wake and enter every day with ever-varying combinations of wonder and dread. It is a flip-flop shoe of an existence. I like what Goethe said: do not hurry, do not rest.

6

Late last year I told the devil I could no longer stay up chatting until five in the morning. He laughed at me and suggested I refrain from refreshing my email every five seconds and not log on to Facebook until well into the afternoon. I thought this was good advice. Thanks, devil, I said, let me know when I can do something for you. A week later the demented lunatic started showing up with his chess board.

7

If you know what you want to be you will be it. If you don't know, then you will spend your days reinventing yourself, discovering who you are. I accept and indeed envy the former standpoint in so many ways. But I am an uncertain person. And rather than rail against this uncertainty I suffer it and endure it and try to harness it, make something of it. And so each day becomes the first day; it allows room for discovery, invention, re-invention, wonder, mystery; all of which are manna for the creative urge and time spent dwelling within the imagination. DeLillo again: May the days be aimless. Let the seasons drift. Do not advance the action according to a plan.

8

I have started several novels. There is the edgy-existential one about the brother-sister assassination squad who must go on the run after taking out a controversial Irish politician. There is the comedy-of-desperation one about the office slave finally tipped over the edge by a boss constantly referred to as the highly-evolved vegetable. There is the life-weary one about the last day in the working life of a barber terrified beyond measure of the imminent reunion with his poet-activist daughter. There is my iffy west-of-Ireland situated *bildungsroman* featuring an as yet-to-be-named antagonist who is more of a genius in dreams than in life. I intend to return to each of them, grant them time and energy, sweat and tears, some blood too. One reason I have started them is because I so enjoy beginnings. That sense of flailing about heedlessly before committing to a singular inevitability. Another reason is that I am all the time hankering to work on the very project I am not currently tangled up inside. Yet one more reason is that I do not want to reach the end – it is a little death. More than little. My solution is this: they are never finished. Merely abandoned.

9

I find every novel I have started or have done some work on (as already noted, there are several) has one all-encompassing definitive centre. But long before I become aware of this there are several, smaller centres which seem to have an elevated notion of their place in the scheme of things and so spend a lot of time fooling me into thinking they are worthy of this singular vital point in space. These various centres – frauds, imposters and infidels the lot of them – declare themselves to me at various moments in a narrative's progression. Some shout and wave and make lots of theatrical gestures. Some are quieter and comfortable enough within themselves not to attract any attention – as though they are aware that I will stumble upon them and act accordingly. And then there is the centre that is very much in hiding, invisible and utterly soundless. Buried deep. A needle within a haystack. An x-mark on the treasure map. This is the centre I need to find.

10

The devil continues to rile me. Not so long ago I was about to read a short story to a packed house. (By packed I mean ten or twenty people). I took to the platform, stepped up to the lectern and opened my book, only to discover the story I had intended to read was no longer between the covers. Convinced that invisible gremlins were playing their usual havoc with my abilities to adequately function in a public space, I flicked through pages, certain that I would alight on the piece I was after. But there was no sign of it. I closed the book, looked out at the expectant audience, half-smiled and took a gulp of the wine that had magically appeared. 'My story seems to have momentarily absconded. Please bear with me,' I managed to say. Convinced that some form of visual trickery was at large I reopened the book. Again, there was no sign of the story. It had definitely absconded. Deciding I should instantly summon and resort to a plan B, I flicked to the beginning pages of the book and to a story I had read many times before, one I knew I could rely on to get me out of a bind – a crowd-pleaser. It, too, had disappeared. Again, I closed the book, took another gulp of wine, deeper and longer-lasting than the previous, did my half-smile which was really little more than a vague attempt to mask the gathering maelstrom inside me, and once again looked out to the audience. One or two were fidgeting in their seats. One or two were actually walking towards the exit. I looked down at the book, checked to ensure that my name was on the cover and opened it again. The entire thing was a swathe of blankness. Then I had a brainwave. I tossed that particular copy and reached for a second copy on the nearby sales table. Nothing. And so it went. My entire oeuvre. Black page after blank page. At some point, satisfied that he had gotten his kicks, the devil decided to release me from this latest torment. At once I jumped out of bed and made a beeline for my bookshelves. I piled the books around me, curled up and swore that I was never setting foot outside my door again. Then my phone pinged through a message. It was the devil, informing me that for one evening only it was buy-one get-one-free in my local pub. At the end of his message he added some sniggering emoticons. I put on my 'isn't madness a fright' t-shirt, grabbed the chessboard and out the door I toddled.

11

I often think of the scene from Lewis Carroll when Alice encounters the unicorn. 'I didn't think unicorns existed,' Alice says to the fabled horse. And the unicorn replies, 'I'll believe in you if you believe in me.' I think there is something magical about this exchange, it contains a world of possibility, more manna for the imagination.

12

Writing is about taking risks. It is a high wire act. A game you lose almost all the time. I remember reading Dostoevsky's *The Gambler*. And when my delay mechanism finally kicked in I remember thinking, gamblers don't gamble because they want to win. They gamble because they want to lose. Later again, I read Bohumil Hrabal's joyous one-utterance *Dancing Lessons for the Advanced in Age*. The narrative is prefaced with a line from Ladislav Klíma: *Victory is made up exclusively of beatings*. Which in turn sends me to the line from Cormac McCarthy, think of the worse luck your bad luck has saved you from. Ha-ha. This is what the devil says in my ear most days. Of course, being Irish, I have an abiding sense of tragedy, which sustains me through fleeting periods of joy.

13

And of course it has to sing. Be it rock 'n roll or moonlight sonata. Swing time or daft punk. Looney tune or Greek chorus. A Miles Davis *Kind of Blue* or 'Bohemian Rhapsody'. And always a quest that quietly insists: don't seek what's there, seek what's not there.

13.5

These are my current writing thoughts. They will change. Sometimes the questions can be enough – that is, if they are the right questions. And now I can hear the devil sniggering again. It occurs to me that I may have to come up with a pet name for him.

Eoin McNamee

WALKING GIRL

We're driving up the west coast of Scotland. We're on a
stretch of dual carriageway somewhere outside Kilmarnock.
Rundown high-rises in the middle distance. Litter on the
road margins. I see someone on the white line. A girl
walking between the two fast moving lanes of traffic. She's
wearing a towelling dressing gown over white pyjamas
with reindeer on them. Slippers. She has dirty blonde hair
drawn back from her face. She has high cheekbones and
grey eyes and there is a bruise on her temple. She's smoking
a cigarette and her grey eyes are fixed on something in the
distance. One minute she is there, then gone, disappearing
in the rear view mirror. My wife doesn't even look at me.
Her eyes, fixed straight ahead, narrow slightly. 'Don't' she
says softly. The only thing she said about it on the entire
trip.

When we get home I've got a phrase in my head. *If there
was a realm of bad choices she would be queen.*

I've been at this for a long time, this suborning of people
into fiction. I've written five novels based on real events

and peopled them with the actual players, fit them in with an architecture which is part real and part fictional. I explain it by saying that these stories demanded to be told that way. I still believe that. But there is something else. I seem to need a certain amount of edge in the telling, a scent of blood if you like, something that could blow up in my face. I've started to wonder how real the risk is. The blood on the floor never belongs to me. When I populate the books with those who lived the events I am writing about, it is their heart at risk, not mine.

I started to write the story of the girl in the dressing gown. It began to get entangled in the story of the women we were in Scotland to visit. My wife's friend from college, grievous events in her past. When the story was finished I showed it to Marie. She was furious. I had been told about these events in confidence and I had breached that confidence. This was her friend, and I had betrayed them both.

She was right. I started to horse trade. I didn't like the way she was looking at me. I would show the story to her friend and discard it if she didn't like it. Marie didn't say anything but her eyes narrowed the way they did when we first saw the walking girl.

My wife's friend is an artist and film-maker – in the business – and got what was going on, though she didn't have to and would have been well within her rights to have been angry as my wife was angry on her behalf. But she wasn't. She said that she knew everything she told me might end up in a piece of work and generously corrected some assumptions I had made in the text.

It doesn't end there though. The artist's responsibility in all of this is a broad debate – but the human responsibility isn't. You're intruding in places that you were never meant to be, taking something that belongs to someone else, smuggling it out of the room and shaping it to your own purposes. You could say that the art, the short story that emerged, is worth it. Beauty is not always lovely, Robinson Jeffers says, and you could say that the steps you take towards beauty are unlovely. A troubled girl is granted some kind of stature by being elevated. But this won't do. She didn't ask for it and will never know of it.

I woke up one night thinking about sin. I went to the dictionary and looked up the word. *A moral offence or shortcoming.* That seemed to fit what I was doing better than anything else. To intrude on the stuff of other's lives is a personal moral offence, and I'll answer for it in those terms. We can slip into the assumption that the writer has a hand in the moral settings of society. That you lead so that others might follow. That isn't the way it works. I don't write for, to or at anyone. I hum the tune because it is there to be hummed. That's the height of it.

In the story of the walking girl, called 'Walking North, Walking Home', a young woman travels across Scotland by taxi to confront a family trauma. She sees the walking girl in her dressing gown. On the way home that night in the snow, having been defeated by her own heart, she sees the walking girl again, many miles from where she first saw her:

> 'Look,' she said. It was the woman they had seen that morning. She was walking on the other side of the road. Still wearing the yellow dressing gown, her hair stiff and ghostly with cold. Tam slowed the car and stopped but the woman kept walking. Her head was high and the light of ruin and of glory shone in her eyes.
> 'Jesus,' Tam said, 'she never stopped. She never stopped walking.'

One of the things they say about short stories is that they should, or might, begin with a person or situation and at the end return to that same person or situation only transformed. This story seems to fit that model, although I wouldn't want to apply it as a rule to every short fiction. The writing is good. The story works. It never occured to me then or now to ask whether the piece of art was worth it in terms of the pain it might cause to others. It wasn't that I was unaware of what I had done, but I was borne along by the imperatives of the work. Thomas McGuane talks about an elaboration of soul, and that is as good a description of writing as I can find. Whether the act of writing, the sin of it, costs you all or part of that soul seems to be beside the point.

Emer Martin

Fiction is the Mothership

Deeply lost in the night. Just as one sometimes lowers one's
head to reflect, thus to be utterly lost in the night. All around
people are asleep. It's just play acting, an innocent self-
deception, that they sleep in houses, in safe beds, under a safe
roof, stretched out or curled up on mattresses, in sheets, under
blankets; in reality they have flocked together as they had once
upon a time and again later in a deserted region, a camp in the
open, a countless number of men, an army, a people, under a
cold sky on cold earth, collapsed where once they had stood,
forehead pressed on the arm, face to the ground, breathing
quietly. And you are watching, are one of the watchmen, you
find the next one by brandishing a burning stick from the
brushwood pile beside you. Why are you watching? Someone
must watch, it is said. Someone must be there.

– Kafka, *At Night*

Stories are made up but they are not lies.

Fiction is the closest way to access truth.

Fiction is the truth unfettered.

Our compulsion to create stories generates in the soft
grey mountain folds and valleys of our human mind. We

close our eyes and our brain fictionalises our thoughts, spews images from fears, manufactures totems from dreams, and scaffolds our understanding with myth.

Story is the overflow of the human mind. Our bodies are indistinguishable from our fellow mammals; for better or for worse, it was always our mind that defined our species. In essence, fiction is our unique attribute.

Stories are serious business: we live, die and kill each other over fictions. We humans, clustered in our fabricated nation states, depleting our resources on the shifting landmasses of a spinning planet, our own works of fiction.

In the beginning, stories leaked from us onto the walls of the caves, they were the spiral scratches on Neolithic stones; they pulsed through ancient hands that squeezed clay into the abundant Goddess shape. All our religions are fiction – holy stories and mythologies that house our spirits. We have danced them, painted them, rhymed them, sung them and worshiped them. Story is the shape of our soul. We are both elevated and controlled by our fictions. The constant playing out of these sacred stories becomes rituals that bind and root us.

Story is the stealing back of the infinite from the finite. Fiction means that we can hide for a moment in a small pocket of eternity as time treats us like shit. Time viciously devours all the pieces of ourselves except that which we have dreamed, released, transcribed and put into form. Therefore, fiction is an extension of the spirit, the demonstration of our faith in the worth of each other and the value of our own existence.

Long ago, the Greeks recognised the cathartic element of performing tragedies in a shared setting. In ancient times, sacrifice was used as a release. In lieu of actual human sacrifice, a tragic story can heal us. Probably the most painful aspect of being human is the experience of grief. The existentialist Prince Hamlet is an expression of Shakespeare's mourning of his own son Hamnet who died at eleven years old. So Hamlet is not really a prince, a man of power; rather, Hamlet is a promising child taken before he had a chance to live. He is a boy, among so many boys, who will never fulfil his destiny. The tragedy is surely that, but fiction is the transformation of the dead boy into a communal archetype of grief. Not only does Hamnet live through Hamlet, but Shakespeare's pain has found that cathartic fictional outlet. And so the unwieldy grief of a genius mind is poured into a shape that now moves by itself, that will continue to resonate over the centuries. It is that grief that still walks out from the obscurity of the wings onto the floodlit stage. As we sit together in the darkness, side-by-side, we are called on to bear witness. Hamlet dying again and again throughout the centuries is the sacrifice that makes us whole. It is the salve for our own grief.

Stories are medicine. The hurt once exposed can be healed by acknowledgement. All my own work is a battle against forgetting those whom the gods forgot; from beggars and refugees in the underworld of Paris; to squatters in London; to broken families adrift on a constricting planet; to women prisoners; to the chorus of hurt voices in *The Cruelty Men*. Voices I heard first on national radio speaking their truth in twenty-first-century Ireland. The Magdalene women, those children who were caught up in industrial schools and those confined in mental institutions at the mercy of the church and state began to reveal their abuse. I read the gruelling Murphy Report and the Ryan Report, and was moved to write the book. Why did I fictionalise them when they were already telling their stories? Once I read their horrific accounts there was no other story I could tell. I wanted to honour their truth in story. Their voices fade in fact and are relegated to newspaper columns and government reports. Fiction lets the painful poetry of their existence enjoin with myth to become something more powerful than us all.

At my book launch in Hodges Figgis on Dawson Street, I recognised many people in the audience. However, there was one elderly woman who sat in the second row and she was completely alone. She clutched the book in her hand and was staring at me throughout the reading with a startling intensity. Afterwards, when I was signing books she told me that she had been a slave in a Magdalene laundry and had heard me on the radio. 'I had to come,' she said. 'I had to get this book.' I was moved and humbled. I knew then the story was bigger than me. It was outside of me. It had its own life. The book belonged to those who had suffered. Their courage and resilience were what inspired me to write it in the first place. Fiction is a communal act.

Fiction can be the voice of the unrecorded. I write because I took form as an ordinary female human child on a small cold island at the edge of Europe, with no access to power and few resources. I wanted to be beautiful but I wasn't. I wanted to be special but I wasn't. I even wanted to sing but I couldn't. I wasn't very impressed with myself. Fiction is what saved me. I could be relieved of being myself and slip inside another's head and think their thoughts. Fiction elevated me. The more books and stories and poems I read, the more steps I took. Literature was the ladder that led up and up to some understanding of what it is to be human; to be mortal yet hopeful; to be doomed yet believing; to be ordinary yet sacred; to be forgotten and yet remembered; to be powerless yet have the power to create.

The reader is as vital to the book as the writer. Instinctively, as an unremarkable child who had no other powers, I understood that I had control and authority as a reader. As Kafka said, 'Someone must watch, it is said. Someone must be there.' If the writer is the guide to bring us into a deep place of contemplation and understanding, then I, the reader, was the empathic witness the guide was longing for. Reading is an act of great love and trust. It is how I survived my unlovely human form.

Story is the human impulse to dream aloud, to bring the dream into a shared place. If this material life was all, we would go grey with weariness. In his short prose poem 'At Night', Kafka proposed that when we sleep we all meet and are finally unified. As a renowned insomniac, maybe he felt he was being abandoned and missing out. I am a good sleeper and could have told Kafka that we do not all actually gather and meet in sleep like he contemplated, but rather we meet in books. It is a profound exchange of psyche. The reader lives the writer's dream in its entirety and intensity. Like aliens arriving on another planet, we can walk around each other's minds, traverse the unfamiliar fathomless oceans, scale strange soaring mountains and share sustenance at the corner tables in cafes tucked away in the exotic cities of another consciousness.

If the space of story is that of the shared dream, then what would it be like to exist in a world with no fiction?

It was Féile na Laoch, festival of the heroes. This special festival only occurs once every seven years in Cúil Aodha, an all-Irish-speaking area of County Cork. On the final day of the festival, seven poets, seven storytellers, seven musicians and seven painters are awarded a heroes medal by the President of Ireland, Michael D Higgins, himself a poet. I was invited to become a hero and I offered to drive my fellow heroes Judith Mok, the classical singer and poet, and her husband, the Dublin poet Michael O'Loughlin. Michael wrote an extraordinary response to Kafka's idea of us all meeting in a world of sleep in his poem 'Sleeping in Prague'. He read it to me from the back seat of my car on the long rainy road trip to Cork. His poem starts with what could be a description of what it is like not to have shared our stories, to be living in a fictionless world:

Torturers know this. Keep us in light
and we shrivel like dead flowers –

keep us from sleep and we drown
like fish in the air, we sway and flail
like sailors on land, like astro-
and cosmonauts walking in space
cut off from the mothership

Judith Mok then said that she too had a poem and read hers to me from the front seat. As I navigated through the tolls she asked me which one was better. Like the diplomatic parent I told them they were both equally good. Michael leaned in to me from the back seat and said, 'Don't worry Emer. Only three more hours of this.' On this journey it was Michael who told me about Kafka's idea of all of humanity meeting in the dream space. His words echoed in my head as we continued through tiny colourful towns into the lush dense countryside of Cork. We arrived in Cúil Aodha, and those of us who were nominated heroes sat in a circle in the local community hall and engaged in a public discussion about the relationship of story to the land itself. The President of Ireland was wearing a three-piece suit with a Maori tie. Peadar Ó Riada, the musician and composer, told stories of Maoris and Australian aboriginal people who travelled to this area and how their belief that story is what brings the land alive is very similar to ancient Irish beliefs. After all, what is a land without stories?

Later, in procession behind the Cullen Pipe Band, we followed the President to Páirc na Laoch, the field of heroes, where the 'Swirling of the Waters', a ritual to remind us of our common heritage, took place. Or, as Michael put it, 'An Irish field, full of Irish people doing Irish things.' We were invited to share our work with the hundreds of people who had gathered. Jovially, the President of Ireland mingled with local people and with some tourists who had happily stumbled on the event. I was struck that his aide-de-camp, an army captain, followed a few paces behind, in full military uniform, carrying the poetry books of the president in his gloved hand. The festival went on all through the night.

The President read his poem about rural women and their resilience. Under the stage lights, I couldn't see the crowd, but I felt them listening. I read the story of a young woman raised in an industrial school who is transferred to a laundry at sixteen. She works alongside her birth mother but neither of them is told the truth of their relationship. At 3am Judith Mok sang a lament in Ladino, the language of Sephardic Jews. It was a fifteenth-century Spanish song about a mother who found her child dead in the cradle and couldn't tell her husband when he came home. The song is a fictional metaphor for the loss of the homeland when the Christians conquered the Iberian Peninsula and expelled Muslims and Jews. A hushed, reverent audience felt the sorrow of their displacement through the centuries. Later I found myself exhausted and curled up on a plastic tarp, clutching a bottle of whiskey, in a cold field in Cork listening to the bagpipes play as I got rained on. I thought of Kafka:

> they have flocked together as they had once upon a time and again later in a deserted region, a camp in the open, a countless number of men, an army, a people, under a cold sky on cold earth, collapsed where once they had stood.

Was I getting too old for festivals? I longed for my warm bed back at the hotel. No doubt, I would give anything to be back in the body of that unlovely child I was as a teenager. I would be more forgiving of her. Then it occurred to me how happy I was to be here in a field of stories. After half a century in human form, I have come to terms with my existence through fiction. No one slept that night. Everyone had a story to tell, whether through poetry, prose, painting or song. And people had flocked together to listen to all these stories. We were no longer separate entities; we moved in one dream. Fiction *is* the mothership. It is where we touch and become known to each other. It is where we stop calculating and advertising and instead reveal ourselves. It is our only way home.

Geraldine Mills

THE WRITING LIFE

'This afternoon has gone mad with figs and heated
sounds,' the poet Lorca wrote, and so it had. Given the
room named after him, with sleeping area and workspace,
I stood on the balcony that looked up towards the *pueblo*
with its white-cubed houses stacked high on the side of the
mountain. Sebastian was in the garden, cutting down the
almond trees. Their blackened trunks, destroyed in a
previous fire, were being reduced to logs of almond fuel.
His chainsaw whined in the hot, Spanish air. Blue fell
through my open window.

The writer as temporary exile, this was my first
international residency, Fundación Valparaiso, in Mojacar
in the southeast of Andalucia. There were eight of us, six
visual artists, one composer and me. We met up for pre-
dinner tapas and took the first tentative steps towards
fellowship. We were served cockles and mussels and
squid, its ink dark enough to write with. We broke bread
together, *pan, brot, chleb*. A ghecko took the last rays of heat
from the wall. I could hear the *grillos* singing each to each.

Morning came, gilding the tiles of my floor, and from across the balcony, Iris, the Slovak composer, had already started the first notes of her new composition. I headed out into the world of figs ripening, red peppers drying on the path. On the dusty walkways around the residency I could see the devastation of the previous year's fire that swept down from Holy Mountain and consumed the valley. The pomegranate tree held up charred arms still bearing its exploded wine apples, their claret jewels turned to ash.

The wind came up at midday, shutters slammed shut. Ideas blew away; I ran after them and tried to tie them down in that room that had been named after their revered poet.

Unlike another poet, Pablo Neruda, I do not know when writing came in search of me, though it seems as if it was there from my first breath. A few months before I was born my mother, gravid with me, was cycling home from town. The sun was at the foot of the sky and a horse jumped over her bike, knocking her to the ground. From the moment I first held a pencil, it was clear that I was going to be a *ciotóg*. The word *ciotóg* not only means left-handed, but also refers to someone who is not quite right. She saw me as different, blamed the horse, the fall from the bike. The animal that had jumped over me had made me cack-handed, gauche, sinister.

School knocked the left-handedness out of me. The evil hand of the devil was locked behind my back and the anaemic tentacle that was my right hand had the pencil forced into it. With great difficulty, letters stumbled off the page, collided, became dirty holes in my copybook when I tried to erase them.

To make sense of the world I was born into, the hand that was forced to write, wrote. It recorded all those living images that were part of this upturned life: the flesh of ripe haws as if they were miniature apples; a wren, with its tiny fan tail in the air, flitting into a hole in the wall; the raindrop becoming a glimmering man sliding down the window pane. I wrote out all that was inside me and when I read it out at school, the nun sent me into the higher class to repeat it. I thought it was another punishment.

Being child number ten of eleven pregnancies, there was always a lot going on in our household, mouths forever opening and closing like swallow chicks in July waiting to be fed, to be heard. I learned very early on that the easiest thing for someone like me was to watch, to become an observer in the drama that was constantly unfolding around the kitchen table at which all life was fought.

Ours was not a house of books. There wasn't money for such luxuries. The most world-changing moment in my seven-year-old life was the day my brother put me on the carrier of his bike and cycled the three miles to Galway city library. Greedy for every story I could find, I devoured all around me, secreting those titles that I couldn't take home with me at the back of shelves, in the hope that they would be there when I returned the following week.

I wrote all through my teenage years. College saw me taking the scientific route where I delighted in a whole new vocabulary, made lists of new words as lengthy as metabolic pathways; words like dendrites, diatoms, carapace. While working full-time in a laboratory, I completed an arts degree at night, re-imagining the lives of ancient Greece: Iphigeneia, Clytemnestra, Laertes.

I wasn't a writer. I was just someone who wrote. Being a writer was something completely different. Writers didn't come from a background like mine. They didn't write the everyday story. They went off to Paris and lived in attics, drank absinthe and wrote masterpieces. Words were my palette. All I wanted to do was draw pictures of what I saw in the world around me, the beauty and the pain, the tiny lacerations of the heart.

Years went by and I kept my world inside me. Then in the early 1980s, the loneliness of motherhood in a sprawling housing estate in Tallaght pushed me into my first creative writing class in St Colmcille's School. Here I was supported by other writers and encouraged to let the words paint pictures for me. Drawing them out of my own history I put them in tentative lines on the page. And when I did I could hear my own voice and it wasn't being drowned out at all. Writing had somehow found me within myself. I wrote as if my life depended on it, not knowing that it did.

I learned to type. I bought my first typewriter. One of the greatest stresses on any writer is finding time to actually write. There never seemed to be any extra hours to fit it in. It was always consigned to the end of the pile after all the other jobs had been done.

One night, while driving home from a reading, an empty hearse overtook me on the road. I looked up at the sky and vowed that I wouldn't end up in the back of that hearse and not have produced something worth publishing. I reassessed my approach to my workload and anything that wasn't a priority was catapulted to the lower pecking order. Furry green things grew at the back of the fridge. A moonscape of fluff congregated under beds. I used my car as my writing space while I waited for my children to finish their dancing or athletics. And when life interfered again and I had to go back into the workforce, I left the house in the morning with a hot water bottle, a flask of tea and got an hour's writing done sitting in a carpark before I headed into the office. This is how I learned that inspiration just doesn't show up. I had to train it to come to me. Day by day stories fell out of the sky and into my notebook.

Today, thanks to publishers who have believed in me, I have published poetry, short stories and a novel, each genre growing out of the gift of an idea that comes from that unknown place. Hungry for stories, for images, the words come, eating up the blank screen. They creep out of shadows or fly in on the wing of an egret to drop temptation at my hands. With the urgency of fire, I set alight an idea across this arid landscape of page, coax it, kindle it, wait for the moment when it bursts into flames.

Lia Mills

ON WRITING[1]

Writing is Where I Live

I mean where the whole *I* of me lives, the plurality, where
all the voices are heard – in that strange, inner, writing
world where there are no rules and the life-supporting,
life-giving condition is language. It is where I am my most
real, my most honest self.

I might be a small bit obsessive about it. No matter what
I'm doing, there's a current of under thought running in the
background – even, apparently, when I'm asleep. I can't
count the number of times I've been woken by a sentence
forming in my head, insisting on being transferred to paper
before I'm allowed to sleep again. I'm not saying those
sentences are brilliant – they might not even make sense to
me in daylight – but I love the fact of them. They are signs.
Something, somewhere is working.

I'm sure there are writers who are supremely confident
in their gift and their mastery of that gift, but I don't think
I know many of those. Most of us are utterly sure of the

importance of what we're doing, but that's a different thing entirely, hard to live up to. The thing of it is that writing is a lifelong apprenticeship. There's always more to learn, harder challenges ahead. The more you write, the more skills you develop, the further there is to fall. It can be nerve-racking. And there's that sickening anticipation of the critical keyboards sharpening in the background, just waiting for you to make a show of yourself:

> Who do you think you are?
> Who asked you to do this, or suggested you could?

Believe me, nothing the critics can say or do to you will even come close to the things you say and do to yourself, giving yourself the dreads.

Why do we do it? Why open our innards and spill them right there on the page? May as well spread them on the street for the neighbours to use as speed bumps, exposed, raw, needy. Ambitious. There's the book you think you're going to write and then there's the book you actually write. No one will ever know the difference but you, but in the gap between them there's a little ghost book that will haunt you for the rest of your conscious days.

So there you are, with the ghosts and the ghost books and the dreams, bending the sentences, crossing lines; language the thread, the guidewire, the rope, the knotted sheet. You live with the voices, their sentences and your own and the ones you make together; the wild ambition and a creeping fear of ridicule; the joy and the deep depression, the emptiness and the fullness, the light and the dark and everything in between. Writing will reveal what you most want to hide (although you might not get the message until much, much later). That's how you live, if you're a writer.

Well, if you're this writer. I wouldn't like to presume.

In *Aspects of the Novel*, E.M. Forster writes that the storyteller in primitive societies was in a precarious position. When they gathered around the fire, our ancestors liked to be entertained, diverted from the sure and certain knowledge of icy winds blowing across the tundra, wolves howling at the moon. They wanted stories of the hunt, of escape from raging bears, of gods – and yes, of fighting men. If the storyteller failed and the audience got bored, they either fell asleep or killed him. Those are the stakes you play for. Reading from your work out loud or putting words on paper, you can sense the flames at your face. They might kill you. You might live forever.

Reading

Do you remember the exact instant when you knew you could read? I don't mean the process of learning to recognise each separate alphanumeric shape, dragging your finger along a line letter by letter, syllable by syllable, spelling it all out word by painstaking word. I mean that immense, life-changing moment when the words stir, lift, form themselves into sentences that speak to your inmost mind and guide you through the world of a story.

When people ask about writing, that is the closest explanation I can come to: it's like reading, but from the inside. In the same way that the combination of language and story pulls you through their lines to the immense inner space of a book, an idea or a character sparks a magnetic charge that attracts you, somewhere inside the inner space of your imagination

Imagination. To imagine. Noun and verb. Light-years beyond conventional time, imagination is both place and action. It's a dynamic faculty that feeds on your response and grows. Have you ever seen iron filings respond to a magnet? Writing is like that. All these agitated little particles – ideas, random thoughts, a word here and there, something you overheard or read: they bristle, fidget, shiver – that's the resistance part – then coalesce into a stream of metal flying in one sure direction.

Apprentice

I wish it really was that easy, all the time. It's a stage every piece can reach, if you're lucky. Then the rewriting, bringing it home. I often get stuck back at the bristling part: all agitation, little flow. Here's the thing: writing is work. A new piece brings its own challenges as well as rewards. What's the best way to make *this* argument? What's the best way to tell *this* story? Long walks, sleepless nights and whatever you're having yourself don't always bring an answer. Each piece is a new question, or a new way of answering an old one; you start from a new position, a beginner all over again. Sometimes I treat myself as a student, send myself back to first principles: haul out the *How To* books and go back to the basics of craft. No matter how experienced you are, however small or large your skills, you have to teach yourself how to solve *this* puzzle. Show-and-tell. That's the challenge, the excitement, the adventure of it.

And when I'm stuck, or lost, or in despair, there is a sure remedy in reading other writers: biography, an interview, an essay, a poem, a chapter written by someone whose insights and energy might ease the tangle I find myself in. What I need is to be in the presence of another writing mind, to recharge the energy of the flagging ectoplasmic forms that inhabit the weird inner space of my reading and writing mind. This is one of the absolute joys of writing – we're in a community that transcends time and space. If I have a question for someone who is light-years ahead of me in terms of achievement, I can still bring my questions to their work and find their answers, freely given. I can have conversations with the dead. I can eavesdrop on characters in novels; I have access to letters and diaries as well as pieces written with my exact dilemma in mind. Those people speak my language; they are my tribe and in their writing they never let me down. The magic of sentences reasserts itself. It calms and restores me, sends me back to my own work: *calm down, you can do this.* It's just work. It's words and sentences. It's paragraphs. Novels, stories, essays – they're not written all at once; *one word at a time will get you there.* I can, actually, do this.

And: if it was easy, everyone would do it.

The Quest[2]

The classic quest narrative begins when the kingdom is in trouble and the hero is offered a chance to ride out in search of whatever saving thing his or her world needs. So it is with writing. The work starts with an initiating idea. It could be character or conundrum, a place, atmosphere or question – all stories and writers have different starting points. The idea stands up in the recesses of your mind and waves an invitation: do you want to come with me and do this thing? Whether and how you respond is up to you, but if you do it, everything hinges on the quality of attention you bring to the task and whether you can stay with it.

You are in a relationship with that idea until you've finished exploring it in writing. As with any relationship, beginnings are a thrill. While you're still fresh, it sparks flashes of possibility, flares of delight, shocks of revelation. You're wide open to it, as it is to you. At that point you'll make time for it, you'll drop everything and run when it beckons. The trouble starts when the daily grind sets in, the continued presence and demands you make on each other begin to pall. It can be hard to stay focussed and alert, to be fully present with this cranky stubborn fossil – it's only a lump of rock after all, it will never yield its secrets, you don't know what you were thinking, what you ever saw in it. Things can turn ugly, violent. There'll be days when you loathe each other. Other ideas will try to come between you. They're younger and brighter. Ditch that old yoke and come with me, they'll say. That's when you need faith in what you can realise together – if you stick it out.

If you don't commit yourself to the long haul, if your attention strays, if you hold back or hide from the deeper implications of what you're doing, neither of you will be satisfied. If you lie, cheat, evade, you're going nowhere, fast. You need to attend to your idea in every sense: care for it, nurture it, bring it what it needs, feed it, wait for it but above all give it your very best attention. There's nothing like the rush that comes when the work suddenly ignites and you're there – ready – and let yourself go with the sheer intensity and power of it.

Writing Life[3]

Years ago I was diagnosed with an advanced-stage squamous cell carcinoma in my cheek and gums. By the time I got the diagnosis, the cancer had spread to several lymphnodes, with perineural invasion. That means that it had also progressed to the space surrounding multiple nerves in my neck. The prognosis was bleak. The proposed treatment included radical surgery to my face and neck to be followed with aggressive radiotherapy. I would get a whole lot worse before I got better. If I got better.

I was working on a novel at the time, so I brought notebooks into hospital with me, thinking that I'd work on storylines while I was there – I wasn't about to let a thing like cancer stop me.

Well.

Before long those notebooks were overtaken by lists: of names, individuals and specialities, options and treatment plans. Being in hospital is a lot like moving to another country – there's a whole new vocabulary to learn, new customs, geographies, constraints and possibilities. I had to record everything so that I wouldn't forget or confuse the details. At the same time I was noticing everything around me with a peculiarly-focussed attention. I wrote down everything that happened. What people said and did, what I thought and felt. The notebooks would eventually grow into a book, *In Your Face*, but I didn't know I was writing a book at the time. I only knew that I used them in a desperate attempt to hold onto something precious – a thing that turned out to be myself. There was a woman on the ward who used to call out a name, over and over, the name of someone who never came. In the book I suggest that the name she calls is the rock she clings to as she drowns. The notebooks were my rock.

Before all this I'd have said that I write because I have to. It's a physiological need for me, I'd have said – did say – like breathing. I meant that, but I meant it from somewhere near the front of the mind. In spite of it I was often at war with myself. I needed and wanted to write but had to struggle to do it, often feeling utterly unentitled, fraudulent – a toxic disempowerment that is the cruel opposite of the authority a writer, by definition, needs. This conflict has tangled personal roots that are irrelevant here, only the fact of their existence matters. Many writers experience similar blocks. If we're lucky we find ways to work against or around them, to hold doubt at bay while we finish a piece. Even if we think, as I did, that we understand the issues on an intellectual level, the effort can be exhausting. It undermines the actual work. This writing was different: urgent, necessary and absolutely mine; a lifeline that anchored me to the world and held a place in the world open for me – not just mind but heart and root.

There was little I could do to help myself through this illness and treatment, other than to find ways to express what was happening in my own terms, to resist medicalese and the standard consolatory euphemisms. Not that I was above euphemism. The first one that dawned on me, the first chink of light, was when I realised that cancer is a word, not a sentence. I would learn that other people had come up with this construction before, but it came to me like a new-minted phrase and getting there felt like shelter. Words and sentences are what I know. I spun phrases and conjured images and sought the right words, a clear expression of everything that happened in terms of its meaning for me.

Writing my illness in this engaged, focussed way, I was not so much telling or describing it as living it, in writing. The phrase 'my mouth is eating me' steadied me. When I put the question *What will it be like to have half a face?* on paper, it looked back at me, perfectly calm. The image of my tumour as a crab gave me a sign to look for and I found it everywhere – in the behaviour and sensations associated with the kind of pain I experienced, the pincer-like restriction of my jaw, the ugly red, the carapace. When I was allowed home for visits we'd walk around the harbours and beaches of south County Dublin. I saw signs everywhere – empty shells, broken claws – and felt enormous pity. One of us had to go.

I was absolutely present in that illness, one big ball of apprehension: nervy, taking everything in. My mind had nowhere else to go. My tools of engagement were: attention, observation, language. In writing I could translate experience to words, images, sentences. I was relatively powerless in physical terms, but there were powers I could summon – powers of suggestion, of association, of imagination and naming.

Somewhere in that labyrinth of experience and observation, of dread and love and awe I came home to myself in writing. It was a while before I noticed: I was happy there. There was no space for the old mechanisms that used to interfere with my work or my sense that I had a right to do it; no room for doubt, vanity, self-sabotage, self-protection or evasion.

Writing with that intensity healed a tectonic fault in my sense of myself as a writer. I realised that the faith and commitment a writer needs are a choice every writer has to make, every day. The many obstacles I had to negotiate to bring my whole self, my full attention, to my work, were absolutely mine to dismantle and discard.

I had been sleepwalking, now I was wide awake.

If there is something that you burn to do – a thing that makes you feel most passionately alive – if you're not doing it – why not? What are you waiting for?

NOTES

1 Some of these passages are fresh, others are extracts from previously published essays.
2 Extract from Lia Mills, 'Passionate Midnights, Perfect Jars', in Declan Meade (ed.), *Beyond the Centre: Writers in Their Own Words* (New Island, 2016), pp 106–116 (110–111).
3 Lia Mills, 'In Writing', http://www.artsandhealth.ie/perspectives/in -writing-finding-a-way-through-illness/; an essay commissioned by www.artsandhealth.ie in 2016.

Sarah Moore Fitzgerald

REFLECTIONS ON WRITING

In which conditions does your writing come into being/flourish? Does mood play a role?

For many years, I believed that I had to wait for the 'right conditions' in order for my writing to flourish, or indeed to happen at all. This is the reason why it took me such a long time to commit to my creative writing – I had some abstract notion that the ideal writing conditions needed to come along and that they included huge chunks of free time, the absence of a to-do list, a clean house and unlimited peace and quiet. I realised eventually that if I was to wait for those conditions to arise then I'd never write a single word. So gradually, over the years I have learned to write under less than perfect conditions. I think I understand now that for any creative endeavour, waiting is folly. 'The water does not flow until you turn on the tap.' I now tell my students what it took me a long time to learn: Write before you're ready to write. Don't wait for the perfect day, the perfect notebook, the perfect desk, the perfect moment, the perfect idea. Because if you wait for those things or if you wait until you think you're ready, you may never write at all.

Which conditions are detrimental to the right concentration?
While I have learned to write in many different contexts (on trains, at bus stops, in the kitchen, in bed). I also have learned that even though I often don't come to my writing until the end of a long working day, still it doesn't pay to leave all my writing to the times when I am least relaxed and least alert. Writing while physically or mentally tired is possible and I've often done it, but if I get stuck, or if I feel blocked, or if I start taking shortcuts then it's a signal that I need to rest. Fatigue can make small problems or plot puzzles seem like insurmountable challenges. Two of my favourite cures for minor writers' blocks such as these are a good night's sleep and a decent cup of coffee.

Does the unconscious come into play, and if so, how? Could you give an example of how something gestated over a certain time? Do the best passages come (un)intentionally?
As an academic who has been trained in objective research methods and the application of conscious, cognitive, deliberate techniques to my work, it took me a long time to learn to trust the role that the subconscious plays in the development of story. It's important to believe in the extraordinary role of the subconscious in storytelling. I'm a careful planner whenever I'm involved in an academic project, but in the case of my creative writing, I've learned that too much planning can stifle the natural emergence of the stories inside us. And I think I've become better at allowing a story to unfold and to be more comfortable with the idea that we are not in full control of our creative processes. Stories are deep within us. A lot of creative work is about silencing the chattering of the conscious mind, to let stories bubble up to the surface, allow our deeply buried ideas to emerge.

Is there a specific childhood memory that is still alive in your work?

Because I write for children and young adults, I do work hard to channel my own childhood self and my early memories. My childhood was very free and rather wild. I spent lots of time camping and boating with my three brothers, and unlike children of today, much of my free time was unsupervised, setting the scene for some great adventures, hazards and discoveries. As I think about it, these are the perfect conditions for drama and I'm sure have helped my storytelling in all sorts of different ways. Place and setting also play a huge role, and because I grew up by the sea, coastal settings seem always to recur or to want to appear in my stories. More generally though, I also work hard to remember how the life of a teenager is often so very intense and deeply felt. It's a unique time in life where people stand on the cusp between childhood and adulthood. It's often struck me that teenagers have an authenticity and a passion that many of us lose over the years. For me, writing is a way of revisiting that extraordinary stage of life and of remembering the experiences and feelings that formed me, and the lessons I learned.

What is your favourite genre and why?

I can't claim to have a favourite genre, and I like to read as widely as I can, but I must confess that from a very young age, the concept of time travel has been an obsession. I've been inspired by a whole range of time travel stories including *The Time Machine* by H.G. Wells; *A Wrinkle in Time*, by Madeleine L'Engle, *Dr Who* and *Back to the Future*, and more. In many ways time travel to me is the ultimate storytelling device. I used it as a central aspect of my first novel, *Back to Blackbrick*, which is about a boy whose beloved grandfather is losing his memory. The boy finds a way to go back to the time of his grandfather's childhood to reclaim important parts of his history. I loved writing that book and after I'd finished it, for a long time I thought I'd never be able to write a story that didn't have time travel in it! But I suppose when you think about it, every novel is like a mini Tardis, whisking us off to a different place and time, allowing us to imagine the world from a different and new perspective.

Gender and Writing

It's often been said that writing is a very gendered process for all sorts of reasons. It's true that many of the women writers I talk to often struggle to legitimise time and space for their creative work. The lack of regard for women's writing (for example in the compilation of many anthologies in which women's writing is absent or under-represented) is troubling too, and there is lots of evidence to show that compared to male writers, it is harder for women writers both to do their work, and to be taken seriously as writers when they've done it. These challenges do worry and affect me. I think part of the response is to keep writing, and keep finding ways to do one's best work. We may not be able to dismantle in one fell swoop the structural inequalities that make writing more challenging for women but we can promote and support women's writing, show solidarity and respect for people's work regardless of their gender or background, and highlight the ways and places in which support is needed.

What is the purpose of writing for you?

Storytelling and fiction writing is a very comforting process for me. With all its trials and difficulties and struggles, writing stories is ultimately my way of imposing meaning on the chaos of life and of making sense of the world.

Mary Morrissy

CHASING THE I-DEER OR THE JOURNEY TO WORK

This deer doesn't just run – it springs. Away out of the frame of your windscreen, leading your eye off the main road, into the wild unknown. This isn't a slowly-meandering deer, or one of a grazing herd; it's alone, head held high, antlers up. It's always seemed to you that those tree-like branches that sprout from its head must be too heavy to be borne. Surely the deer should topple, carrying this cathedral of bone aloft, but it doesn't. Particularly now as it's become bipedal, pushing off its hind legs, its front legs powerfully tense. Sure-footed, isn't that what they say? This is the idea deer. The i-deer. Your turn to pounce. You feel the excitement of that first reckless leap ...

But as soon as you surrender to the i-deer, you lose that airborne sensation, the feeling of being in another element. You feel more earthbound than ever. You're pretty sure the i-deer came this way so you follow faithfully and find yourself in a dark tunnel. Alone. No light ahead or behind. You abandon the car and go on foot. You have a pit helmet with a torch attached so you can just about see where you're going once you've adjusted to the night blindness. You feel your way with your feet, one ragged step at a time. There's no sign of that i-deer, of course – it's as if he's evaporated. If you stretch out your arms you're sure you'll feel the encrusted walls of the tunnel, but when you do there's nothing solid there. Only the sooty darkness and the faint light of your own head to guide you.

Back in the car, you careen out into an unfamiliar landscape made hazy and insubstantial by the sun's brilliance. The brightness makes it hard to get your bearings. There are distant unfamiliar mountains shrouded in heat haze and you seem to be in the foothills. There are trees and, in the zebra sun dazzle, you think you see something move out of the corner of your eye – the i-deer? Is it? It might be but it looks different now and you can only get a sidelong view as it flees into the undergrowth. You've no idea where you are. Is there a map in the car? You reach out to scrabble in the glove compartment, one hand clutching the steering wheel. Suddenly the car swerves as if the road is icy, but it can't be, it's high summer outside. Or was a minute ago. Now you're a bull rider trying to control the car as it bucks and sways trying to throw you off. Remembering old advice, you resist the temptation to apply the brakes. You hold your writing nerve.

Oh God, what is this, a humpbacked bridge? You're travelling too fast now. You see yourself and the car airborne like in those car chase movies, all four wheels off the road; the kind of airborne you don't want. The car will never withstand this treatment, the shock absorbers will be shot. This is high voltage stuff and your car, well it's a bit ramshackle and bears the marks of several other journeys of this kind. A dent here, a scrape there, a shattered windscreen once. You're not sure how much more it can take. You lean into the bend before the bridge and make it over.

After all the alarms and excursions, it's quiet for a bit. You travel on through a featureless valley. The dull, flat country of mid-project. The speedometer doesn't seem to eat the miles as before. You get to wondering, why are you doing this? All for an i-deer you only got a fleeting glimpse of. And what's this coming up? The red triangle, the exclamation mark warns you of danger ahead, something you can't see. But everything about this journey is unseeable.

The road turns into motorway. Thank god you're done with those small by-roads with their twists and turns. The signs tell you that queues are likely, but at least the motorway is straight, the road surface good. All you have to do is cruise now, stay in lane and you'll get to your destination, though you're not even sure what that is. But you feel you must be on the right track. There are so many other drivers here. But is that a good thing? Are they all like you, following i-deers of their own? The i-deers may travel in herds and you may think you see them all over the place, but, in fact, they're an endangered species and, of course, there are culls from time to time. Some regard the i-deer as a pest. And there's another worry. Will some other hunter end up snagging your i-deer? But you can't think about that now.

The motorway exit signs whizz by and you look at them longingly. Everything off road looks so attractive. A cup of tea, oh yes, and a nice meal, plus a ready-made escort to keep you company. This is what the rest of the world is doing while you're running after an i-deer. Refuelling – that's what you badly need now. You're tempted but if you stop now you might never return to the chase. You press on, running on empty.

Oh look, an airport! On a whim, you take the exit. Maybe this is your destination? The sense of lift-off reminds you of the start of the journey, airy escape combined with a terminal, an end point. Once, when you were having your eyes tested for a driving licence, the doctor held up his left hand above your head. How many fingers am I twiddling, he asked. You couldn't say. You've a blind spot, he said. Is that going to be a problem, you asked. *Not unless you encounter low-flying aircraft*, he said. You can hear the rumble of jet engines overhead but they're hidden in cloud. Or are they travelling in your blind spot? You duck, just in case.

The road narrows. You brake, then check in the rear-view mirror. But look, look what's on the back seat. It's a doe. How did that happen? It's not the i-deer you spotted earlier. It's smaller and it doesn't have those magnificent antlers but its eyes are brown and intelligent and it has some lovely white markings that the i-deer didn't have. It's not what you imagined and if it were a dress you bought on the Internet you'd send it back. On the other hand, it's your very own i-deer, you can reach out and touch her, and she's safely inside your car. She seems extraordinarily tame. But is that a good thing?

There's a roundabout coming up. It's decision time. Which exit to take? The doe is fast asleep in the back seat. Will she do the trick? You've grown fond of her, you have to admit, and a bird in the hand etcetera. Or could you do better? Is she just a wee bit *too* tame? Not the wild creature you saw initially. Should you cut your losses? Go all the way around, repeat the journey – maybe get a bigger, better I-deer, closer to the first one you saw? Or can you have both? Keep this one AND go back?

Should you go back?

Should you go forward?

Or should you just stop?

You go on.

Paul Murray

Ghost Stories

For a long time I shared a rented house, and I would write in my room. I was working on a novel, writing it by hand, adding the pages every day to a pile stacked at the foot of the desk. The novel became very long, well over a thousand pages, and after a certain point, because I slept on a futon, the manuscript would seem to loom palely over me from the other side of the room. It was like being haunted. I slept very badly in that house.

I have an office now, and a door I can physically close on whatever it is I'm working on: but physical barriers have a limited effect on a novel-in-progress, which is to say, I still feel, quite often, as if I'm being haunted. William Gaddis once described writing a novel as like having a friend in hospital – every day you go in hoping he'll have improved, and every day, there he is, in the same moribund state. This image captures the sense of powerlessness a long writing project can induce, but not, I think, the dread.

Once you've gone a certain distance into a novel, it starts to permeate everything in an alarmingly spectral way. You think about it all the time – washing the dishes, at the cinema, trying to sleep. It insists on your attention, in the same obsessive way that a ghost might, in order to direct you towards some terrible crime. Working on a book can feel like uncovering some awful disharmony, like you've broken the seal on a forbidden temple and the only way to set things to rights is to complete it. That's a lonely task and no one can help you with it: you may have a reader or an editor who will speak to you reasonably and kindly. But no one else can see the ghost. So it's just the two of you, haunter and haunted: one increasingly sleepless and desperate, the other languishing in a strange netherworld, crying out for peace.

If that doesn't sound crazy enough, let me take it a step or two further. In my own work, I find myself coming back to worry, in both senses of the word, at the same theme or group of themes. There's a death, there's someone struggling to cope with the death, the death or the absence is so powerful that it takes over the living world in a way that verges on the supernatural. If the process of writing the work becomes a kind of artificial haunting, it almost seems as if I'm creating working conditions that in some strange way mirror the situation I'm trying to explore in the book.

This particular praxis is most likely mine alone. Clearly though, writing novels is quite a strange thing to do. You are literally making problems for yourself: you are using the best of yourself to create the most difficult, intractable problems you can think of, and then driving yourself crazy trying to solve them.

But those difficult, intractable problems are the same ones everybody deals with everyday. Being haunted isn't quite as unusual an experience as we might think. To be alive is to be in the presence of death; to exist in time is to feel life slipping ungraspably by you. That is no picnic. It's a state of affairs, furthermore, that life in the twenty-first century is singularly ill-equipped to deal with. We live in a moment when the vertiginous scale and swiftness of time are brought home to us with a ferocity never before experienced in human civilisation. On the one hand, we're confronted left and right with iterations of what purports to be the future. On the other, thanks to the cameras we carry around with us all the time, we're constantly deluged by, not to say drowning in, the past. The present has never felt more precarious, and that's before we even start thinking about climate change. This may be what Derrida means with his term 'hauntology'. The whole thrust of neoliberalism, or necro-capitalism, or whatever it is we're living in now, is to distract us from the moment we're in: to lead us away from the ghost, big or small, that is haunting us. Death is not a friend to the market: there is not a single product, not on the whole of Amazon, to fix death. Someone who has realised that everyone they love and every most cherished moment will disappear in the river of time and be gone is notoriously difficult to persuade to buy, for example, a power flosser. Hence the incessant distraction, even as, ironically, the market leads the entire planet deathwards.

Simply by not being connected to the Internet, a novel is radically different from other present-day cultural artefacts. Reading a novel, even a bad novel, puts you in a different relationship with time. You read it over days or weeks or months, at a pace you set yourself. It does not have a timeline, it is not going to disappear from Netflix. It is in a dialogue with you and you alone. In that way one could argue reading a novel becomes a political act. Rather than hook you up to a multitudinous, anonymous They, whispering their promises of corporatised assimilation, reading presents you with yourself. The form is embattled and will become more so because we are less and less able to be with ourselves. Instead we would rather dissolve ourselves in the noise of the crowd, even though that makes us unhappy. The precipitous decline in public discourse, the rise of hate speech, the unabashed worship of greed and violence of the last decades – these seem to me to go hand-in-hand with the modern-day inability to pay attention, which is the first step towards empathy.

I feel very privileged and very lucky to be able to work as a writer and to be able to pay attention on a full-time basis. I take it seriously: I don't start work particularly early, but I show up everyday and I stay there till it's time to go.

It's not easy to resist my phone, my Internet connection, 'the world outside tugging ... with all its golden hands', as Edith Wharton put it. It's not easy to be by myself all day, listening to who- or whatever is haunting me. But even on bad days, when the words won't come, when the story resists me, when I can't seem to coax it out of the fog – I still feel like I've learned something. I think it was Joseph Brodsky who said that your job as a writer is primarily to show up. If you're not at the bus stop, you can't catch the bus. You show up at your desk every day and you hope something will happen. It's a little bit like being a medium at a seance, sitting at a table, calling into the void, hoping a voice will respond. When it does, it's the most electrifying thing. You feel a connection to the universe that is very profound. I'm not sure I'm persuaded that every love story is a ghost story, but I think it works the other way around. You come to love your ghosts, even when they're terrorising you; there's nothing like death to make you feel alive, and there's nothing like a pale spectre hovering over your bed to wake you up from your slumbers.

Éilís Ní Dhuibhne

SWIMMING IN NOVELS

What I Like

The writing I like best is that which seems to successfully describe people's emotions: their desires, their passions, their dislikes, their hatreds, their fears, their disappointments, their happiness. It is focussed on behaviour, interaction, thought and feeling – in response to events of ordinary life. I don't like action movies or action literature. Life involves sensational and dramatic events, but when these are huge – murders, war – subtlety is too easily lost. Car chases, shootouts, explosions drown out the beating of the human heart, submerge the quiet conversation and silences between people in a bath of noise and bathos.

Ordinary

Is there such a thing as an ordinary life?

These are the lives we happen to live ourselves, the life we have been born into or the life that we have somehow found, as we grow up and old. Ordinary life in Calcutta is different from ordinary life in Moscow or ordinary life in Dublin. Ordinary life in the seventeenth century is different from ordinary life in the twenty-first. The ordinary life of a very wealthy person is different from the ordinary life of a homeless person who sleeps in a shop porch on the street, even if both the wealthy person and the homeless live in the same city and the same time.

The only ordinary life is your own life.

I have always though mine was extra-ordinary. Which it is, like everyone's.

Place

Life is lived in places.

We are influenced by where we live. You cannot be a Dickensian pickpocket in a glen in the west of Ireland. Not only what you work at, but how you think, feel, interact with others and with the surroundings, how you behave, is affected by where you find yourself. Fiction which abandons place entirely is not for me. I like descriptions of cities, towns, houses, mountains, woods, rivers, oceans. I want the author to translate place to words in a way which enables me to imagine I am in the place described. I want to feel the air on my skin, the rain or the sun, to smell the flowers or the garbage or the dinner, and to see things. Images can effect this trick, the painter selecting what she sees, recreating it on the canvas or the wall of the cave. That words, sounds composed of phonemes, or black marks on a page, can perform the same operation beggars belief. It is alchemy, the transformation of things to words and the reverse, the transformation the reader creates, re-translating words to things. The signifier to the signified. This is the most mysterious and magical aspect of writing, reading, talking, listening. When I write 'chair' you see a chair. When I write 'red chair' you see a red chair. When I write 'little red wooden chair' you see that. When I write 'little red wooden chair with carved back and turned legs' you see that. The more detail I provide with words the more detailed the image you see – but you will probably not see what I see, when I write, 'chair'.

On the other hand, when we read *The Little Red Chairs*, the title of Edna O'Brien's 2015 novel, what do we see? The almost twelve thousand chairs which were put out on a street in Sarajevo to commemorate those killed there during the siege? Or a few red chairs in a doll's house?

The latter is what I see, for some reason, when I read that title. And when I see a chair, sitting in the corner of my living room, I see at the same time the letters 'c h a i r'. I see the word and the thing at the same time, and it is like this with many things. I see the word in English, first, and at the same time as I see the thing itself.

English

But, sometimes, these days, I get bored with English. Once I adored this language and its literature. And, indeed, English is a rich language. But age has withered her infinite variety. This language is a victim of its own success. It is worn down by overuse; a car that was once gleaming in the driveway, like the red car in Raymond Carver's story 'Are These Actual Miles?' but whose engine now has too much mileage on it. So alive that it seems half dead.

I read a novel a day, in English, and every novel is drawing on the same old creaky well of words. Sometimes I think this sacrilegious thought: *There is too much English on this planet*. Chaucer, the father of English literature, wrote in a language that few people spoke and less could read. In 1400, it is estimated that the population of England was about 2.5 million. According to the source one uses, it is estimated that between 300 and 360 million people speak English today as a first language, and 20% of the population of Earth know it as a second language. About a million books, mainly in English, are published annually in the USA alone. Chaucer's linguistic context was closer to that of a Dane writing in Danish today, or a Bulgarian writing in Bulgarian, or perhaps an Icelander writing in Icelandic, than to today's writer of English. (In the fourteenth century Chaucer had many more potential readers than an Irish writer in the Irish language has today, but that is another story). His language wasn't a mass-market lingua, verbal Coca Cola, but something more unique. Good wine, like the stuff he imported from France.

It is not his fault that he was giving birth to the written language that would eventually become the Lidl, the McDonalds, the Starbucks of the modern literary world.

But my mood can change. A sparkling book can arrive on my bookshelf. Caitriona Lally's novel, *Eggshells*. Molly McCloskey's novel, *Straying*. Writers with the rhythm of ballet dancers, good imagination, deep emotional and intellectual intelligence. Their English sings.

It still happens.

I have been more or less bilingual – in Irish and English – from early childhood, within the peculiar linguistic situation of Ireland. I have no special linguistic gift – I don't have a fine-tuned ear and I have to work hard to remember grammatical paradigms. On the positive side, I'm quick to 'pick up' a language if I'm surrounded by it, and I think this is a result of early bilingualism – something which needs to be pointed out to the enemies of the Irish language in Ireland. (I've always noticed, at international literary events, that the Irish speakers are the ones who also speak French and German and other languages – we aren't afraid of 'foreign' languages). These days I find myself more and more attracted to other European languages and enjoy reading them. Not because the stories or ideas are better – although they are usually quite different, in subject matter and attitude, from Irish/

English/American fiction – but just because the words are new to me and therefore seem full of energy and possibility. It's hard work, of course. Reading a language I don't know automatically, I have to pick up each new word, like a pebble from the garden, and figure out its shape and its sound.

I write in two languages: English, my mother tongue (literally – my mother was an English monoglot) and my father's language, and my language at school, Irish. My command of English is stronger, and when I began writing it didn't even occur to me to write in Irish. But by a sort of accident, I got drawn back to this language. And once I started, I felt at home in it. And, yes, I feel there is a certain obligation to write in Irish if one can. Millions of people can write in English, and only a handful in Irish. My family, in my father's line, have been Irish speakers for hundreds and hundreds of years. I don't feel like being the one to break the linguistic link. And I provide the link with my books.

Plus. It is a challenge. It's fun. I feel liberated when I write in Irish.

Swimming

I went to the sea. To Donabate, a small town and beach in north County Dublin. First you drive on the M1, a very busy motorway, where the speed limit is 120km per hour; it's stressful, it's horrible. But after five minutes, you turn onto a narrow road, lined with trees, which threads through the flat fields of north Dublin. Golden corn fields, fields of potatoes and fruit bushes. Huge sky full of puffy cumulus clouds like a painting by Constable. There is a sandy light feel to the landscape here, unlike the more sombre hilly landscape of the south county. A holiday feel. The beach is sandy but empty because it is an overcast day, not very warm. My friend and I undress in the shelter of black rocks, and then walk out, out, across the wide sand, to the water. It feels cold. It *is* cold. I wade around for five or ten minutes, and then start swimming. After a minute or two it feels less cold and after five minutes quite comfortable. The water is calm and feels soft on my skin.

An island, Lambay Island, is on one side, and Howth Head, Bray Head and the Wicklow Mountains, far away on the other. The Sugar Loaf, that triangular mountain, is clearly visible. Into the water terns dive, with their sharp, determined plunge slicing through the surface.

Not Writing

For three days, no writing. Shopping, housework, preparing for house guests, collecting them from the airport, cooking, entertaining. I fit in some reading – my ongoing novel in Bulgarian, of which I read three or four pages a day, frequently referring to the online dictionary, and two novels in English, which I read as fast as I can since both are for work, rather than for pleasure – although both give me plenty of pleasure. I've managed some walks also. I've written several emails. But no writing.

My life has always managed to squeeze writing into the margins, and now I suspect I organise life in that way.

Perhaps I don't really want to write at all?

I want to go for walks. I want to learn Bulgarian. I want to read other people's writing. I want to cook, talk, watch drama serials on television. Sleep. Go for a swim. But do I really want to write?

Writing a Novel

I enjoy inventing scenarios and worlds, and immersing myself in them. Sometimes I have found that writing a novel is not all that different from reading a novel. I open the manuscript – which is not a manuscript, but a document on my computer – just as I open a novel, and move into the world inside the covers of the book, or whatever the equivalent on the laptop is. Out of 'reality' and into that other world. Some writers describe this experience as 'making time stand still.' A novel or a story can freeze time, and in writing it one is unconscious of the passage of time – but, of course, a carpenter is unconscious of the passage of time when making a chair, or a surgeon ... I imagine ... when extracting an appendix. Writing is like moving into a different place, for a while. Moving into a dream, a daydream. Into the sea of the subconscious.

Some writers work very slowly, and describe the experience as agonizing like squeezing blood from a stone. That always sounds impressive to me. If it is so painful, the result must be wonderful! But I have to admit that I don't find writing agonizing, and never have. It is true that I'm reluctant to start. I'm lazy about it, and I don't know why, since I'm not really a lazy person otherwise. Perhaps I'm reluctant to let go, to plunge in? To read what is there waiting to be written? Once I get going, however, I write as easily as I read. It is as if I am transcribing some text from ... where? A dream?

That does not mean the result will be good – nor does it necessarily mean the opposite. But at some stage, sooner rather than later, I have to hop back onto land, into the 'real world' and apply critical structures to my fiction world. That is enjoyable also, but in a more workman-like way.

It is like excavating a big chunk of stone from the ground, and then chipping away at it until it takes the shape (a) its essential nature demands (b) I want it to take.

Dreaming and working are the two essential aspects of creating literature which are at odds with one another. On the one hand, you must let go of inhibitions – that is hard. On the other, you must apply them – and that is also hard.

Dreams

Talking of dreams. This reminds me of various 'truisms' I have come across, in my life, about writing fiction. Often these take the form of prohibitions:

Never describe dreams. They're boring.

Don't write about writing.

Don't be confessional.

Write what you know.

Don't write what you know. Make it up.

All these rules are wrong.

There are no commandments about writing. The only rule is to write what you want to write – or, as we say, more importantly, to write what you 'are compelled to write.' Do it as well as you can. Hope for the best.

A Room of One's Own

Yes.

You need it.

That is all that needs to be said about this.

Mícheál Ó Conghaile

WRITING ... IN IRISH

I remember not being able to speak English. Growing up in
the 1960s on a small island, Inis Treabhair, off the coast of
Conamara, Irish was the everyday language of its
dwindling population of about forty people. Six
households in all. The reason I remember so clearly not
being able to speak English is the summer visits when our
cousins from London and Galway city would come to
spend a few weeks with us. I must have been three or four
years old. They spoke only English. I spoke only Irish. But
we got along and played together communicating with
each other as children from different backgrounds do. I
picked up some English from them and later would learn
at school, where every subject except English was taught
through Irish. I entered the island national school in 1966
and there were twenty one students on the rolls there.
When I left in 1975 the number had dwindled to five. The
school doors would be locked for the last time in 1980, the
numbers having fallen to two.

The same fate awaited life on the island. In the 1870s when its population peaked, 171 people lived there. The last native islander, Patsy Lydon, left the island a couple of years ago to live with family members on the mainland, bringing an end to island life which had gone on unbroken for at least two hundred years. From that moment on kitchen lamps would remain unlit at night and hearths would remain cold. Dampness would spread and decay would set in. Life on the island is now silent, now left to birds, animals and insects.

So much dies with the death of an island or island life. Even in the future if other people come to live here the chain or the link to the original inhabitants will be forever broken. It was they and their forefathers who named and knew every field and hillock on the island, its strands and inlets, shores and big stones, the surrounding tides and currents and waves they had to navigate in all sort of weathers. The joys and pains of hundreds of years of continued life. The local lores, songs, poems and stories. And the language – the language that brought everything to life. In this case it was Irish. We have a phrase in Irish, *crua chaint*, which means hard talk. And there was and still is great respect for a person who is a good speaker, who has a way with words, who is, as we say in Irish, *abalta* or able. We say about such a person, *tá a theanga ar a chomhairle féin aige*. And while the word *comhairle* normally means advice it also means council. In Irish we use the same word *teanga* for both language and tongue. What the phrase really sums up is: he can do anything with his tongue. Twist it this way and that way without even thinking and the words just role off his tongue naturally. The artistic beauty of the language coming through in a magical, fiery way. Gripping the listener by the throat, the language itself is very often just as important as the story that's being told – just like great writing.

Even today I don't feel at home speaking English because I have spoken Irish nearly all my life. When I talk in Irish, I can ramble away at ease. No need to think. When I speak in English, I have to think before I speak, and sometimes I have to search for the right words. Sometimes, an Irish word reaches my lips or even slips out of my mouth before I can stop it. So I feel a lot more at home talking and writing in Irish.

We are all aware of the great contribution the Irish language has given to the English language as it is spoken in Ireland and indeed beyond. It makes it more colourful and rich. It may seem small, but it's like the yeast in a cake making the English language rise and expand. Into fullness and goodness. Greatness. Most of our great writers in English have taken advantage of this and it has enriched their writings and world literature in English. The likes of Joyce, Beckett and Heaney come to mind. They all dug deep and mined for golden nuggets here and there and they delivered the goods. Of course in Irish we have our own great writers. The likes of Ó Cadhain, Ó Direáin and Ó Ríordáin who immersed themselves fully in the language, its history and lore.

And they did that against the same odds that Joyce, Beckett and Heaney had to face. But with one big difference. As Ó Cadhain said it's difficult to write in a language that will probably be dead before you. But that did not stop him from giving it all he had, like all great writers. And he knew where he and indeed many other Irish language writers were coming from:

Tá aois na Caillí Béara agam, aois Bhrú na Bóinne, aois na heilite móire. Tá dhá mhíle bliain den chráin bhrean sin arb í Éire í, ag dul timpeall i mo chluasa, i mo bhéal, i mo cheann, i mo bhrionglóidí.

I'm as ancient as the Hag of Beare, as old as Newgrange, as timeless as the hornless doe. Two thousand years of Ireland, that filthy sow, echo in my ears, in my mouth, in my head, in my dreams.

Irish is a language with a long unbroken literary tradition in this country – or at least in part of the country. A language which has been spoken here for about two thousand years, long before English arrived. In Irish even the most basic words are expressed so differently. Please, in Irish is, *más é do thoil é/If it is your will*, and thanks becomes *go raibh maith agat/may you receive good*. For over seven hundred years now both languages have lived side by side in this country, in people's hearts and minds. Writer and scholar Fr Peadar Ó Laoghaire (1839–1920), called it *an dá arm aigne* (the two armies of the mind). They have competed and bounced off each other over the centuries, but they also infiltrated and enriched each other. An army can fight and kill but an army can also defend and protect. And help the weak survive.

I write in Irish not because it's my native language or to promote the language (although I do that in several other ways) but because it is the language I can better express myself in. Writing and art is about expressing yourself or the human condition or whatever it is you want to express. I would write in English if I could express myself better in English, but I can't. It is, after all, my second language, although most Irish language writers are not native Irish speakers. But I think in Irish. I am at home in Irish, writing in Irish. Writing in English, for me, would be writing from somewhere else, away from home. I often describe it as like waking up in a friend's house and being left on your own there. You're getting your own breakfast but you don't know where anything is. You keep opening cupboards and drawers before you find exactly where things are, before you know what you're looking for. If I were writing in English I would be the same way, looking for the words here and there, and not knowing where to look sometimes. In Irish I know where to find them, at least most of the time. They are at hand. Nearby.

We had no television on the island so we had lots of time to read. With no electricity, we had to read using gaslight, flash-lamps and candlelight. I remember writing stories when I was in national school – in English funnily enough! My mother bought us a typewriter and I remember writing a little novel and typing it on little folded pages which I bound together in a little book with staples. I coloured the cover and all. *The Adventure of the Shabby Man* by Michael Joseph Connelly. I was under the influence of Enid Blyton's books. I was also a publisher before I knew it! Later in secondary school, when I was about 14 or 15, I wrote poems and sent them off to the weekly newspaper, *Inniu*, which had a column/ competition entitled 'Na Filí Óga.' (The Young People). FNT, the company in Mayo who published the paper, also published books. I remember getting some of the books as prizes and reading them. That was the first time my poems were published. Going to UCG really opened my eyes and broadened my mind. I started studying literature and began to write short stories seriously when I was eighteen or nineteen. My first collection of short stories was *Mac an tSagairt* (*Son of the Priest*). Some of the topics were controversial at the time, over thirty years ago. Subjects like abortion and suicide, which are still big in the news in Ireland today. Of course people complained. People said that the book should have been burned, but I don't think anybody went that far. Not in public anyway. In the mid 1980s *Comhar* published my short story 'Gabhal na gCloch' which is about homosexuality and male rape and there was outrage from certain sectors who referred to it as *brocamas* or dirt. Ireland and Conamara have come a long way since then, of course, but not without pain and suffering.

As a writer, the best thing I have brought with me from my own home and from being an Irish speaker is a knowledge of the different shades of the colour of words and a sharp ear for the spoken Irish language – or I should say languages because there are different levels of the Irish language spoken in the Gaeltacht. I would often ask myself:

> How would my father, or my uncle who lived with us, or my mother or the neighbours say such and such a thing if they were talking about what I'm writing?

The same applies to the characters from the Gaeltacht that I create — how would a teenager in the local bar, for example, say this or that? Normally, when writing conversation or a play I would stick to that, even though it might mean mixing some words or phrases in English through the Irish. There are times when the word in English is a lot stronger than the word in Irish, because of the influence of the language. It can hit a lot harder in certain cases, and make the character more believable. If the English word is used in the Gaeltacht it sometimes has a stronger register for me as a reader and a writer than the Irish translation, which might not normally be used everyday and might only be found in dictionaries or among learners of the language. Literature is bigger than any one language. If a writer can or has to go outside his own language to create something better, stronger or more precise, he should do that and reach that higher level of power in his writing.

I am a night person. I never in my life got up early in the morning to write. Sometimes my writing day might not start until seven in the evening or later and continue into the early, and often late hours in the morning. But creative writing is draining and demanding and for me I often feel that four or five hours writing is a day's work. Re-writing is different, as is translating. While translation is not easy, you have at least a road map to follow and you stick to it, more or less. So a day translating a play or short stories could easily be a ten hour day. But when you're writing a play or a novel you're not always sure where you're going. There is a choice and you can go in different directions, sometime the wrong direction, which is ok if you realise that and turn to find the right way. I would never write more than 2,000 words daily if I was working on a novel or a play, but with a translation I could end up with more than 4,000 words.

I'm never devoted to just one project at any one time. Normally I have three or four books on the go at different stages. At present I'm putting the finishing touches to a novella, *Sa Teach seo Anocht* (*In this House Tonight*), rewriting some plays that have not yet been staged, drafting the outline of a new play and also some short stories and poetry which will one day be part of a collection, I hope. I'm also translating short stories into Irish.

This allows me to give a good timespan to each project. The first draft of my novella was written four years ago, and I have left it on the shelf and returned to it many times since then. I have at least twenty drafts by now and I keep making changes – to the better I hope – with each rewrite. Each project normally takes four years and I believe they are the better for it as it gives them lots of time to simmer in my mind. It is probably the only advantage an Irish language novelist has over an English language novelist in Ireland who (if they are with a big publisher) have to meet deadlines. There are small advances for Irish language writers and deadlines may be ignored. After four years I'm usually tired of a project and get the feeling it's time to let it go. There is not much more I can do with it by that stage. I am also losing interest and am much more interested in the next project or working on some idea which might or might not end up on paper someday.

I never read my own books. I would hate it if I had to. In the first year or two after publication I would be rewriting in my mind if I read a page here and there – saying to myself why did I write this or that. After that when there is some distance between me and the writing of a book I feel it's not part of me anymore and I'm not interested. While I write for myself, I'm not one of my own readers. That is for other people, hopefully. Sales of Irish language books are small. A book which sells a thousand copies (and very few do) would be regarded as a bestseller. My books have sold 400–800 copies each on average, except for one title, *An Fear a Phléasc* (*The Man who Exploded*) which has sold over 4,000 copies since it has been placed on university courses. But there are other rewards outside of monetary rewards. As an established writer I often get invited to readings and festivals. I have done several readings in North America, Asia and many countries in Europe, as well as throughout Ireland and the UK. I have worked as writer-in-residence in several universities. A man told me once he read my book on Christmas Day, which is a day people don't read just any old book but one they really set aside and are looking forward to reading. People sometimes tell me that they see life different after reading one of my books, that they have learned something new about life, that they see an aspect of life in a different way. Word came to me once of a woman who read my play *The Connemara Five* (*Cúigear Chonamara*) on her hospital bed the night before a major operation and it helped her through that night. This also is why I write.

I am now the author of over twenty books and several translations. Yet I always have to start with a blank page and a pen, several pens in fact. While I have learned a lot over the years, it can still be scary and uncertain as I do not always know where I will bring the story, or where the story will bring me. Sometimes you just have to go along with your characters, as they know themselves better than I know them sometimes! Unlike my first book I am more aware of the potholes and pitfalls that are on my writing path and will obviously try to avoid them. It's like going on a journey with the characters. I'm with them in their good times and bad times, which are a lot more plentiful. I laugh and cry with them. Their pain is also my pain. As a writer and creator I need to believe in them and have a feeling for them, and live part (at least) of their lives with them. They take over my time, my life and my world. And they are often good company for me – often better company than real people. Hopefully they are also good company for the limited number of readers who read stories and books ... in the Irish language.

Billy O'Callaghan

THE NATURE OF STORIES

In July of 2016, I was in China, travelling by train from Beijing back to Shanghai after a couple of weeks spent exploring some of the northern part of that ridiculously-vast country. Still an hour or so out from Shanghai, we crossed over a small, dull thread of river. I'd been watching the passing landscape and keeping check on the horizon, hoping that the sea would come into view, and feeling surprised at just how much I missed the sense of it in my life, contemplating, I think, the notion that when you're born within smelling distance of water you carry some need of its presence with you always.

The river had nothing much about it to speak of, except for a little wooden boat, some six- or eight feet of scrap lumber nailed together to create a high-sided trough, but in the few seconds that it took to pass in and out of my field of vision an entire story fell on me.

I can remember the sensation, the breathlessness of the moment, as if it had been just waiting there for me to pass. I felt at the same time knocked stupid and heightened. I suppose because of the soothing tranquillity of the train, I'd been daydreaming, and thinking a dozen or a thousand thoughts at once; but in that instant, something about the sight of the river, the boat, or maybe the thin yellow-white fall of the light on the water, bound all my strands of thought, conscious and otherwise, together in a particular and specific way, much as how I imagine stars are formed.

I had a notebook in my backpack and struggled to keep up with how fast the story came. I kept getting in the way of it and having to cross out words and whole sentences. At the station in Shanghai I got off the train and transferred to the subway, hitting the rush hour crowds so that the carriage I boarded was packed almost beyond breathing space. I kept scribbling, stooped down and using the bodies around me for balance and the top edge of my suitcase as support. By Heathrow, some fifteen or twenty hours on from that first moment on the train and fit nearly to drop, the story was done, the essential rags of it, anyway, which would be stitched together over the following couple of weeks, the edges trimmed and seams refined.

With neither intent nor expectation, I'd written a new story called 'The Boatman'. The links within the final text to China, or to that river boat, were almost non-existent, yet something in what I'd seen or felt in that moment on the train helped prompt a deeper and more personal story into being. The finished story, fictional though it was, seemed so much a part of me that I refuse even now to believe it hadn't been smouldering away inside me always, biding its time, waiting to be told. But I also have to wonder, if I'd not been on that particular train in that far corner of the world at that precise second, whether the story would still have been written, or written differently. Would it have been lost to me, and maybe picked up by somebody else, to be slanted the way they needed to see it?

In the manner of its arrival, 'The Boatman' was very much an anomaly, and while my life would be so much easier if all the stories I want to write could drop into the world so complete and with such speed and assurance, it also doesn't matter that the opposite is far closer to my reality. The truth is, I'm not necessarily chasing easy, and I seem to get as much from the actual forging of the work, the struggle of getting it into a shape I want and need it to be, as I do from its completion. Once a story has gone as far as I can take it, there's a feeling of relief and, I suppose, of accomplishment. But it doesn't last and probably shouldn't. Because there are so many more stories to tell.

If my stories are at all a reflection of who I am – and I can't help but feel that my better ones are – then it is probably correct that they should come slowly and without certainty, that every sentence needs to be wrestled into place. I am not writing autobiography, except in the sense that what comes out, when it comes out well, speaks of how I see the world, and also my place in it, however peripheral that might be. What I hope for, and strive for, is something that reads as truthful, even when it doesn't always match the facts.

Where the stories themselves come from is, I'm afraid, imprecise. To paraphrase the Greek poet Seferis: a lion is made up of the lambs he's digested. Generally, my starting point seems to be with theme. The elements of life that most trouble or haunt me start to coalesce. Some make themselves apparent over a long stretch of time; a few – rootedness and exile, isolation, love and its absence, loneliness, time's passing, guilt, and the ability to endure in the face of deep trauma or turmoil – feel permanent. And it's from this slow fog, largely, that stories emerge, vaguely tormenting, looking to be explained, or made sense of or put together in a way that becomes bearable.

The feeling that sits me down over a page is probably, more than anything, one of being lost, or of not belonging fully to the world around me, and it's in the writing, in the process of dragging strands together, that I find myself and, at least for a while, can feel secure. If something keeps me away from whatever I need and want to be working on, emptiness pervades. It's gotten so that, after some twenty years of putting myself constantly to the task, stories have become my compulsion. Without their detail in my day, a void opens. It's not about therapy, or healing; it's about having somewhere to be.

Like almost everyone, my mind is most of the time a muddle of worries, dreams, hopes and fears. Life has its beautiful days and its occasionally-terrible ones, and the equilibrium is ensured by routine. Every morning from 7am until around noon, unless I absolutely have to be somewhere else, I sit down and try to get my thoughts on paper, sifting them for grains of story. Stopping to make tea, to water the flowers on my small apartment balcony, to feed the magpies and jackdaws that come to perch, but bobbing always in and out of the work, keeping my head within it, standing occasionally to read a paragraph, walking it around the room, as if that should make a difference.

Language excites me, the way it can layer meanings into itself, even seemingly in its most simple state, and how it feels 'off' if it should be forced to carry a syllable too many or stand a syllable shy. Painting has brush strokes, music has notes and rests, but both are so much more than the sum of their parts. So it has to be, too, with language. Words are old magic, and the best stories, poems and novels cast spells that crack eternity and let the light come streaming in. On good days the sentences sing to me in the stillness and I glow with them. On the days of struggle I sit there and ache, trying to pull the story along, trying to kiss it back to life, slow to take no for an answer, stubborn as I am in most things. But whether the mornings flow or feel mired, I am, for those few hours, the happiest version of myself because that's the part of the day when whatever mask I feel the need to wear falls most easily away and I can get somewhere close to the truth of things.

As a child, until the age of about seven, we lived with my grandmother, my mother's mother. She died in her early sixties, which by today's standards is no age, but to my young eyes she was ancient. If we are shaped to a large degree by our backgrounds then mine is as ordinary and as simple as it gets: poor, working-class. For all of those who went before me, education, at least of the classroom variety, was not prioritised and, apart from in the most basic sense, not really an option. But I suppose there is more than one way to be taught a lesson. My grandmother wasn't at all a writer, but the tales she told, and the way she told them, lit a fire in me that burns to this day. What she imparted was a love of stories, a passion for them, and a sense of their worth, making it clear that existence would be less without their magic. At some critical point in the telling, her voice always softened to a murmur, and sitting at her feet, my small fingers fumbling with the buckles of her shoes, I'd lean in to catch the words, and I'd see her eyes shining with wonder in the cold light and feel that I was being let in on all the secrets of the world.

I got them all, stories sworn to be true, of hauntings and apparitions, of Jack O'Lantern and the Banshee and the fairy fort half a mile up the hill from our house, but also of her own schooldays, and the Black and Tans, and about her own father, who was born in the workhouse with nothing more than his name, and who'd gone into the Munster Fusiliers in order to feed his family, survived the fronts of two wars, the Boer War and then again, in middle-age, the First World War, coming through the bloodbaths of Loos and the Somme, only to be broken finally by the death of his fourteen-year-old son, my grandmother's brother, Jimmy, after the child had taken a bad fall from the back of a pet goat. The parts I struggled to comprehend were explained with patient care, and even as young as I was, I gradually came to understand, probably without really thinking about it, that while the walls of my world might have been flat and grey, the surfaces weren't necessarily all there was to see.

That start, my early education, set about filling my reservoir and primed me for the books that followed. And living a two-minute run from the local library ensured that I was well nourished. In the years that followed I read everything I could get hold of – partly out of a desire to feed my curiosity; partly, I think, seeking the sense of awe that I'd experienced with my grandmother's stories. I found it, too, again and again, being held spellbound by the notions of treasure islands and Arabian nights, Transylvanian castles and hell-hounds haunting the Devonshire moors. These books, and a thousand others, kept me dreaming.

My childhood wasn't anything like the poverty endured by previous generations, but neither had it much in common with the affluence enjoyed by the generations that followed. Growing up in Cork in the 1970s and 80s, at least in the version of it that I knew, a place fairly mired in recession, an older mindset still prevailed. You had your level, and for the most part didn't expect to rise above that. Even when I finally began writing, tentatively in my teens and more seriously in my twenties, I did it without believing for a single minute that it was something the likes of me could ever actually do. As far as I was concerned writers were mythical creatures. I knew, of course, that Frank O'Connor was from Cork, and my grandmother used to talk about Lennox Robinson, the Abbey playwright, speaking with a kind of reverence not about his work, which I doubt she even knew, but the fact that he'd been born in Douglas, our village. For me, though, they were too much like schoolwork and too long dead to feel quite real. The writers I was drawn to seemed of a different ilk, or at least weren't so obviously black and white. Their names existed on the covers of books – usually slightly exotic-sounding: Hemingway, Steinbeck, Bradbury, Michener, L'Amour, and even, later on, say by my mid-teens, the likes of Mailer and Updike – but were galaxies removed from the world I knew. Certainly no one in Cork had such names. And measured against their novels and short stories, my own early writing was small and hesitant, defined by shyness and insecurity. Looking back, maybe what kept me going was that I lacked even the least expectation of success. For a long time, I felt like I was just writing to fill the space beneath my bed. I hadn't yet learned how to get down to the heart of what mattered in a story, or how to tell it in the way it needed to be told. And I thought, foolishly, as many do, that I lacked material. Time cured me of that notion, at least.

That boy has long since grown, and I've learnt a lot along the way, mostly from the mistakes I've made. My education has been the life I've lived, the places I've seen and people I've known, and also the stories I carry with me from my grandmother, and from my father, who being one of sixteen children knows some that could put your hair standing on end and some that would break you clean in two.

I continue to devour books, and the notion of not being in the middle of a novel is incomprehensible to me. And while my tastes have grown, broadened and deepened, the sense of awe at discovering something great has never waned. The masters, the many gone and the precious, treasured few still living – writers like John Banville foremost among them – still working to produce monumental art, make me feel inconsequential as a writer, and I wouldn't wish it any other way. I like that such books set the bar so out of reach, because while they inspire, and in their best moments reawaken, my sense of wonder, they also help focus my attention and steel my resolve. Because when I am burning up with a story, I understand then that it is ok to sit down to write it purely for myself. I am my audience. Of course, once it's done I hope that people will seek it out and read it, but during the writing process I am not thinking about outcomes. There's the story, for better or worse, and nothing else. And in that way, I keep myself honest.

Nuala O'Connor

THE ANXIOUS WRITER, FREED

If mood controlled my writing output, I might never write a line. I'm not blessed with a happy genetic makeup – I lean towards the melancholic, doleful and introspective side of things, all of which may be the very reasons I'm a writer. I'm a shy, introverted loner and while books have always been dear companions, writing is my sanity. I've been writing since I was a child – poems, stories, diaries – all in response to my great love of reading. The novelist Pat Barker reckons writers are arrested within some childhood loss; she says, 'I think in a lot of writers ... there is a damaged child who never gets a day older. And I think that's possibly why we do it.'

I have an organised mind and, because I write full-time, I use my love of order to make sure that I write regularly. Like any regular practice, I don't think about my mood, or my health, when I go to write. Writing is my job, my discipline, my habit, so five days a week I go to my desk and I write. I work in sickness and in health, as it were. My somewhat rigid personality means that I like routine, and my Catholic upbringing means I feel guilty if I'm not doing what I'm supposed to be doing, so I go to my desk and I produce. There are downsides to this: enormous anxiety when I miss a day's writing. Even, I'll admit, anger if the path to my desk is thwarted or upset by apparent trivialities, like housework or the demands of other people. The upsides: I write a lot and by doing that, I feel I improve. Added bonus: I always (always!) feel better, more human – more humane, even – during and after a writing session.

On days where I don't write creatively, because my other writing workload is large and/or I have a deadline for mentoring, reviewing or non-fiction commitments, I feel like I'm shirking. Even though the other work is part of my writing life, and I have agreed to do it, I have difficulty accepting that. In an ideal world I would just write creatively and not be distracted by peripherals but, really, I know that all of the other stuff adds to the pot and I just have to work on my preciousness about time.

Having said all of that, I can and do write anytime and anywhere. Yes, I now have a dedicated space – a beautiful, wooden writing cabin in the garden – but I write when I walk, in the car, on planes, in waiting rooms. Anywhere that I have the freedom to let my mind wander over words and ideas and pluck and store them. Up until this year I was writing in a corner of my bedroom, but it felt unhealthy to spend the majority of my life in one room, so I had my writing cabin built. It's a haven, a gorgeous, sacred space that is all mine. It wasn't exactly necessary but it was much wanted and I love it.

I find it hard to write when there's excessive noise in my vicinity and constant interruptions. I don't like anyone to come near me when I'm working. When my kids were much younger, I dreaded school holidays because the children wanted *me*, and *I* wanted my desk and my escape into fictional worlds. Now that the youngest is nine years old, I am freer to write in peace. The family knows to leave me alone when I'm writing.

I have a low boredom threshold. I like to be always occupied but, as I age, I find I need to learn how to down tools and just be. It's necessary for writers to have solitude but, for me, as an introvert, it's also important not to neglect the outside world and off-page human interaction. Given a choice I might stay in my writing cabin, nursing my hermetic tendencies, and not go anywhere. Thankfully, the call of the world is loud and seductive and travel is the great unsung perk of the writer's life. I love to travel and see new places (much as I might dread going beforehand) and I always return to my desk alight with new images and ideas for work.

Writing is so woven through me now that, apart from family, it's the biggest part of my life. I often neglect other things in its favour (e.g. socialising and maintaining friendships that have no connection to writing). Inevitably, perhaps, most of my friends are other writers – there's a communion we share that is instant, valuable and nurturing. Fellow writers so often *get* me and my concerns. I will go to a literary event quicker than any other cultural one; it's a matter of prioritising what's important to me, I suppose, though I've begun to check myself lately as I find I'm slipping into a mode of living that may not actually be healthy: self-imposed isolation; not engaging with anything that doesn't seem beneficial to my work, or immediately interesting; being a bit hysterical about protecting my writing time. I want to try to connect more with my community, with real life, and balance it out with this bubble I've chosen for myself.

Does being a writer mean that I relentlessly catalogue my life, my emotions and my experiences as art? It probably does. Is it an unceasing commitment? If it is, it doesn't tire or bore me, as most things do. I can't, for example, easily watch TV for hours at a time, or patiently sit through long plays or continue to read dull books. I'm twitchy, my brain is continually conversing with me, creating narratives around every small thing. I don't write down most of it, but it's always there, that loop of thought/connect/possible story fragment. The unconscious clearly plays a part in this. I go to bed thinking about my work-in-progress and, in the night-fog, I'm often offered a key to whatever knotty issue I'm trying to unravel in the narrative. Sometimes it's difficult to remember these dream-offerings but, often, they come back to me and I mull over their usefulness and implement them if they fit.

Siri Hustvedt has said, 'The making of art takes place in a borderland between self and other. It is an illusory and marginal but not hallucinatory space.' I sometimes feel like this, that I hover above what I'm doing as I write. Pleasing word clusters, phrases and plot twists seem to occur as I write. I'm not much of a planner, anyway, so I rely on an organic, as-I-write dynamic that is probably controlled by my subconscious.

The purpose, or meaning, of writing to me is to explain the world to myself – my understanding of it – and to tell myself stories. It's also to expose and examine the vagaries and compulsions of humans, as they appear to me. And the act of writing is closely linked with my health and well-being. I write in order to stay sane and relatively at peace with myself and the world. When I don't write, I'm unpleasant even (especially) to myself. Writer's block is not an issue for me; I never seem to run out of things to feel excited or intrigued by so, luckily, fallow periods are rare to non-existent.

My ideal reader is someone who is not afraid of discomfort, who understands that humans are flawed and stupid and kind and mad and, therefore, that characters in stories are also all of those things. I have no interest in writing about paragons or reading about them. Show me mucky, confused people struggling through and gaining small triumphs and fucking up splendidly. They're the characters I want to read and write about.

Research suggests that women see the world in a more detailed way than men: apparently we see more colour, more nuance. Whether that's true or not, and whether our alleged emotional variances stand up to scrutiny or not, I feel that I do see and feel the world differently from, say, my non-writer husband. At a party, I will (usually accurately) gauge the emotional temperature of the other guests very swiftly; I can see who's down, who's fighting, who's content. I notice people's outfits and jewellery. I hear conversations that seem to pass my husband by. Maybe I'm just nosy, maybe it's because I'm introverted, or maybe it's just that I'm a writer and therefore obsessed with minutiae, but I seem to engage more with my environment than my husband does. He calls it passion, I call it sensitivity. I really don't know if it's because I'm female or not, but I want to understand and *know* the meaning of things; I seem to care – often too much – about everything. I experience the world viscerally – women's bodies are sites of so much action, and we negotiate the world through them, and surely that feeds into the writing.

The act of writing for me is a soothing, bindless thing. In life, I'm organised, I plan things and I control my time meticulously. When I write I enter a less taut headspace. In the act of writing I loosen up, I forget my worries, I'm a little chaotic and unguarded. I trust myself in the written word – I trust my word choices and my instincts and my unconscious acts. I don't want, or need, anyone else in my mind. I don't need cheerleaders and I certainly don't need naysayers. Getting the words down is the most important part for me. I know that I can impose order later. I enjoy editing, I like to 'pause in holy fear', as Hilary Mantel said, then dive in and improve things. But the first draft is the place of greatest immunity and abandon and in it – in the moment of writing – I'm resolutely free, and that's what I love the most.

Mary O'Donnell

HOW WRITING FINDS WHAT IT NEEDS

Interior space, exterior space, and mood as securing agents of creativity

As a child, everything creative – although nobody referred to it as 'creative' in the 1960s – occurred during periods of relative quiet. Whether I was drawing and colouring, or writing, or playing the piano, a level of isolation from the main activity of the household was automatically an agent. I enjoyed this, and was aware of a certain feeling which could overtake me as I occupied myself with any of these activities, and a pleasurable sense of very deep absorption.

It has continued in this manner down the years. When I was a full-time secondary school teacher (1985–1988), I gradually realised that the busy schedule of a working school, and the pressure on internal energies, were not ideal as means of developing new writing. For that reason, I *very* occasionally took one day off work if I sensed that a new piece of fiction was on the brink of my consciousness. Writing took, to my mind, first priority. I could write poetry at weekends, but fiction required a level of attention not restricted to weekends. This says nothing about the order of importance of either genre. To write a novel takes over one's time and energies, full-time. When one is not actually writing the novel, one is thinking about it, and finding and securing the delicate balance between detaching oneself from ordinary life whilst being 'in' it. Carrying out one's daily business is sometimes challenging. If too much time passes between putting the novel aside and taking it up again, one has to return right to the beginning, because everything is forgotten! And with novels there's always invisible trouble brewing in some corners. It's like spinning plates, and everything must be kept in the air, nice and taut, spinning and making sense of my writer's inner gravity, until completion. This is just how it worked for me. Poetry, on the other hand, can be at least thought about and noted down in all kinds of ways (in my experience), in one's iPhone for example, by voice memo or whatever. The thing with poetry is to catch the wisp of a moment in the air, almost as you pass it by, like a butterfly or dragonfly. Once caught, it can be left with its beautiful wings in your notebook (or head) until you have enough time to jot down a basic draft and develop it.

Over the years, despite having a perfectly good study or workroom in which to write, I find that the home I live in has grown exponentially in terms of my consciousness of it. There is something about putting down roots in a specific place that is not always helpful to sustained work, unless one's workroom is slightly at a remove from the home, perhaps down the garden. Up to the time our daughter was born twenty-five years ago, neither I nor my husband bothered very much with domestic tidiness. In the years after it, however, I found that a 'nesting instinct' – to my surprise – emerged, and I enjoyed the notion of making a pleasant space in which to raise a child. It's not so much about tidiness, per se, as creating an environment in which a child can be physically and mentally free. But the downside of this for a writer like me is that a house that is a home can also become a kind of doppelgänger which haunts our waking minutes and consciousness. It follows me with things it imagines I need to do, attending to it as if it were an Other, but one which makes capricious demands on the Self. It's very easy to be diverted from writing, especially on a morning when one isn't so confident about the actual work to be done, to suddenly become preoccupied with something like hanging out the laundry. (These are things I never thought I'd think, say, or write!).

For that reason I sometimes work at night when the house – the presence which reflects back many different energies – is asleep. I know that when the house is creaking in silence, or when I can hear a leaf gently blow against the window of my study, that I am truly alone and beyond haunting by this place now at peace with itself.

Solitude is the only true space in which writing can occur for me. Whatever mood is dominant in my personality is also affected by the place in which I find myself working. As a writer I cannot bear emotional disharmony, and have never understood the writers who thrive on emotional *Sturm und Drang* with those closest to them. This does not infer that I live on a calm plateau in which feeling does not occur. In fact, it is the opposite, and all life's experiences have tended to flow through my skin (this is how it feels), some of them lodging with sufficient obstinacy as to connect with my unconscious Self.

It is, for example, how my third novel, *The Elysium Testament*,[1] began: an awareness of the brittleness of the taught habits of love, especially maternal love, and how we practice these after the death of a child. In that novel, interior and exterior space play a significant role and space itself aspires to 'character'. Where else do we have our experiences but within space? And as we respond to those experiences, we use and abuse our spaces, we destroy them or exalt them, as needed. Human unhappiness can be regarded as an abuse of space, it can be a destroyer of how we perceive the space we inhabit. For example, it is possible that the human spirit and attitude is not suited for the average restrained dimensions in which the majority of people live. Yet technically, most crime against women and children takes place in what we call a home. Domestic violence against men also takes place there. It is perpetrated by a violator capable of exploiting the privacy of the contained building. In this way, the spaces in which our experiences might ideally flower, instead, are abused and diminished.

The place and position of writing in my life

Occasionally, I've exhorted my daughter when she was a student and a little bored during the summers to go out and find some young fellow 'to pass the time pleasantly with', as I put it, which was basically what she wanted to do anyway. I saw it as a question of learning to live with what encounters we have, and to enjoy the moment. Some encounters are important, some are not. There are times when we need to think, and times when we must do and simply *be*.

For me, living involves finding something meaningful with which to 'pass the time' as we mature, grow, and until we die. I wasn't telling my daughter to be trivial, but to accept the periods when what 'blows' in the wind may actually be worthwhile in between the other activities of her life, and to accept such things without too much judgement.

I can't say that writing always passed the time 'pleasantly' for me throughout my years of writing and publishing, although sometimes it did. It was not, after all, a pastime or a local romance. I took it deadly seriously, believing in the idea of authenticity of being, and was very influenced by my early readings of what had been offered at university, of Nietzsche, Thomas Mann, anti-semitic

German literature, Alfred Döblin and Elias Canetti. Not a woman author in sight! But these men encapsulated the creative freedom I aspired to. This was how I envisaged myself, an Irish version perhaps, at some point in the far future.

Essentially and on a philosophical level, such writers began to half-answer the many questions which had been tussling through my head throughout my teen years, largely unanswered within my milieu.

My thinking was this: if there were these published authors who were using characters to deal with the nature of existence, and it was not directly philosophy but even so engaged with philosophical questions, then perhaps there was also room for me to try this out. I was naïve, of course, in the Ireland of the 1970s: any woman starting to write had a very hard struggle to gain fair recognition and equality of stature with the pantheon of male writers, the rows and rows of 'greats' who loomed over us, wagging patriarchal fingers, or else ignoring us entirely. The exception to all this exclusion was the writer David Marcus, the late editor of 'New Irish Writing' in *The Irish Press*, who gave equal space and more to the female voices now rising on the horizon.

The place and position of writing in my life had been insulted – as with so many other female authors in Ireland – by the long resistance of canonical writers to include our voices in any discussion of the art and act of creativity, and of course (notoriously now) by our exclusion from certain significant anthologies. These exclusions remind me that writing was so hugely important in my life, that it had never just been how I would 'pass the time' on earth, but that it was a raging force of expression that did not want to be refused its space in the world and was frustrated by the attention to gender and not to *voice*.

But away from the politics and gender awareness and canonical inclusions and exclusions, I am, thankfully, a little independent republic! My instinct is to invent fiction (long and short) and to experience the making of poetry as it filters through my unconscious Self and upwards and out into the conscious world. My instinct also is to go out and actively seek things that will nourish me creatively, intellectually, and in a less visible way. There is a seeking soul within all of us that beckons towards byways we had not expected to visit, but which we arrive at, explorers landing on new territory. My job as a writer is not to colonise that territory (the word revolts me for its historical and contemporary resonances), but to simply pause in wonder, and allow fragments, hints and imaginary scenes (and sometimes memory too plays its part), to rise up from the source within the Self.

Enter, the magpie unconscious!

When writing *The Elysium Testament* in the mid-1990s, I was conscious of this novel emerging from several different directions. Over the months preceding the first pages of the first draft, I had been collecting quartzes and a few fossils, simply because I like them; that led me to read a book called *Follies and Grottoes*[2] which I also enjoyed. I had a vague notion that the character in my about-to-be-written novel would be involved in some kind of restoration. Then I heard a story about a local woman whose son had been accidentally impaled on a gate. At the time my own daughter was still an infant, and I was very attuned to protecting her, as any parent is. The abduction and murder of an English toddler called Jamie Bulger by two very young boys was also on my mind, and affected communities everywhere at that time. It fed my anxiety, but filtered into my writer's anxiety, I believe, and what emerged gradually had been gathered, magpie-like, with an incomplete sense on my part of what the final result would be.

I believe the unconscious can create great dramas, enhanced by the realities we encounter. These dramas can be anything along the spectrum of human feeling, ranging from comedy to tragedy. In the case of this novel, the question of how to proceed after a child's death was to the fore, and how to proceed as a woman, if her art – in this case, the woman undertakes a major commission to restore a Victorian 'fake' grotto on an Irish country estate – may have in its way contributed to this loss. Unconsciously, this story pushed forward and onto the page from all the described directions. I had no conscious idea of how the story would actually be unveiled, so much as the main, pivotal events. Nor had I any sense of the full range of characters until I had finished the first chapter. I was led by my unconscious, together with a writerly instinct, to move forward and place my trust in the act of creation and invention.

On the purpose of writing

I rarely consider writing in terms of its purpose, but if pushed, I believe it may have something to do with relieving the odium, the sense of isolation and loneliness, and inner despair which afflicts most thinking people at some point (for some more than others) in life. It offers pleasures, obviously, and complex processes and situations in which the human mind and soul can romp in private, without fear of judgement. When I think of *The Rings of Saturn* by W.G. Sebald, or *From the Mouth of the Whale* by the Icelandic Sjøn, or to move from literature to film, with the Icelandic film *Rams*, written and directed by Grímur Hákonarson, I know something striking and special, which also relieves anxiety, occurs for me in such works. In the case of the film, two isolated and incommunicative brothers are locked in a serious dispute which escalates when one of them conceals the fact that one of his sheep has the contagious disease Scrapie. But the story is about the two sides of primal love and hate between these two brothers, and how love eventually triumphs in tragedy.

I am drawn to the little I have read of northern European and Nordic and Scandinavian writing and realise that, for me, it acts as a balm on my life. Perhaps this notion of consolation is the naïve response of many western Europeans who love to sit back comfortably and watch *Wallander* driving along bleak coastlines, or who digested the novel *Miss Smilla's Feeling for Snow,* delighted at the knowledge that there are so many different words for 'snow', but I believe it is something more. I associate the far north with marvellous legends and myths of both life and death, but I also associate it with a pragmatism and social democracy and striving for a general equality that has sometimes been missing within my own culture. Ironically, the Swedish poetry I have read displays moments of playfulness and inventiveness that goes against all the stereotypes of what it is to be 'Swedish' in mentality. Yet for their absolute seriousness in terms of subject and formal experiment I am drawn to the Swedish Tomas Tranströmer, and the Finnish Eira Stenberg. Writers who recognise the essential solitary journey of each of us as individuals, can connect with others who recognise this. I like the seriousness of the far north, the deep gloom that is sometimes acknowledged by the writers. Such writing can automatically exclude the millions who enjoy stories which do *not* deal with 'the journey', so much as the sometimes socially tranquillising ups and downs of romance or crime, and that's ok. I don't mean to cause offence by using the word 'tranquillising', but for me, that version of storytelling is as remote from the epistemological as a girl balancing on a circus pony is from the Serbian performance artist Marina Abramović. So, there is an epistemological purpose to good writing, which some readers are drawn to, and that is equally due respect. We read what we need, perhaps. My hope is that something I write might reach into someone's soul and allow them to say something like 'Oh. Of course. That's why I felt like that when ...' or 'So I'm not alone after all, there are other weirdos like me!' or even 'I enjoy her beautiful words. Clearly, this writer enjoys beautiful words.'

Mostly though, we writers are like professional liars in our storytelling and poems. We are following a millennia-old habit of being the tribal storytellers, and in order to tell the tales we must remove ourselves from general society. When we return we hope we have something that will convince the rest that although life is harsh – birth, sexuality, death and landscape all inscribe marks on our psyches and we bear witness to this – this person has written words which act like a balm and tell them that all is well. All is process. We are helplessly, hopelessly, part of that process until the day we die.

NOTES
1 Mary O'Donnell, *The Elysium Testament* (Trident Press, 1999).
2 Barbara Jones, *Follies and Grottoes* (Constable, 1989).

Roisín O'Donnell

MY PATRON SAINT

1983. There's a patron saint for everything, if you search hard enough.

1987. I have a friend. A toxic relationship, I'll admit, but one I have no desire to escape from. Francis has been with me my whole life.

Even as young as five years old, sitting on the rough tartan sofa in my granddad's terrace house in Derry city. Late December cold. Smelling the warm salt of yesterday's soup, watching the coal fire sending tiny fusillades of sparks onto the carpet. A little boy with ink-black hair sat on the blackened stove, swinging his legs and smiling at me. 'You know there's a lion trapped in the chimney?' he said.

'There's not.'

'There is. Swear to God. Where do you think that roaring's coming from?'

I looked into the hot coals and saw feline faces staring back. Francis kept on swinging his legs and telling me stories, placing dragons under the stairs, eyes behind the windowsills. Sometimes his stories frightened me. Whenever anybody walked into the room, he vanished.

1989. People thought Francis was cute. Cute, the stories and lopsided poems, illustrated in squiggly pencil crayon, stuck on the fridge door by my proud mammy. Poems tacked to the kitchen walls of our house in Sheffield, paper wilting in the steam of dark night windows, words melding into each other. Cute. Me and Francis hand-in-hand, too young to be taken seriously.

He came with me on my first day back at school after the summer holidays, the building reeking of disinfectant, pee and fresh-dried paint. 'Tell you something funny,' Francis whispered, 'The principal has painted the whole school magnolia. Soon all the kids will be wearing magnolia uniforms too. Imagine!'

'My Magnolia School', I wrote. It's the first poem I remember writing. Cheesy as hell (I was six years old), it's about a principal who goes berserk in her insistence on monochrome neutrality and introduces magnolia shoes, magnolia skirts, magnolia blackboards. I showed it to Francis and he laughed.

Was it loneliness that drew me to this oddball, whose black eyes could speed up time and who hung bat-like from my ceiling when I least expected it?

I was an only child for the first seven years of my life, until my sister arrived on a snowed-in February night. But up until then, the house was always full of kids. School friends hanging off the garden swing, sleeping over on the travel bed with its curly, squeaky springs. I was hardly ever alone because of Francis with his sticky smile and gap-toothed eagerness to jump on the sofa beside me and tell me his stories.

1990. Places we liked to go: the heathery sprawl of countryside around Sheffield city, where ice-age rock formations had been abandoned across bracken and fern-dense hilltops. The terrifying Victorian mansion of a childhood friend. Attic, basement, wild-briar garden. A posh dump, my mammy used to call it. Spiders and naked bulbs, ghost stories we'd use to scare the crap out of each other with. Out in the white peaks, the canyon of Dove Dale with the loud splutter of its stepping-stoned stream. Monsildale Valley arched over by the old railway viaduct. Ladybower Reservoir, where on summer days the spires and rooftops of a drowned village jutted through the blue. 'There's people still down there, in the drowned village,' Francis told me, filling my head with images of bulbous, floating faces. He loved scaring me.

1992. Francis came with me to Ireland almost every summer. Sometimes if there wasn't enough money to go to Derry, we'd take a family holiday to Wales instead (still in my imagination, Wales is a type of fake Ireland). Francis skipping and jumping beside me on the P&O Ferry, memorising haikus, riddles, impossible tongue-twisters.

1998. How much time is *too much time* to spend with a lover?

Francis was never banned from the house in my teenage years, but he wasn't exactly invited either. At some point during my early teens, my relationship with Francis had gone from *cute* to *worrying*, in my parents' eyes. I guess they thought there were better options for me than hanging out with a skinny goth kid with a dodgy sense of humour.

Aged fourteen, I read *Romeo and Juliet*, *The Colour Purple*, *To Kill a Mockingbird*. Francis and I re-read each word by torchlight. At school and at home people started to talk to me about career options. When I closed my eyes to think about these questions, all I could see was Francis' face, the stories on his lips, the feel of his paper-pale skin against mine. Like all teenage romances, our love thrived on the elicit thrill of secrecy. I stopped telling people about Francis. Notebooks shoved under the mattress, words scribbled after the last light in the hall had been switched off.

Cold nights in the city of steel, when the water running from the bathroom tap was like knives of ice between your fingers. I'd open my window for Francis, who'd scoot up the drainpipe to clamber in, shake the frost out of his inky hair and hold me. Pressed against the penumbral warmth of his chest, he'd lock his fingers into my hair. Time would melt away. Seven-hilled city smouldering, orange lights like piles of smelt in the background. On another hill, the dirty-white scar of Sheffield's ski slope.

2002. When I moved to Dublin to study at Trinity, Francis came with me. As first year undergrads, we were inseparable. Detached from my family's questions by the growl of the Irish Sea, I was able to spend all my free time with Francis and he loved it. Half the time I couldn't even get to sleep in my tiny attic at the traffic-roaring Portobello crossroads, because Francis kept me awake all night with his teasing. Whenever I turned off the bedside lamp, Francis would flick the light back on to reach for me. Our desire turned us both into insomniacs, but I didn't mind losing sleep over Francis.

At this time, Francis' pale skin was webbed with indecipherable tattoos, whose greenish tentacles seeped into his inky hair. He had a comma-shaped eyebrow piercing and black full stops of earrings which lent his face an edgy look. Francis wanted to be daring and to shock people but he didn't quite have the nerve. Beyond the tattoos and tentative piercings, he was a sickly-looking young man who always wore trailing gloomy clothes to blend into the shadows and barely dared to show his papery face. Only one friend in Dublin (an English girl I trusted) knew that I was living with Francis. Most people saw my cheap white runners, tight mini-skirts and anxious eyes and they looked through Francis as if he wasn't there.

2003. Septembers of my college years. The first autumn mists sending that almost sexual buzz, the rush of a story not yet written. And with Francis Dublin was my playground. There were shards of brilliance hidden at every crooked corner, and the city played out like a film before my eyes. Willows skimming the muddy path of rowdy mallards in St Stephen's Green. Back-to-back seahorses laughing on lampposts along the Liffey walls, silver paint chipped and flaking. Everything in Dublin was new, and I simmered with secret confidence when I was with Francis. By day I'd attend lectures in the Arts Block and wander the streets until they started to become gradually familiar. At night I'd retrace my steps back to my attic overlooking the Grand Canal where dirty swans floated between sunken trolleys and crushed beer cans. I probably would have been lonely on those nights if it hadn't been for Francis who kept me company, made me laugh and held me in my sleep.

2004. Even bleak Dublin days were brightened by Francis. Ghosted, often waiting on phone calls from a Dubliner who slept with me and then never called, I poured out the story to Francis who enjoyed it so much that he made me retell it from five different angles. When people discredited my Irishness by pointing out my accent and calling me *English*, Francis hugged me until my bruises healed. Even when I got homesick, missing my parents and the gentle familiarity of the Yorkshire hills, Francis blotted my face with kisses until my tears had ceased.

Francis was never annoying and he was never boring. Chameleon-like, he adapted to suit my every mood.

Of course, our relationship was not without problems.

'Why do you never *feed* me?' Francis announced one day, 'You spend all your time in the library now and you leave me *hungry*!' I apologised and tried to sweet-talk him, but that didn't work.

'I know you only really like it when we're at home alone together. But I can't afford to heat the flat all day,' I explained. 'That's why I go to the library. Why don't you come with me, Francis?' I suggested, 'It'd be great.'

'*No,*' he replied, 'I am not going to the bloody library.'

'But Francis,' I said, locking my arms around his neck, 'Come to the library ... it'll be fun.'

Scowling, Francis pulled away. This was the thing about Francis; you couldn't convince him to do anything he didn't want to do, or to go anywhere he didn't want to go. You couldn't cajole him or persuade him. It just didn't work. What Francis was second-most afraid of was criticism (what Francis was most afraid of was himself). Once at the Trinity writers' group someone dared to make a mildly sarcastic comment about Francis's tattoos ('trying a little too hard, perhaps?') and Francis fled the seminar room and didn't come near me for a fortnight.

2005. 'Not the desk,' Francis moaned, 'let's sit on the bed or the sofa, or anywhere, but not the feckin desk.'

'Alright,' I said, 'ok.' (Since I was a teen, I have always had a desk and Francis has always refused to sit at it).

Francis loved late nights and he adored early mornings. Shortly after sunrise we'd bask together on the wide windowsills of my Georgian student flat or stroll along the canal in the almost-day. At the extremities of day and night Francis's eyes were alive with ideas, but he hated afternoons. Many afternoons, Francis would get scared of things that weren't even there and I'd have to stroke his hair and whisper to him that everything was ok.

'You don't *love* me!' Francis shouted at me one day and hurled a paperback at my head, 'Am I even *on* your list of priorities? Am I even bloody *on* the list?'

'Of course you're on the list, Francis!' I told him, reaching to take his hand, 'You *are* my list! For God's sake, it's only you *on* the list!' but Francis turned away.

'I *used* to be top of your list ...' he said to his frowning reflection in the window, 'But now I'm second, SECOND!'

'No, Francis, it's not like that,' I pleaded, but he stormed out of my apartment and I didn't see him for days. Sometimes Francis' absence came as a relief. My essay grades improved and I could do things like laze away an afternoon on the lawn in front of the Pavilion Bar without worrying about Francis.

2006. I was sheltering at Front Gate waiting for Francis on a damp day when the Trinity cobblestones were marbled with rain, when a short man with swarthy skin approached me, 'Excuse me madam, do you know where is the Book of Kells?'

'I'll walk you there,' I offered and he ushered me under his gleaming umbrella. The Italian was newly arrived in Dublin from Verona. Forgetting all about Francis, I took this charming stranger on a makeshift tour of the city streets, on a route which inevitably ended up back in my bed. He was easy to be with, and dating him was like taking a holiday from myself and all that messed-up stuff with Francis. Leaning my head on his shoulder at Parnell Street cinema, sitting on the worktop while he cooked lasagne with the pouting, frowning concentration of a five-year-old building a Lego tower, I felt the giddy joy of normalcy. This is what twenty-somethings were meant to be doing; relaxing and enjoying life. On Saturday afternoons when I would normally have been sitting on my bed arguing with Francis, I lingered in the Italian's river-view apartment, dressing, undressing, re-dressing against a backdrop of water.

At first, Francis was quite turned-on by this development in my life; he liked it when I tried new things. On nights when I wasn't with the Italian, Francis would keep me awake till all hours while I related every detail of my latest romantic encounters. But the more time I spent with the Italian, the more Francis slipped away, and I saw less and less of him. Then whenever we met, Francis would just stare at me and refuse to talk. Francis and I spent awkward nights in my bedroom, both of us sitting there without touching or saying a word. *Sod him*, I thought to myself, *I don't need him at all.*

But what started as a slight scratch under my ribcage soon spread into a body-wide ache. I'd wake up in the middle of the night sweating, scared that I no longer knew who I was and petrified that I'd never see Francis again. One night I phoned Francis, 'Look,' I said, 'You know I need you, Francis, but I also deserve a life. Why won't you let me have one?'

Francis just hung up.

It was becoming clear that I would have to make a choice: love or Francis. I couldn't have both. The Italian was caring and tender, turning up with bunches of yellow roses in crinkly cellophane, and telling me stories about the history of tiramisu given to soldiers by their Venetian lovers. Meanwhile, everytime I glimpsed Francis across campus he was doing something destructive like tearing down signposts or beating himself up.

One time, when I was on the bus going down the sunlit Rathmines Road, I saw Francis walking towards me with his hands in his pockets. He looked gorgeous. My stomach lurched when I saw him. Lovesick. Now I knew the meaning of this phrase. The bus was going too fast for me to get off, and before I could help it, Francis was just a dot on the horizon behind me. I was suddenly nauseated by the idea that Francis (*my* Francis) was on his way to meet somebody else.

'I can't do this,' I told the Italian as we sat by the Liffey, 'I need my space.'

'*Space?*' he squinted at me, rubbing his head, 'Space for what?'

I need space for Francis, I thought, but I didn't say that.

I left the Italian sitting on the boardwalk and set off to search the streets for Francis. I looked in all our usual places; the deserted cricket ground at the far end of the Phoenix Park, the cavern-like coffee shop in the Georges Street Arcade, on my bed and on the sofa, but there was no sign of him anywhere. And the more I searched for Francis, the more I realised how much I needed him, and the further away he seemed.

2009. For years after I graduated, Francis refused to return.

Lost and tired, I drifted across continents.

Things which I thought would summon Francis: moving to Catalonia, the rattle of chestnut shells across cobbled streets, the smell of roasted *castanyes* and marzipan *panellets*; getting lost in the hot metal-tasting maze of the Barcelona subway; Brazil, a pre-dawn landing in São Paulo airport, skyscrapers rising up to swallow the plane's wings; Caraguatatuba with its white curve of beach, its jungled hills that looked like the humpbacked form of some oceanic monster; Derry city, walking along the river, tracing the steps of my ancestors. Imagining women's heels clacking along steep streets on their way home from the shirt factories, sunken U-boats dragged up the Foyle. None of this appealed to Francis. At times, he'd text me. Short, barely comprehensible messages which I rarely replied to.

So I fell into primary teaching, partly as a path to a stable income and partly for fear of never doing anything else. The late nights and early mornings once occupied by Francis were now taken up with lesson plans and student observations. My mind fell into a type of stupor. I'd stare out of the window, thinking about Francis but unable to conjure up a single word to say to him.

2012. And it was years later that I looked up and saw Francis leaning in the doorway of my empty classroom. He looked like crap. His eyebrow piercing had gone septic, his cheeks were flushed and a torn leather jacket hung off his sunken shoulders like a raven's ragged wings.

'What do you think *you're* doing?' Francis said.

'Working. Earning a living. Helping people,' I replied, indicating the tiny yellow-legged chairs, the overturned pots of broken crayons and the little rail of multi-coloured backpacks.

'You? *Helping* people?' Francis kicked over a wastepaper basket and walked out.

Just then, my Senior Infants charged back in, scrambling, elbow-butting, pencil-fighting, making me feel miniscule in the face of their tsunami of noise. My attempts to gain control over the class were failing fairly spectacularly, and clarity dropped over me with such gentle reassurance I wanted to laugh out loud. The next September, rather than looking for another temporary contract at saint-something-or-other-national-school, I took a job teaching English to international students at the university. Life was easier. I was getting more sleep.

'In my country,' one of my students told me, 'if a couple kisses under the first snow of winter, it means they will be together until their hair is white.' Stalled in the middle of a lesson on the Present Perfect, I imagined a young couple dashing from the sliding doors of a glassy office block, running towards each other through spiralling flakes. A warm feeling spread from my belly, the pleasure of a story unfurling. I looked up and saw Francis sitting beside two bored-looking Italian girls who were painting their nails at the back of my classroom. For once, Francis looked relaxed and well-rested. I mouthed at him, 'hi.'

2013. A late summer day, walking through the blonde sway of dry summer grasses in the Phoenix Park, the city held in the dusty caul of an August heat haze. Francis fell into step beside me and casually opened the conversation with, 'So, what's new with you?'

'Nothing exciting,' I told him, 'Just work and the kids at school and living in the furthest flung corner of Dublin, where everybody is from somewhere else. Nothing worth talking about.'

'We don't have to make up mad shit,' Francis said, 'It's your life. We can talk about that.'

And we did. We talked all afternoon and long into the night.

For the first time ever, I introduced Francis to someone. I took him along to a creative writing workshop where the teacher, a well-known poet and editor, looked at me and raised an eyebrow, nodding towards Francis, 'How long have you known this guy?'

At this time, Francis was dreadlocked, bearded and hooded, and sat with his hands between his knees. At home, after the workshop we showered together. I sat behind him, trimmed his dreadlocks, kissed his shoulders. 'Come on, Francis, it's time to stop hiding. You're in my life. Ok. I finally get it.'

2015. Those days Francis was more beautiful and more selfish than ever. He'd filled out, become more confident, got more tattoos and started to wear brighter clothes. We were infatuated with each other and hardly had time for anyone else. When I brought Francis out in Dublin, he started to attract some attention, holding circles of people enrapt with his mad stories and conversation. He was taller, stronger, more eloquent but just as likely to scarper. We went to literary festivals, stood under hot spotlights in theatres and arts centres and answered questions about our relationship. Francis loved it.

For a brief and glittering moment, it seemed we would always be this way.

May 2016. Francis stood beside me one day as I opened a brown box, lifted out the first book and ran my finger over the title. The strange alien-feeling of my name on a bright book jacket. My inner thoughts turned into a holdable object. All I could think of were my doubts about certain stories, and of last-minute edits which had occurred to me too late to be included in the final manuscript. Nothing had prepared me for the feeling of nakedness, of my thoughts being exposed to the world. The thought (and I don t know why this hadn't occurred to me before now) of reviews, and of my friends and family reading the book. Francis ran into the en suite and retched over the toilet. All I could hear was him muttering, 'crap, crap, crap.'

2016. I was still teaching to pay the bills. Sometimes my colleagues would find out about Francis and give me looks which might have been jealous or suspicious or downright freaked out. 'You dark horse,' they'd say. Presuming that ... what? That my life with Francis involved sunset cruises and roses? That my relationship with Francis was *easy*?

All my life I'd felt like a wave pulled by lunar gravity. I'd presumed the lodestar tugging me all those years was Francis, but I was wrong.

One late May afternoon, I took a deep breath and looked at him, 'Are you ready?'

He nodded. He was wearing a black jumper embellished with silver calligraphy and page-white skinny jeans which he'd worn for our latest literary festival. His attempt, I suppose, to be different and stand out from the crowd. 'It's ok,' he said, 'you can do this.'

I stooped and lifted the white plastic stick from the bathroom rug where I'd flung it in a moment of panic. Lines and squares and circles and sweet Jesus, I didn't know which line meant what. I reached for the box, pulled out the instruction sheet. It was all in some language I didn't even recognise. Shit. *Öppna förpackningen I samband met tatt da skall* ... Where was the English? Words loomed and swam before my eyes. *One band: you may assume to be 'not pregnant.' Two bands: you may assume to be 'pregnant.'*

I sat down on the bed, watching the

two

mauve

bands

deepen colour before my eyes.

It felt like someone just pressed the 'pause' button on my life.

Francis took my hand.

2016, mid-December. According to my pregnancy app, my growing baby was the size of a cauliflower and could even dream. I imagined the child's eyelids twitching with REM. What do unborn babies dream of? Black-and-white photos from my child's twenty-week scan were pinned to the kitchen noticeboard. Sometimes I'd stare at them, like photos of someone in a far-away war, trying to imagine life and movement into the static images. At these times, I never thought of Francis.

Other times, when I was sitting on my bed deep in conversation with Francis, I'd forget about the baby. Forget to feel her kicks and rolls, to imagine her turning in her sleep. When I realised this, I would turn away from Francis and concentrate on my belly. It was a sense of re-earthing. I'd feel guilty for having ignored the baby. Unborn, unseen and yet already she was my lightening rod.

2017. Blood behind sealed doors and the particular pressure of waters being broken. Pre-labour ward, behind hospital-blue curtains, the sub-aquatic thud of fast prenatal heartbeats. I'd been induced, and so far nothing was happening, but I knew what lay ahead. From behind one side of my curtains, quasi-orgasmic moans and from the other side, a woman whose squeals sounded like a trolley with a stuck wheel. Francis sauntered up to me while I lay there waiting for the pain to start. I threw a book at his head.

The night before Valentines Day, 2017, my daughter was born. At last, Francis and I had something in common.

2017, mid-March morning. Jazz hands, fingers splayed, waving rapidly to and fro as if my daughter has been startled from sleep. Tiny fingers conducting invisible air flows. Eyes that shift between the brown of fresh turned earth and the grey of ocean storm.

And I am not meant to feel like this. I'm trying to be cool and not to write about motherhood, but here's the catch; parenting is walking into a forest for the first time. How can you avoid writing about that?

'Bees! Flowers! Horseys! Can she see them? Hold her up! Look, little love! Clippity-clop, horseys!'

No one can write like this. It's hardly the material of highbrow literature.

I take Francis aside and tell him, *'We are in some serious shit.'*

But Francis, in a baggy blouse, doesn't care. His tattoos have faded from his skin as if erased, and his piercings have healed over. His face is relaxed and calmly confident. He's no longer trying to impress anyone. He suddenly wants to know things like the names of wildflowers and how to identify birds from their song.

Summer 2017. We've had our moments. All these years, it seems we've rarely been on the same page. But one thing Francis and I agree on; my daughter is all we want to talk about. After she's gone to sleep (and sleep is rare, sleep is fleeting), we sit watching her. Francis is as smitten as I am. And there are times my daughter looks at me with a particular concealed humour in her storm-grey eyes (they never settled into a definite colour) and I see my mum looking back at me. We could be hunting for bees in the garden or reading bedtime stories, but when she looks at me like that I am transported miles away. Decades of wisdom in her baby face. Like all babies, it's as if she was born knowing everything. Skipping ropes between red brick Derry terraces, the swing of a lilac paisley skirt along a London street, makeshift sledges charging down a Sheffield hill, the snow marshmallow deep, our family story written in white engine spray catscombing the Irish Sea.

Before my daughter arrived, I worried that becoming a mum would mean the end of my relationship with Francis. Instead it's as if we've just met each other for the first time. Gone are the teenage fumblings, the stupid arguments. Francis is less flighty and also less concerned about what other people think. A thin blonde dressmaker in an alteration shop once told me, 'Once you've given birth, you are not prudish any more. You don't give a crap who sees what.' An elderly friend of my mum's once peered into my daughter's pram and said, 'Congratulations. Now you will be worried until the day you die.'

The change in Francis came about so slowly, it was almost invisible. An abandonment of arrogance. A slow kindling of empathy, making it easier for us to grab a quick coffee together during my lunch break, or chat on the phone during my daughter's afternoon nap. His hair grew past his shoulders and his form softened. I've re-read the texts he sent me during the time I spent living abroad, and we laugh about these texts and discuss them at length. Even though Francis still hates afternoons, out of necessity he's learnt how to be more pleasant at this time of day. We Skype. We message. We make it work. Now the metamorphosis is complete it's hard to know how I didn't see it. Francis sits on my bed, watching the baby attempting to crawl.

'You could keep your name?' I suggest.

S/he says no. 'I'll just change the 'e' to an 'I'.'

I shake my head. 'Oh Jesus, Frances.'

2018. An unbelievable summer. Unrealistic, even. Weeks of dry, hot weather have left the lawn a dry wasteland. 'HAY,' my daughter says as she runs helter-skelter across the grass in an abandonment of gravity. Aged eighteen months she is discovering the magical algorithm of slotting words together. TEDDY BEAR. MAMMY'S ROOM. PURPLE SHOES. It makes her seem less like a baby and more like an actual person. It's possible to have an almost-conversation with her. Frances and I spend weekends like this, talking and being stunned by the sudden gush of language.

These days my daughter is my priority. Along with full-time work, sometimes that leaves little time for writing. Words are squeezed into the margins of my life, condensed into the corners, but that's not necessarily a bad thing. Frances is always by my side, seeing everything and storing it in her inexhaustible memory, waiting for the pilfered minutes, late at night or early morning, when we finally have the chance to sit on my bed and talk. At this point we're just two friends who have known each other their entire lives. There's an honesty between us, neither one trying to show off or prove anything. Frances sits behind me and rubs my tired shoulders.

'So? What's the latest story?'

Saint Francis de Sales, a bishop of Geneva, died in 1622. He is known as the Patron Saint of Writers.

Nessa O'Mahony

WHEN A POET TURNS TO FICTION

In the autumn of 2015, I discovered something new about
myself as a writer. It wasn't the fact that, after twenty years
of writing poetry, I was now embarking on a new
adventure – my first piece of long fiction. It wasn't that
after forty years or more of reading crime fiction, I was
finally taking the leap into writing it. It was the actual time
of day that I chose to sit at my laptop and begin the
arduous task of filling the empty screen with words, much
as I'm doing right now. Now it is late in the day; the other
tasks preoccupying my fretful brain have been put to bed
and the mid-Autumn light is fading. Back then it was early
dawn, the sunrise not yet breaking through the trees at the
end of our garden and the house still quiet, other than for
the relaxed breathing of my husband in one bedroom, or of
our dog at the foot of the stairs.

I would like to say that I had deliberately chosen 5:30am
as an auspicious time at which to start this new project.
That the strains of Eartha Kitt's 'new dawn, new day' were
running through my head as I opened the laptop and

watched the screen flicker into white space. But that would not be honest. The choice was entirely hormonal; the combination of menopause and underactive thyroid had rendered my bed uncomfortable those past few months. It was harder work staying put beneath the duvet than it was climbing the stairs to the attic room and beginning the day's work early. And the advantage was that I could get a head start with the novel before the rest of the world began posting status updates or tweeting themselves into existence.

So I found the house to myself (almost), the headspace to myself (completely) and a spare ninety minutes each day to try out this new type of writing, this mad challenge I had set myself. And it felt utterly appropriate that I should try out a new way of storytelling at an ungodly hour. The very repetitiveness of the task I set myself – to get up at 5:30, write for ninety minutes, produce a thousand words a day (a teacher had pointed out that writing five-hundred words a day would produce a novel in six months and, literalist that I was, I wanted to test the hypothesis) – was utterly at odds with the way I'd written poetry all those decades. I'm a very responsive poet – unlike those who sit and wait for inspiration to strike I need a stimulus, and usually find it from a morning walk, a beautiful landscape, an existential threat in a doctor's waiting room, that sort of thing. I never expect it to turn up like clockwork or to keep regular hours.

But novel writing felt very different. I seemed to enjoy this diurnal rhythm, this regularity. As I typed the chapters grew in number, the characters developed, the conversations became livelier. As the page numbers climbed the story itself felt more solid, more substantial. It could also be mercurial – one slip of a storyline and I was sheafing back through printouts and notebooks, trying to remember who was supposed to have done what to whom and whether they still could take that action if I'd killed them off earlier. So there was a lot at stake in keeping track of this accumulation of words.

The mornings built up into weeks, into months, through redraft after redraft. The pile of pages got bulkier, then the task of typing 'The End' came into view. One day that finally happened. Having spent two decades as a poet, I was now a novelist.

Then another strange thing happened, something that requires me to be especially honest with you now. Something changed about my self image as a writer. I felt more confident about this bulky pile of paper with a punchy title and the requisite amount of suspense, than about the four slim volumes of verse sitting resentfully on my book shelf. Please don't misunderstand me. I'm quietly proud of the books of poetry I've published, the journals I've edited, the critical studies I've contributed to. But I'm a little abashed too. Poetry isn't something you can chat about with the neighbour or engage in small talk with a stranger at a party. And when somebody does tell you they've read your book, that it was like looking inside your head, you quake a little.

But novels are different, and crime fiction is different again. Everybody knows somebody who reads crime fiction, don't they? It's the sort of thing you buy your grandmother for Christmas, or a favourite aunt for their birthday. It's not an embarrassing habit, something to keep quiet about. It even has commercial potential, so all those grey-suited people who tutted over the life wasted to poetry can have nothing to complain to me about now.

Thus I went into the valley of death in search of a publisher with my head held high. The lengthy wait for a response to a manuscript was no different to what I'd experienced in the poetry world – it was only a matter of time before my confidence would be vindicated.

And so it proved to be, though not in the ways I'd imagined all those months ago before I was a published author. The book found a home; I found myself having lots of conversations with people about the story I was writing, and the sequels I might be planning, and the potential for TV adaptations. Friends seemed more delighted for me, now that I was a real writer of books that they might actually read. My family could actually look me straight in the eye and admit that not only had they begun my book, they'd finished it too. And recommended it to their friends.

Before, I had been a poet. Now I was an author. I had never understood all those introductions of such-and-such a person as 'author and poet'; I'd always thought the two were inextricably linked and needed no differentiation. But now I understand. An author has an audience. A poet has other poets. I like having an audience. That doesn't mean that I won't shortly return to the quieter landscape of poetry, to wrestle with images that capture whatever existential crisis I'm currently grappling with. But for now I am enjoying the concept of popularity: the novelty of writing in a different way.

Joseph O'Neill

THE WRITING HABIT

In which conditions does your writing come into being/flourish? Does mood play a role?

First of all, I don't have an office. I don't have a routine, either. If I'm lucky, I have a few hours in the day that are open to me and that may or may not result in me going to a coffee shop and writing something, or tinkering with something. My books are really written when I displace myself from my daily environment by leaving town for a couple of weeks – to Flagstaff, to Montreal, most recently – and really giving myself the total freedom to immerse myself in the fictional world I'm trying to create. I get more done in ten days than I'd get done in ten months at home.

What place does writing have in your life? How does it interact/interfere with life, or does life interfere with writing?

I'm not a habitual writer. I never have been. In the days when I wrote poetry – my first love! – I produced very few poems. As for fiction (or nonfiction), it seems that I don't have the desire to write a lot of it. That's something I half regret, because why not be prolific? It would certainly be a good career move. But it can't be helped. When I ponder why this might be the case, I usually conclude that life is to blame – the absorbing demands of family, of teaching, not to mention the political emergency that has characterised American life in recent years and which has captured so much of my energy and attention. But increasingly I arrive at the rather gloomy conclusion that the problem isn't life. It's me. I just don't have a lot of writing in me – writing that passes muster with my inner censor, which is to say, writing that would be deeply interesting to me as opposed to professionally good enough. That last challenge – finding something of interest to oneself – becomes harder as you grow more experienced and more alert to self-repetition, more sensitive to the problem of making work that is in a deep sense superfluous. But the real challenge is an emotional one. My work may not seem emotional, but I am indeed one of those writers who draws material from the proverbial emotional well, bucket by bucket, and perhaps that is one reason I'm not prolific. I'm exhausted.

Which conditions are detrimental to the right concentration?
Actually starting to write – exiting one's ordinary consciousness, one's ordinary preoccupations – is the first hurdle. Then concentration is required to not revert to ordinariness. The only way I successfully do that is by total immersion. I do have a lot of difficulty achieving and sustaining this immersion, and that's one reason why I invariably use a nicotine product (but not cigarettes, which I quit years ago).

What exactly can a wo/man's specific ways of perceiving bring to writing?
The reality of the gendered standpoint has been persuasively articulated by the likes of Susan Bordo, and I don't think I've ever doubted that, in pretty much any

society, male subjectivity can differ as such from its female counterpart. I'm very wary of essentialist ideas, in any realm, but it must be true as a general proposition that women and men can offer qualities or insights that are peculiar to their social and biological existence as gendered beings. What these offerings might be, I can't say. I certainly wouldn't want to devalue a writer who deploys a point of view that differs radically from the autobiographical point of view. Of course, we have examples of writers successfully leaping across the so-called gender gap, although I suppose you can't help noticing, first, that only the very best make it intact to the other side; and second, even if you were to make it safely over, you'd probably be ambushed by ideologues determined to push you into the chasm you've just negotiated.

Of course, the wo/man binary contained in this question has come under severe pressure, particularly here in the USA, and no doubt we'll see more writing that reflects this development. It'll be interesting to see how that goes.

Is the literary translation of life into stories/poetry/drama somehow an unceasing commitment? Could you give an example of how that works?

I don't think the commitment need be, or can be, unceasing. It can probably be turned on and off, like intelligence. That said, I do think that you can't successfully translate life into text without total artistic and emotional commitment. If an author has taken some kind of shortcut, even a little one, you can usually feel it.

Does the unconscious come into play, and if so, how? Could you give an example of how something gestated over a certain time? Do the best passages come (un)intentionally?

The unconscious comes into play whether you want it to or not. I want it to – I count on it to. My 'thoughts', my 'opinions' – in the context of making artistic work, these must be treated with a degree of suspicion. Why? Because opinions and thoughts are, by their very structure, second-hand and banal.

What is the purpose of writing for you?
We already have plenty of books in circulation, certainly enough to be reading and re-reading for a human lifetime. Simply adding to that corpus would seem to be fairly pointless. So I suppose the purpose must be a private one, having to do with private needs.

What should your writing do to the ideal reader? To society?
I'm not sure, on either score. These certainly aren't questions I ask myself while I'm writing, when my only concern is whether the text I'm making feels right to me. In any case, and to paraphrase Antisthenes, I see readers everywhere, but nowhere do I see your ideal reader.

What is an ideal sentence to you and why? Are there any metaphors which are central to your perception/work?
The word that comes to mind, here, is 'accurate.' An accurate sentence is the ideal. Accuracy, in this sense, isn't (merely) a question of precision – of an achieved state of affairs in which the sentence operates as a satisfactory verbal counterpart, or cutout, of its object. I mean 'accurate' in its etymological sense, 'toward care' (*ad* + *cura*). An accurate sentence tends toward care – of language, of justice, of reality.

If you were to describe the act of writing in one scene, would that be a curse, a relief, bliss, a struggle, or all of these?
All of the above, with only 'struggle' as a constant.

Sean O'Reilly

SAVING SOULS

A good few years ago now, I was asked if I would be willing to meet for an informal conversation with a readers group in a Dublin library. Back then it was news to me that there was any such thing as a community reading group. The librarian tried to reassure me the group would have read one of my books and they would have lots of questions. And my job would be to provide answers; why you wrote the book, just to talk to them about yourself, according to the librarian.

A month later, I found myself in a second-floor room in the library with a group of twelve elderly women and seventeen chairs. There was a hot water urn, cups and saucers and paper plates of biscuits. My name was written on the white board in weak green marker. The windows overlooked the entrance to a shopping centre. Pretty quickly it became clear that most of the women had not finished the book. The main character was too unsympathetic, the atmosphere too disturbing. None of which seemed to spoil their enjoyment of being there talking to the writer about himself. One woman, however, kept trying to bring the discussion back to the book itself. She was a small woman in a long knitted cardigan, with a lovely smooth pale face and quick dark eyes. I couldn't place her accent, thought she might be English. The other women ignored her questions by talking more loudly about something else. I thought they might be suspicious of her for some reason. Perhaps she was new to the group.

The session fizzled out rather than ended. The women left their chairs and began to talk among themselves around the hot water urn. Only the small lively woman had any interest left in me. She asked me to sign her copy of my book. Her name was Joan. She had no smell. She was very curious about what she called the imagination; it amazed her – this power to create something out of nothing. I remember trying to be as honest as I could that not all of it came out of nowhere, but she seemed unconvinced. I began to land a question or two on her instead. And slowly, it became clear that Joan was a nun.

Or to be more precise, she was a retired nun. Sister Joan had spent her life working in what used to be called the missions. South Africa, Calcutta, Latin America, New Guinea, teaching the wisdom of Jesus. As we talked, I was struck by the way she described people, no matter who they were, the poorest of the poor or those profiting from it, and her gentle but playful sense of humour. I told her she should try to write those stories down. Oh I used to, she said, with a dismissive wave of her small soft ringless hand, but it was only for myself, only to remember.

Privately I was asking myself who did I write for, while I pushed Joan to tell me where this record of her adventures was now. Oh, she said, don't be calling them that. She wouldn't have the ability to write about anything more than the everyday boring stuff. Nothing like your imaginative writing.

Joan, it turned out, was a diarist. And a compulsive one. Every day of her life after she left Ireland at nineteen, she had kept a diary of the entire day's God-given events. The sights and sounds of a Johannesburg shanty town, the street kids of Calcutta, the favelas, the freshwater swamps of New Guinea. Right up to the last few years which she had spent in New York's Upper West Side. Until eventually the story came to its natural end with her departure home to her retirement in Dublin.

I was now imagining, in the corner of a clean, spartan bedroom, an old-fashioned trunk plastered with stickers from exotic places, and inside book after book of this woman's life.

It was the cost, she said suddenly. I couldn't justify the expense to myself.

What expense did she mean?

The price of shipping all those diaries back to Ireland.

I couldn't contain my shock that she had left them in New York, told her that the money didn't matter, we would have to get them back somehow. I even promised to help her.

Joan smiled kindly at my spurious fervour.

No need to worry, she said. They were only becoming a bother anyway.

I reminded her that she was talking about the story of her life's journey, her very soul. Then a terrible idea struck me: had she thrown them away, a dumpster in some alley?

Not at all, she said, firmly. I was relieved but only for a moment.

I incinerated them, she said. A bin obviously wasn't safe enough. She had burned the lot. Up in smoke.

Her brazen young eyes betrayed no regret.

David Park

LOOKING FOR LIGHT

I only ever won one academic prize and it came in my first year of primary school so I must have been about five years of age. My memory is standing in front of the class with my back to the blackboard and I am reading Brer Rabbit aloud. The elderly teacher is Miss Brownlee – how readily we remember the names of those who were either kind or cruel to us in our childhood – and she is so pleased with my reading that she gives me a silver sixpence.

All writers begin as readers. But even when my independent reading began with comics, I approached them in the same slightly Calvinistic way that still pertains to the written word, so I had no interest in superheroes or supposedly humorous caricatures. What I wanted were 'true' stories subsuming me into the realities of their world and whose words also transported me to different places opening up inside me. As someone who spent thirty-four years in classroom teaching, one of my few formal insistences was the sacredness of the book as an object, so please never ever throw, annotate only in pencil if you really must, and never turn down the corner of the page. Let me give you this bookmark instead.

Despite coming from a very different religious tradition, when Seamus Heaney spoke of coming to his desk like an altar boy in the sacristy getting ready to go out on to the main altar, I instinctively understood what he meant. I am someone who enjoys humour and do my best to avoid pretentiousness or expressions of ego in all its public forms, but when I come to write I believe I am engaging in something that is more serious than the impulse to entertain, that it requires my best self and that it will be irredeemably cheapened if I undertake it motivated by the wrong impulses, or – although I am reluctant to use the phrase because there is a risk of sounding priggish – an impure heart.

Why do I write? I write because to be at my most well, my most healthily alive, whatever it is that is inside me needs to find creative expression. I find this expression in other valued ways such as playing sport – hitting the sweet spot of a ball is as pleasurable as a perfect sentence – and through engagement with the arts in general, but it is in writing that I am most fully expressed. I do not write constantly. The need ebbs and flows. When the impulse compels me I am writing essentially for myself. If anyone else reads what I have written or takes pleasure in it, or best of all is moved by it, I am pleased and grateful but I think of that as a bonus and not what drives me to undertake the work.

During those years as a full-time teacher I produced seven of my eleven books. Looking back I do not fully understand how I managed to combine a demanding job with writing. Occasionally younger writers who find themselves in a similar situation ask me for advice on how this can be done and I have to struggle to produce something useful for them. Although the best writing can produce something mysterious, even mystical, I believe in avoiding conceptualising the actual process in such a way. So I just sit at my desk and do it. I struggle only to offer some coherent explanation of my writing process, any analysis of what is actually happening. I used to envy writers who could do so eloquently but not anymore and I am happy and consider myself fortunate that much of what happens on my page is instinctive and does not yield to intimate analysis on my part. There are conscious decisions always being made but at some deeper and more important level I am working in an intuitive way, feeling my way towards the light, step by step through the shades, looking for handholds in the imagination.

To combine full-time work with writing you need to develop the capacity to move easily between different worlds. The daily-lived life and the purely imaginative life are not polarities but parallel existences and the writer needs to move seamlessly and quickly between both. If it helps, think of those children who enter that cavernous wardrobe, rummage round for a couple of minutes then step out into the snow bright world of the imagination. Let it be as sudden as that.

The great paradox of writing fiction, of course, is that it has to be true – true in its emotions, psychology and narrative, true in its fidelity to the world as it is – not how we would like it to be. And above all true in its language. Writing a novel is difficult because it is easy to come up short on one of these truths. I always want everything I write to meet these criteria. That is the enduring challenge. A first page of any lifted book will always reveal whether there is any genuine prospect of the writer reaching these goals – it is not possible to disguise a falling-short.

Having lived through Northern Ireland's Troubles and now writing in a post-conflict society, I am also conscious of the connection between art and the political and social landscape in which we find ourselves. In *Birds of Heaven*[1] Ben Okri has written that:

> Nations and people are largely the stories they feed
> themselves. If they tell themselves stories that are lies, they
> will suffer the future consequences of those lies. If they tell
> themselves stories that face their own untruths, they will free
> their histories for future flowerings.[2]

In Ireland we have often been guilty of telling ourselves lies – in the world of religion, politics and indeed through many of this island's deepest cultural mythologies. Writers – imperfect, deeply flawed and with the deep regrets harboured by all humans but who seek to present alternative visions, however difficult – have an important role to play in any future flowering.

In the literary world I am seen perhaps not as an outsider, but as something of an outlier, someone not fully absorbed into the centre ground. Earlier in my career this would not have been my choice and was possibly a legacy of my teaching career and my absence from the frequently publicised, but now I am happy to exist on the edges, coming in on occasions and stepping away again. For most of my writing career I described myself as a teacher, not a writer, because I have always been conscious of the resonances involved in calling myself a writer and it was something to which I always aspired, rather than ever felt I had finally achieved. When I retired and was no longer a teacher, I was eased into using the word 'writer' to describe myself and am happy now that it seems to fit without obvious worry or self-consciousness.

Although I no longer have any traditional or formal religious faith, the legacy of my evangelical upbringing continues to linger across my writing. I find myself still influenced not by theology but by Biblical images of transcendence and transfiguration, of personal redemption and atonement. Increasingly I am aware that what I want to do as a writer is to take what seems irredeemably steeped in the shadowy, earthbound confinements of human existence and, for better or worse, find some moment of illumination. It may well be a transient moment and it does not matter if the shadows form again soon after.

I grew up with my ear held to the language of the Bible and one final lasting influence of those days is a love of the stories involving miracles that hold such symbolism for anyone who writes – water turned into wine, the dead brought back to life and with a particular resonance for someone who has entered his sixty-fifth year, a child born in old age. To write is always to believe in the possibility of the miraculous. That is the one enduring faith, even now as the years advance, even now in this world in which we live.

NOTE

1 Ben Okri, *Birds of Heaven* (Phoenix 1996). The quotation is taken from the section 'Aphorisms and Fragments' which itself is derived from 'The Joys of Story-telling', a talk that was delivered to the Cambridge Union in June 1993, a series of 'wise sayings' about the importance of story-telling and narrative.

Siobhán Parkinson

CHAIRSHAPED

I visit schools a fair bit and I work with children on writing projects. Because they are children and especially because they are at school, where learning to read and write is the central activity from which most other scholastic activities derive, they take the word 'writing' literally. As soon as I say 'writer', 'write', 'writing', they pick up their pencils. Writing is a thing you do with your fingers, laboriously. A kind of handicraft. They look very suspicious when they hear I write on a computer. They are usually too polite to say so, but I can tell they think that's cheating.

They are even more suspicious when I tell them we're not going to write anything, not for ages. We're going to talk. We're going to make stuff up. We're going to imagine things. We might have an argument. We will definitely have a laugh. We might even – sharp intake of breath – throw most of this week's ideas out the window next week and start again in a new place. Clearly they think that is going backwards. They are remarkably attached to the first ideas they have – even though they must, at some level, know that anyone's first stumbling, exploratory moves to do or make anything are unlikely to survive the process and are only moves to be made, ideas to be had, in order to be thrown out so that the creator can go on to have better ideas, make more nimble moves.

Whatever about writing as an activity they might, however grudgingly, agree to participate in, they are implacably opposed to the idea of rewriting. When they hear the news that most writing is actually rewriting, they are appalled. They cheer up immeasurably, though, when I tell them they won't need their pencils. I'll type it all up as we go along and I'll make the amendments we agree also. The cheat is suddenly ok. They think the work has been dispensed with. Hah!

What I do in the classroom seems at odds with what I do privately when I sit down to write at home in my own study. I don't write communally, as I ask the children to do. I don't begin by talking, except, of course, to myself. But these methods I use at school, I begin to realise, are indeed versions of how I proceed myself, only obviously they have to be adapted to a situation where there are many writers, not in a hushed and hallowed study but in a noisy classroom.

In my study I sit alone and think, sit and tap, sit and look things up on Google, sit and think, sit and tap, sit and sit and sit and sit and then it is – how could it possibly be? – lunchtime, and I've rattled out a thousand words, or squeezed out a hundred and thrown fifty of them out. I will most likely throw the remaining fifty out after lunch and start again. And I've forgotten to stand up and move around for a few seconds every now and then, so my body has taken on the shape of my chair and straightening up is a slow and creaky business. I know I ought to go for a walk after lunch – not just because I need the exercise, but because I know from experience that walking is a kind of peripatetic writing; all kinds of solutions offer themselves, as I walk – and yet I don't want to walk. I want to get back to the writing. I'll just finish that paragraph. I'll just take half an hour and then walk, I tell myself. And then I look up and it's dark, and my body is chair-shaped again.

This private, unrelenting grappling with words looks – is – quite different from the public contention I ask the children to take part in in the classroom. And yet it is the same. The arguments, the struggles, the jostling to be allowed to keep one's pet idea, the temptation to throw the whole lot over and sulk for the afternoon – it's all there, only now it's going on, mostly inarticulately, in my own head, and I am playing all the parts: the pushy one, the sly one, the smart one, the beguiled one, the creative one, the amazed one, the shy one, the exasperated one, the delighted one.

The conditions for writing are time, space and three meals a day. A deadline is also very useful. Mood plays no role. If one relied on mood, nothing would get written – ever. Detrimental conditions are conflicting obligations, and they are many. Life is complicated. Writing, for all its problems and challenges, is at heart rather simple. It's just a question of getting chair-shaped in pursuit of whatever it is that the subconscious throws up – and it does throw things up, eventually, if one sits and thinks and sits and taps for long enough. At least, that is how one finds the material. Then there's the application of the craft. Shaping the sentences, building the paragraphs, beating out the dialogue, structuring the story, tuning the narrative voice. This is the part that has to do with being a writer rather than any other kind of artist. It is engaging with language as a potter engages with clay or a dancer engages with dance. As an editor, a teacher and a translator, I come at this craft from different angles, in my own practice and in more public engagements. These commitments are – unlike the life stuff – not in conflict with the writing, but rather feed into it. One learns from one's students. One learns from the authors one is editing or translating. One even, oddly, learns from oneself. One hears oneself explaining a concept or a skill to a student, and suddenly a solution to an entirely other problem proposes itself.

Most of my writing is for children. This is not a choice, much less a career move. It just comes out that way. I don't draw on particular childhood experiences – nothing, I suspect, is less interesting to today's children than adults' memories of childhood. What I do remember is much more general but also, I think, more useful: I remember what it feels like to be a child. And for all the changes there have been in the experience of childhood over the fifty-odd years since I was a child, the essential emotional weather of childhood is, I believe, constant from generation to generation.

As to the purpose of all this, even as a children's writer, I don't think of myself as primarily a storyteller. Fiction involves story, of course, but I find the idea that the true and only end of fiction writing is storytelling futile and depressing. The story is a way of structuring the work and a supremely useful way of engaging the reader, but that's a technical consideration. Not that I think little of the technicalities. Puzzling out the plot and drawing the reader into the web of the story is immensely absorbing work, and the better that work is done, the better the fiction is likely to be. But whatever it is that I am about when I sit chair-shaped and eke out my words, it's not storytelling.

Sentimental as it may sound, I would have to say that the true purpose of all this is – enchantment.

Glenn Patterson

FROM THE HEART

I have quit writing 783 times, most recently at nine
minutes past eleven yesterday morning. I have so far
managed to start writing again an equal number of times,
most recently at one minute into yesterday afternoon.
Every one of those 783 times has felt like the last.

In the intervening fifty-two minutes yesterday I played
guitar and had a shower. Played, to be precise, 'Laugh At
Me' by Sonny Bono: *after my fashion*, I should say. And for
the removal of any doubt I should also say that the 'and'
before 'had a shower' should be read as 'and subsequently'
rather than 'and simultaneously', just to dispel that image
from your head, though in truth I am sorry for any
shower-related images I might have put there. Truly.

I have four guitars in my study – in order of acquisition:
an Ashton acoustic, a Telecaster with a Stratocaster neck,
an Epiphone sunburst semi acoustic and a black Les Paul
copy, which a friend built (and painted) purely to see if he
could in fact build (and paint) a guitar and – satisfied that
he could – at once gave away. The Telecaster with the

Stratocaster neck (although I suppose there is a fifty-fifty chance it's a Stratocaster with a Telecaster body) is also a self-build – somebody else's self, that is – bought on eBay when I was still too embarrassed to go into an actual guitar shop, because I was a very late starter and a very slow learner. The Ashton – the first bought – came, eight or nine years ago now, from my wife who had grown tired of hearing me say that one of these days I was going to get myself a guitar – I really, really was – just as soon as I had done a bit of investigation into which guitar I ought to buy. I am the sort of person who will not even buy a *Which?* guide until he has read up on which *Which?* is best, though I am also the sort of person who falls in love with things at first sight, which (I interrupt this sentence to apologise for all the whiches; it's the kind of thing that normally makes me want to quit), which, as I say (and apologise again for doing so) is where I went wrong with the first guitar I ever had, back when I was eleven.

My Gran had sent me $20 from Canada for my birthday. I gave a dollar to each of my three older brothers – that was the family convention – which left me with seventeen, or something in the region of £8.50. Somewhere there is a graph with a long list of years up one side and the price of an acoustic guitar across the other on which you could precisely pinpoint the year I turned eleven. But your lives being as short as mine and your interest (on which I already presume much) possibly a good deal shorter, I will save you the bother: it was 1972.

I don't remember the shop – it was probably in Lisburn, where my dad was from, rather than Belfast, which by 1972 more resembled a collection of bomb sites loosely held together by buildings – but I do remember the guitar: pale, pale blond wood body and matching neck. To 1972-me it was perfect: that might have been the same birthday I bought a cream-coloured tank top. I was already working on my singer songwriter stage costume.

In the way of love at first sight, I didn't see the sticker on the inside of the guitar that said 'Made in Hong Kong'. I didn't look too closely either at the red plastic tuning pegs. And it played all right, or sounded as though it would have played all right if I had had the first idea how to do more than strum the open strings, or had known anyone who could show me.

A year later I started secondary school. The school had its own music department – was well known for it – and offered after-school lessons in a whole range of instruments, including guitar. A couple of people in my class signed up for them, my parents couldn't understand why I didn't. Because I couldn't reach in through the strings to pick off the 'Made in Hong Kong' sticker, which was now the only thing I could see when I looked at the guitar, that and the red plastic tuning pegs, which I couldn't change either.

So I told them I had lost interest.

I stopped talking about being a singer songwriter.

I started talking about being a poet.

Then about being a playwright.

Then I stopped talking and actually wrote something, a short story.

I wrote a couple more.

Eventually I wrote a novel.

Shortly after that I started quitting writing and starting again.

And then it was 2008 or 2009 and I was in my late forties and talking about wanting to play guitar again – about needing to have something else to do than sit in my study and (guitar pun alert!) fret when I wasn't writing, and then the Ashton arrived.

And the others followed.

And now here I am one day on from the 783rd quitting trying to hold at bay thoughts of the 784th.

Here is the thing about quitting writing: it's absolutely real.

Occasionally, it's true, I have thought it might be a symptom of age or of a stage in a writing life that has never brought much in the way of commercial success and that shows little prospect of changing. Recently, though, I found a copy of a letter I had written to my agent in 1995 – on one of my first computers, it must have been – in which, a month after the publication of my third novel, seven years after my first, and still in my early thirties, I said I didn't think I wanted to go on writing. I'd lost heart.

Heart.

That – not confidence – is the word. Confidence is in the mind, heart is physical. You can actually feel it go out of you. A void opens up between your throat and your stomach. You – I – slump.

None of this that you are struggling to write, your body seems to be saying, is in any real sense necessary. Let it go.

In the past I have gone around my study gathering up everything associated with whatever it is I have been working on and packed it away in boxes.

Yesterday I simply turned my chair around and picked up the guitar and played 'Laugh At Me', not out of self-pity, but because 'Laugh At Me' is the closing song in a stage adaptation I have written with Colin Carberry of our film *Good Vibrations*, which has been in rehearsals these past several weeks in Belfast's Lyric Theatre. I have been watching actor/musicians at close quarters, with just enough knowledge that I can work out most of the time the chords they are playing: C, F, A-sharp and G, in the case of 'Laugh At Me'.

With writing there is always the feeling of falling short: surely, surely after thirty-odd years I ought to be able to do it better than this? With the guitar I already know I'm never going to improve, not really. I was too late starting, getting over my embarrassment. Everything that I manage to stumble through therefore feels like a small victory.

There is a wonderful passage in Patrick Hamilton's 1941 novel *Hangover Square* (subtitled *A Story of Darkest Earl's Court*) in which the central character, Bone, whose life is beginning to unravel, plays a game of golf for the first time in years. It comes back to him as he goes round the course, alone, that this is something he can do, that he enjoys:

> His face shone, his eyes gleamed, and he felt, deep in his being, that he was not a bad man as he had thought he was a few hours ago, but a good one. And because he was a good man, he was a happy man, and if he could only break seventy he would never be unhappy again.[1]

And he does break seventy, he shoots sixty-eight – on borrowed clubs (I have not the first idea about or interest in golf, but Patrick Hamilton, as all good writers should, gives the reader all that is needed to feel it as his character does) – and his happiness doesn't survive beyond the next four pages.

But, oh, while it does! The relief.

I wasn't playing guitar in the shower yesterday, but I was singing – starting at 'Laugh At Me' and working back through the *Good Vibrations* songbook – more distance put between my 11:09 slump and me, though I would still characterise it as a practical, rather than tactical, shower.

A couple of years back I was working on the libretto for an opera called *Long Story Short*. The composer told me that the first draft was fine, or at least the narrative – the recitative – was. 'You still need a big aria, though,' he told me, late on the night we had met to discuss it: 'by tomorrow, if possible.'

After three hours – three hungover hours (the more he talked about the need for an aria the more I drank) – I had written two words, 'you' and 'may'. I went and stood under the shower for half an hour – a tactical retreat – and when I came out, wherever my mind had gone while I was standing there, face turned to the water, I still had two words, only now I could see how 'you may', repeated and riffed on, would form the core of the aria. It's called 'Seven Seconds' and totals one hundred and twenty words. But it's still 'You May' to me; still the shower aria.

When I walked back into my study at just after noon yesterday the first thing I noticed were the guitars, lined up not in the order that they had been bought, but in the order that they had last been played. Usually this would mean the acoustic – the Ashton – furthest from my desk, in the corner by the bookshelves. The truth is, acoustics are always harder to play for novices like me than electric guitars – more pressure required to hold down the strings, more force to strike a clear chord. And for all that I loved the gift of that first guitar, I have always much preferred the feel of a couple of the others.

Towards the tail end of last year, though, I was writing an address for a conference at the Ulster Museum in Belfast, in the course of which I referenced both the American folk singer Woody Guthrie – who painted the legend 'This Machine Kills Fascists' on his acoustic guitar – and a song from *The Wizard of Oz* that goes by the name of 'Optimistic Voices'. I asked one of my daughters to paint a line from that song on my guitar so that I could bring it with me to the conference. She did it – freehand – beautifully.

And I found myself again picking it up, trying to wrench Woody's 'This Land is my Land' out of it to begin with, but carrying on from there. So that was the one closest to my chair when I had turned around to play 'Laugh At Me'. The closest one when I sat back down and decided for the 783rd to give writing a go again.

'Hold on to your breath, hold on to your heart,' the line painted on my guitar runs, 'hold on to your hope.'

It's been a day, I long ago stopped holding my breath, and I'm not about to run yet to hope, but I am holding on to heart, sitting at my desk, writing this.

NOTE

1 *Hangover Square, A Story of Darkest Earl's Court* (Penguin, 1956), p. 145.

Nicola Pierce

CHASING GHOSTS

In 1845 Lord John Franklin led an expedition of two ships to the Arctic in search of the final chain of the Northwest Passage. Franklin captained *HMS Erebus*, while his more experienced second-in-command, Frances Crozier, took control of *HMS Terror*. This was the largest and most sophisticated expedition that was ever put to sea – with twenty-four officers, one-hundred-and-ten men and three years of food including plenty of vitamin C. There was no way they could fail. They set sail from Greenhithe, England, on 19 May, believing they would be home before their food ran out. When they failed to return, or send any news whatsoever, the Royal Navy sent out a search expedition. This was the first of over thirty searches made between the years 1847 and 1859.

What happened to the expedition remains a mystery. All that is known for certain is that John Franklin was already dead before that first search was launched and that his was not the first death. By June 1847, the men were dying for no apparent reason. Legend surrounds the fate of Captain Frances Crozier, thanks to some Inuit who reported that he was the last man to survive.

There are stories that you are meant to write, the igniting spark something you read, overhear or see on screen. Yet in order for that spark to flame into life, you must recognise it. The same goes for your characters. And I was hooked on the story of Franklin and Crozier.

On learning that the Maritime Museum in Greenwich was running an exhibition of Franklin artefacts, I booked my flight, and it was there that I found my theme, thanks to a line from *Christian Melodies*, the book that had belonged to one of Franklin's officers. It sat behind a glass case and was opened to the first page where I read: 'Home – there's magic in that little word'. I happen to believe that most stories are about finding a new home or returning to an old one. Being lost from home, this would be the theme for my novel. Franklin's men were lost from a second 'home' after they were obliged to abandon the ships and attempt to walk to safety. What should have happened did not – the summer ice did not melt away as it usually did, a phenomenon that had not even been entertained. Similarly, the *Titanic* might have made it to New York if only Captain Smith had allowed for the consideration that it might not.

I was in my hotel room in Greenwich when I felt a lump in my right armpit. It was big, maybe the size of a Cadbury's Creme Egg. I resolved to see a doctor when I got home. I had no idea that what I was returning to would be changed forevermore. The lump set up an impasse between me and the life I had led up to that very moment of finding it; it was my own iceberg. As with Franklin's expedition and *Titanic*'s maiden voyage, what should not have happened did – I was diagnosed with early stage III breast cancer.

The deadline for my fifth children's novel was less than three months away. On the wall of my workroom hung A3 portraits of some of the main players: Captains John

Franklin and Frances Crozier and the two ships, *HMS Terror* and *Erebus*. I always do this. It is a daily reminder that my characters were once flesh and blood and that I have a responsibility to them. They become my confidants. Whenever something annoys me, I will turn to them to roll my eyes heavenwards.

I remember sitting at my desk, feeling utterly lost.

I had just finished Antonia Fraser's memoir, which dealt with her husband Harold Pinter's death from cancer. The day after my diagnosis, I was restless and unable to read, which upset me. I stumbled through that first weekend, feeling as if I was wrapped up in a thick duvet and the world around me was on mute. I picked up one book after another, but I could not be transported by another writer because I was held hostage by my own drama. Like a character pinned to the page, I could not step away from the knowledge of having cancer.

Perhaps the most frustrating element about the Franklin expedition is that, aside from one short note mentioning Franklin's demise, all their writings were lost: their diaries, letters and, consequently, their voices. Descriptions of their dwindling numbers and final days survive thanks to a handful of Inuit witnesses. I was newly aware of the power of words. Well, here were my footsteps in the snow, my marks upon the ice-white screen. In a Facebook post, I included a description of my efforts to locate the X-Ray department during a hospital visit:

> As I walked through a crowded corridor, I clearly heard a line of conversation from two male nurses: 'It was on the Titanic ... there was a little boy ...'
> I stopped still and stared after them. That one line got me down the stairs until I finally found the waiting room.

My first novel for children, *Spirit of the Titanic*, was narrated by the ghost of a fifteen-year-old catch-boy (junior riveter), Samuel Joseph Scott, who had fallen to his death two years before the ship went to sea. That possible overheard reference to my book was my sign that I could do this, I was still a writer and not alone in this place. This is the wonderful thing about characters: they are always with you.

Quite unexpectedly, I was haunted by the need to communicate my situation on Facebook. Really, Facebook? I had never used it for personal material before. Was this an ego trip? Would people think I was showing off, about having cancer of all things? I did not want to talk to anyone; no, what I wanted was readers, if only just to know that they were really there, which would in turn mean that I, the writer, was still here.

Apart from anything else, I was hugely gratified for this rare urge to write. I had never felt a passion for the actual act of writing. First drafts were a constant battle against myself. Meanwhile, some other writers talked the talk, that they must write in order to breathe and so on. To my surprise, however, a love for writing is what emerged over the next few months as I provided frequent updates to my story, on Facebook and Twitter, choosing an angle, a tone that incorporated humour and sincerity for my new character: a middle-aged cancer patient. Writing helped me feel relevant, while social media kept me in the reader's sightline.

I tried in vain to meet my novel's deadline. By the time I started chemotherapy I had managed 50,000 words by clinging to routine (2,000 words a day) while my usual life began to disintegrate. It took some time to accept that I had to release most of what I held dear. Franklin's ships spewed out their crew to fend for themselves. In the absence of flowing waters and men, *HMS Erebus* and *Terror* were now useless. If I wasn't writing, was I still a writer?

Certainly, my identity as a children's writer was being corroded with every email I sent, cancelling events. The life of a children's writer involves being available to do events throughout the school year and, as a writer of historical fiction, I felt a particular dependence on them. I worried how my books would live without my constant showboating. My last two novels were about 300-year-old battles. What youngster would bother to open them if I didn't put in a personal appearance to lead them to the first page?

Naturally, I had believed that I could continue working throughout the five months of treatment, but only because I had no idea what lay ahead of me. Captain Frances Crozier was on foot in the Arctic with the remains of his crew, having abandoned the ships to the ice. Well, I had to leave them there as I too got lost in a fog of my own. I lacked the stamina to keep us all buoyant. He and his men were heading towards disaster, but I had to maintain their blissful innocence just as I had tried, initially, to maintain mine, that I might not have cancer or maybe just 'a touch' of it. A taxi driver had told me about his wife only needing an operation and she was cured. I stole hope from where I could get it, as Captain Crozier must surely have done. I imagined him at the helm of his ship, gazing at the stars in the sky and believing, like me, that anything was possible. The important thing was to keep moving forward.

My days tumbled over each other with more hospital appointments, more clarification, more cancer than they expected. No, I could do nothing for Crozier. My diagnosis held him fast as surely as the ice did. Guilt propelled me to opening up the manuscript every so often, but I could do nothing with it. To attempt to edit or add anything at all was like trying to lift a bag of sugar with a tea spoon.

It is now October, and I would like to finish the first draft before embarking on six weeks of radiation, which gives me approximately five weeks. I have forgotten much of my research and am nervous about finding my way back to Crozier. I feel as lost from him as he must have felt in that white hell of an Arctic winter. Yet, I think about him every day, which gives me hope as this is how every one of my books came into being before a single word was written.

I must retrace my steps, trusting that my cancer journey will add to my telling of his, that not a single day was wasted. I suppose what we share is the need to believe that one step and one word after another will eventually make all the difference, enabling us both to reach home, wherever that is.

Kevin Power

MY FIRST NOVELS

The first novel I ever wrote was called *SubZero*. The capital
Z in the middle of the title is, I'm afraid, *sic*. It was a
thriller about a man who stole an experimental submarine
– the *SubZero*, of course – from the US government and
went to hide out in the Arctic Circle. I was thirteen. I wrote
it on lined refill pad paper – the sort I used in school. I
plotted the whole thing out very carefully: each chapter
was summarised on a blue index card ('BATTLE WITH
AIRCRAFT CARRIER' and so on). I stuck these cards –
there were nine or ten of them – up over my desk and got
to work. I wrote the most exciting chapters first. Then I
went back and filled in the gaps. The finished manuscript
was seventy pages long. It still exists, somewhere – buried,
mercifully, in the middens of paper that fill my office. I
must remember to burn it before I die. Probably the best
thing about it is that I named a fictional American
submarine the *U.S.S. Eamon de Valera*. Oh, and I thought
that high-ranking naval officials were correctly addressed
as 'General.'

My second attempt at a novel was called *Lake of Fire*. (I named it after the Meat Puppets song that Nirvana covered on their *MTV Unplugged* album). It was partly inspired by the shooting at Columbine High School in Denver (which happened during my final months in secondary school: April, 1999), and partly by the movie *Natural Born Killers* (1994). The setting was an imaginary fast-food restaurant in an imaginary American suburb. Here, two men – one black and one white – enter with assault rifles and start firing. Unable to commit suicide, they barricade themselves inside the restaurant. Police and media arrive. A siege develops. The gunmen, preaching their anti-establishment cause, become culture heroes. Obviously, my writing had grown slightly more sophisticated in the years since *SubZero*. But this is not to say that *Lake of Fire* is a good book. For one thing, I ran out of energy. After 50,000 words, the story petered out. For another, I lacked experience, both technical and actual – I had never visited the United States, and I modelled my highly adverbial prose style on that of the crime and science fiction novels that I then mostly read.

But the quality, or otherwise, of these 'novels' is not the point. When I think about them now, what I remember is how enormously, luminously *happy* I was writing them. I was particularly happy during the writing of *Lake of Fire*. I wrote it over the course of my summer break from college. I worked every night from midnight to 2am, writing on thin, smooth, unlined paper using a Parker fountain pen. In eight weeks I filled two hundred pages. I scarcely remember what else I did that summer. I absconded from the real, empirical world. For those eight weeks the fictional reality of *Lake of Fire* was incomparably more vivid and compelling than the base materials of the undreamt world could ever be – my room, my family, my house, my street, my village. The same was true of the writing of *SubZero*. What I was writing was, in the strictest sense, rubbish. But to me it seemed supercharged with meaning. I had found the thing that I most wanted to do. Writing was joy.

I dislike being asked *Why do you write?* because it seems to me that there are too many possible answers to this question, none of them entirely satisfactory. Why do I write? Vanity. Neurosis. A love of language. A love of storytelling. A habit of daydreaming. My usual answer has to do with the inner life. A writer is someone whose inner life exerts a mysterious and irresistible *pressure*. It must be decanted, this inner life – into sentences, paragraphs, pieces, chapters, books. Certainly I feel this pressure. The world inside my head is highly importunate. It won't leave me alone. It must be *uttered*. In this sense, everything I write is an *utterance*. A book is the most satisfying kind of utterance; an 800-word book review, the least satisfying. But any utterance will do. The joy is in the uttering. This is what I discovered, writing my first, awful novels. The more you learn about writing, of course, the more difficult it gets. Acquired skill impedes the flow of utterance – the more you know about writing, the less happy you are with what you write, even as you write it. It becomes harder and harder, in the doing, to discern that original glimmer of joy. But it is the memory of that glimmer of joy that lures you back to the desk – to the refill pad, the fountain pen, the laptop.

To become a professional writer is, in this sense, to enact a fall. Your juvenilia are composed in a state of innocence. In that prelapsarian time you can write seventy pages about a stolen submarine and consider it a triumph. Publication (which means, in practical terms, taking money for what you write – introducing the economic aspect) means expulsion from paradise. When I write nowadays – sure as I am that what I write will be full of faults and errors – I sometimes catch myself pining for the simple pleasures of my very earliest stints at the desk, when the dreamed world poured unhindered onto the page, or seemed to. In those days, of course, my inner life was a relatively simple thing. Now it is tangled – it is an adult's inner life, having passed through various straits of experience: love, work, sex, money, grief, depression, anxiety. Decanting it onto the page is a correspondingly tangled process. Nowadays, too, I must write in order to live: my mortgage, and my soon-to-be-born daughter, depend on me continuing to produce publishable work. I have turned a childhood pleasure, undertaken in innocence, into a career. This is a blessing, but a mixed one. To write purely for the joy of it is the prerogative of the amateur. In other words, it is a luxury. And no grown-up can afford a luxury like that.

Nevertheless, when I sit down to write, as I do every day at a desk in my office at home, there are really two of me. There is the professional writer, who has developed in himself certain habits and skills – knowing, for instance, when an unfinished piece must be left alone for a few hours or days; sensing when the time has come to bring a paragraph to an end – and who works in full consciousness of his obligations (to his craft, to his readers, to his bank account). And there is the innocent amateur in search of joy – the joy that reorders the world as he transcribes the fictional dream. He sits with me, or beside me, or inside me, urging me on. He is me, and I am him – we make up one writer, the two of us, or perhaps we make up a writer and his own mysteriously inspired and story-besotted ghost. We write our sentences together, and always, between us, there is the unspoken hope that as we write the next word, as we try to give form to the dream, we will be – as we were before, back there in Eden – surprised by joy.

Heather Richardson

BEEKEEPING

Years ago I was on holiday in Portugal and went on a jeep tour to explore the forests and little farms that lie inland from the sparkling resorts of the coast. In the heat of late afternoon we arrived at a dilapidated smallholding where the farmer kept bees and sold honey. He directed us into a windowless outbuilding where honey was extracted from the honeycombs and decanted into glass jars. When he'd finished his demonstration I turned to leave, and froze. The room was so dark that I hadn't realised the air was alive with bees. I'd noticed the buzzing, of course, as I'd watched the farmer at work, but that was only to be expected in such a spot. Now, though, standing in the darkness and looking out through the open doorway into the glare of Portugal in high summer, I realised that I would have to walk through what seemed – to my inexpert eye – to be a swarm of bees. Don't panic, said the farmer. Walk slowly. Don't flail at them, or try to swat them. They won't sting you unless you scare them. Just walk.

So I walked, s-l-o-w-l-y, fighting the instincts that were telling me to scream and thrash around like a woman-in-jeopardy in a low-budget horror movie. Once or twice a bee bumped into my bare arms, but no stings were stung.

When I think about my process as a writer, I think of that walk. For me, ideas are like those bees – multitudinous, ceaselessly in motion, distracting – and I spend most of my life wandering through their buzzing. Like the old Portuguese farmer, I'm all but oblivious to them, and try to get on with my work regardless.

This is the problem with ideas. There are just too many of them. Every writer who has ever lived has had an imagination seething with ideas that never went anywhere, and even a writer with the sternest work ethic and the longevity of Methuselah will not be able to turn a fraction of their ideas into pieces of literature.

To take the bee/idea analogy further – and at this point I must advise apiarists to stop reading, as my misunderstanding of bees and beekeeping will probably infuriate you – not every bee can found a colony, and not every idea can develop into something worth reading. The farmyard of my creative inner space is littered with wreckage. Half-built hives that I've abandoned in frustration or apathy. Crumpled piles of chipboard and beeswax that could have been marvellous if only my design had not been incompatible with, you know, staying upright. And buzzing aimlessly through the carnage, disconsolate solitary bees wondering where it all went wrong.

Sometimes – very occasionally – it works. And perhaps rather than poke through the detritus scattered around the farmyard of failure I should examine the successes. I don't, of course, mean 'success' in the sense of best-selling publications, because that's a pretty flawed way to judge if a piece of writing works. By 'success' I mean the novels, short stories and poems that got finished and feel aesthetically complete. Some of these have been published, and some haven't.

Here's the thing about my relationship with writing. I never really want to do it. I'm not one of those writers who take every opportunity to get words onto paper or computer screen. Stephen King says a day without writing is like a day without sunshine. For me a day without writing sounds just dandy. So why do I do it then? Well, I've noticed that when I don't write I'm troubled with just about every downbeat feeling going: discontent, gloom, restlessness and all the other symptoms a psychoanalyst might identify as resistance. When I force myself to write I feel the better for it. I suspect the root of my resistance is that I have conflicting notions of what literature is really for – or more specifically, what the literature I create is for. At heart I'm a utilitarian: literature should entertain the reader, offer them escape, excitement, novelty, consolation. But also, at heart, I'm an adventurer: literature should challenge the reader, unsettle them, bend their minds. A divided heart, at cross-purposes with itself – no wonder I struggle to write at all.

But back to the honeybees. Every successful colony needs a queen bee. Queen bees are made, not born. They start life as a regular baby bee, but with a very particular diet they grow up to be a queen. They lie around having loads of bee sex and producing thousands of offspring while the drones and workers do the hard work of making honey and building honeycombs. Sometimes their colony will be in the human-made confines of a hive, and less often they'll build their own wild and wonderful nest in some nook or cranny of an old tree. So if the ideas that actually come to something are queen bees – fed and supported by an army of lesser ideas – the shape they take will depends on whether the colony is feral or domesticated.

The trick, I think, is to let the ideas take however long they need. For me that's often a very long time indeed. I let them buzz around me for years. Sometimes they'll bump into me, or land on my hair, but I let them do their thing until I notice that one of them has – by some mysterious process of selection and nurture – become a queen. She needs a place to nest, and that's the moment when I finally pay her some attention. What support does she need to establish her colony? The containment of a hive, or the organic folds and hollows of a tree? This is the key question, and most often the answer is the hive.

I find words, phrases, voices and images come easily and plentifully, but structure is hard, and it is structure – the home I choose for the idea – that will make or break it. I've spent too much of my writing life trying to come up with my own take on structure, only to end up creating something unwieldy or unstable. Often, when I thought I'd devised an original way of storytelling, I've found that someone else has done it before, and better. Lately I've come to appreciate the elegance of archetypal story structures – three acts, five acts, the arc of the genre novel – and found that, in fact, they are the most pleasing way to let those queen bee ideas develop and prosper.

And yet, and yet ... My adventurous heart is still beating, and now and again an eccentric idea flies off into the woods and I follow it, wondering where it will settle, and how it will grow, and what it will look like when it's done.

I've come to terms, I think, with the fact that I am several different writers. My creative inner space might be untidy, but there's room for all of us in there. It doesn't trouble me that most of the ideas buzzing around me will never come to anything. It's enough that some of them already have and, hopefully, more of them will in future. When I'm stuck – wrestling with my reluctance to write, perhaps – I take myself back to that hot afternoon all those years ago. Standing in a dim Portuguese room looking out through a doorway dancing with bees. And the air is sweet with honey.

Debbie Thomas

IN HER WRITE MIND

It's 9am. As faintly successful author Davinia Thomp sits down at her desk, the camera zooms through her skull and inside her head to reveal the stage of a chat show. At the front, two armchairs are jauntily angled. The host walks on, a stag beetle with huge mandibles protruding from either side of her mouth. As big as a black bear, she totters upright on her two hind legs to audience applause.

CRITTICA: Good morning ladies and gentlemen, boys and
    girls, parents and teachers, agents and publishers, book
    critics, enemies, writers who provoke envy or disdain
    and, oh yes, readers if we ever get that far. This morning
    I'm delighted to welcome to *The Write Time* (*she pauses
    for a tinny jingle*) a very special guest. Famous for her
    sensitive skin and nervous tic, she rarely gives
    interviews. So a round of applause, please – not loud
    enough to scare her off and not so quiet that she feels
    unwanted – to Anima. (*There's muted applause as a silver-
    grey cloud wafts onstage and settles in a trembling mist on*

the armchair opposite CRITTICA. *Sitting in her chair,* CRITTICA *arranges her shiny black wings around her like coat-tails*): Welcome, ah … should I call you Ms Anima, or Miss or Mrs? Or how about (*she grins at the audience then back at the cloud*) Anemia? You look a bit peaky. (*The cloud shrinks and dulls a little*).

ANIMA (*whispering*): Anima is fine.

CRITTICA (*rubbing her front legs together*): Ok Annie, let's start with your social life. You don't mix much. Why did you agree to this interview?

ANIMA (*pulsing as she whispers*): I'm usually busy in my garden watering the plants. But now and then I come out to gather more seeds on my breezes.

CRITTICA: Seeds?

ANIMA: For new varieties. I collect all sorts: snippets of conversation, strange road signs, physical oddities like, say, those ridic- … remarkable antler things either side of your mouth. (*There's a ripple of laughter from the audience.* ANIMA's *voice gets louder, more confident*). They could blossom into something quite marvellous. Let's see … (*The cloud reshapes in a way that suggests she's turning to the audience*). Don't you think Crittica would make a great villain in a children's story, with her shiny black body and twig legs? How about an alien posing as a brooch that clings to shirts and sucks out hearts with those crazy mouth-branches? (*More audience laughter.* ANIMA *grows bigger and dazzling and rises above the chair*).

CRITTICA (*snapping*): They're called mandibles. (*She leans forward and wiggles them menacingly at* ANIMA). And their job is to grasp and crush. (*The audience sniggers.* ANIMA *shrinks, dulls and drops back to her seat. Confident she's regained the upper hand,* CRITTICA *buzzes her wings and relaxes back in her chair, crossing one hind leg over the other*). So Annie, tell us about this garden of yours. The space where you tend what you call your plants, and what I call (*she holds up a foreleg and stage-whispers behind it to the audience*) the feeble seedlings that will probably die long before they can bloom and spread into the vast forest of literature that already chokes the publishing world like the brambles that choked the castle of *Sleeping Beauty*. Dammit! *(She claps a front claw to her mouth)*. That's just the sort of overblown simile-within-a-metaphor that I'm here to prune.

ANIMA *(glittering and trembling)*: Prune? I trim nothing in my garden. Who knows what might blossom? Besides, there's beauty in every plant, from ornate roses to pithy grasses and the simplest moss: even in the weeds that weave around stems or wander and wonder down winding pathwa–

CRITTICA *(raising all but her hind legs, like four policemen holding up traffic)*: Stop! That kind of rambling is exactly why you need me: to cut you down to size, stop you puffing up with hot air and nip your nonsense in the bud.

ANIMA *(turning green)*: Clichés. Oh no. I feel sick.

CRITTICA: No pain no gain, dear. *(The audience titters as ANIMA turns greener)*. The point is, without me any plants worth picking would be lost in your jungle. I'm here to clip and arrange them so their colours will dazzle and their barbs sting.

ANIMA *(returning to silver as she warms to the theme)*: And their leaves tickle. *(She reshapes to address the audience again)*. You love a good giggle, don't you?

CRITTICA *(rustling her wings in irritation)*: Oh, now you're being childish. Grow up.

ANIMA: Why? It's the child's depth of feeling I long to stir: the thrill of snow on the tongue; the vanilla-fumed hope the ice-cream van brings; the night terror when pins and needles are really tiny witches landing on your skin. Those are my sources and driving forces.

CRITTICA: Rhyming too – for goodness sake! (*She stands up from her chair and snaps*). Pull yourself together.

ANIMA (*shrinking and whimpering*): How? I'm a cloud. It's my job to waft. But your carping and mockery just drag me down. (*She drops to the floor and dulls to grey*).

CRITTICA (*looming over the cloud and clacking her mandibles together with a 'critticky, critticky' sound*): Always the victim. I told you I'm here to help. If you really believe your plants are worth growing, stop whingeing and get on with it. Get a backbone. Get a grip. Because if you don't ... (*she lunges forward*) ... I will. (*Her mandibles reach down for* ANIMA *who's hovering just above the floor. The audience gasps. But the pincers merely clutch each other as the cloud slips through and drifts to the back of the stage where it cowers, a tiny, ash-grey ball. Turning to the audience with a wail*): No, I've lost her! (*She covers her face with her forelegs*). Why did I get so carried away, too big for my carapace? (*She drops down on all six legs, like a proper beetle, and pulls her legs and head under her carapace. From inside comes her muffled voice*). Without her I'm out of a job. (*Her wings flap feebly. She snivels at the front while* ANIMA *whimpers in the back corner. At last* CRITTICA's *head and legs poke out. She turns to the cloud. In a cracked voice*): Please, Ms – Mrs – beautiful Anima. The stage is yours. (*Silence*).

ANIMA (*whispering from the corner*): Promise?

CRITTICA *shrinks to the size of a sheepdog. Slowly* ANIMA *floats forward. She hovers at the front of the stage. There's the sound of short, gasping breaths, getting longer and deeper.*

ANIMA: Breathe ... and breathe, and ... ahhh. (*She expands and regains her silvery glitter*). At last, my space. Listen. (*She pauses*). Hear the silence. (*Another pause*). See the garden. (*She pauses again*). Smell the soil, touch the branches inviting me in. (*Her voice is rising*). The bushes, the brambles, the leaves and colours – browns and greens, oranges, yellows, pink and blue and lilac (*she's growing and turning every colour she speaks*) turquoise, cadmium, café au lait and ultramarine, fuchsia (*now huge, she's rising, sounding shriller and scared*) vermilion, amaranth, falu, sunburst, blinding scarlet, exploding cherry and ... (*shrieking*) bloating and floating and climbing and rhyming and – Crittica, help me, I'm burning up!

CRITTICA *has shrunk to the size of a cat. Her solid blackness is strangely calming against* ANIMA's *outrageous colours. In a meek voice*: Help? Are ... are you sure? (ANIMA's *shrieks become fainter as she floats to the ceiling. With a whirr of wings,* CRITTICA *takes off. She flies up and hovers near* ANIMA, *fanning her wings to cool the fiery ball. At last* ANIMA *starts to shrink and descend, returning to rest as a silvery cloud a metre off the ground.* CRITTICA *flies down and resumes the horizontal beetle posture. She's now the size of a hamster*).

ANIMA (*panting*): Thank you. And please – stay. I need you there to bring me back down to earth. But gently. And only when I ask. (*The camera zooms back out of the head. At her desk, Davinia Thomp runs a hand through her silvery hair, furrows the beetling cliché of her brows and begins to write*).

William Wall

AVOIDING THE DAILY DRAMA OF THE BODY: WRITING AND ILLNESS

Still's Disease is a kind of Winter. It settles on the bones and
the joints with a wintry determination: pain and misery are
the signatures. The pain makes you feel cold all the time. You
sit by a fire or a radiator, no matter what the season,
husbanding warmth. Warmth eases the joints the way a warm
January day softens the budding branches. But there is no sap
rising: knuckles and knees swell but it is a false Spring; the
buds are galls, like the white hollow oak-fruit that the gall-
wasp makes. You call for the doctor and the doctor comes
with his bag in his hand and he looks at you with a kind of
pity because he knows the truth. This is your disease and he
can't take it away from you – *(Unpublished essay by the author)*

I fell ill at twelve years of age with what became a lifelong
illness and at the same time I began to write. Ever since
then I have tried to untangle those two strands of my life
without success. Would I have become a writer if I had not
become ill? Did the illness somehow cause my writing? Is
writing a therapeutic process for me? I realise that I have
experimented with ways of expressing this intensely-

personal experience in a public context, by metaphor and analogy, for most of my writing life, bearing in mind what Susan Sontag said, that illness accrues metaphor to the point of cliché ('Illness as Metaphor').

So how does the experience of physical pain express itself in writing?

In my fiction I have avoided direct approaches (more about indirect approaches later) to what Sontag called 'the kingdom of the ill', and the same is largely true of my poetry. One exception is my poem 'Q' which appeared first in *The SHOp* and later in my collection *Fahrenheit Says Nothing To Me* (Dedalus, 2004). I wrote 'Q' sporadically over many years, often in hospital under the influence of heavy medication or fever. It is three-hundred lines long so too long to quote in full, but for a flavour of the style, here is the opening section:

> Q conspires with God
> who appears in a green
> gown and wears latex.
> He leaves no forensics.
>
> Scalpel, he says.
> Q says: Say please.
> Clamp, he says.
> Say please. Chainsaw.
>
> God is mechanics
> and the triumph of engineering
> and Q thinks
> he is filling up with dead bits.
>
> In the aftermath
> he is ecstatic,
> drifting between death and sleep
> awash with pain.
>
> It's a good one, God says,
> a beautiful piece.
> Give me a spare rib, he jokes,
> and I'll give you a prosthesis.

The dreamlike (or nightmare) imagery and erratic structure enabled me to distance myself using humour, especially ironic humour and self-deprecation. The narrative, if that's not too extreme a word, is formed by loosely-connected passages paralleling the time between a surgical procedure and death. Along the way, the character Q falls in love with a nurse, discusses God with his surgeon, hallucinates flying and some kind of destruction of the hospital, meets 'the good cripple' (the kind of religious person who preaches acceptance of God's will), argues with God, writes his will, and dies. It is not intended to be a coherent narrative but a portrait of a mind in torment:

> Here lieth a crook
> that was once straight as larch,
> claws once piano,
>
> legs marathon,
> ramrod spine,
> too much neck,
> relict of Q
>
> awaiting judgement

However, I have never been able to write directly in prose about my condition, fearing the kind of sentimentality that often shows in 'misery memoirs'. The epigraph to this essay represented one attempt at writing it – incomplete and unpublished.

I have come to the conclusion over the years that my illness most clearly expresses itself as a certain dark twist in my work – in stories that deal with isolated people, characters in physical or psychological pain or even dying, but also in the darkness of my five novels. Although all of the novels focus on political or social issues by accident rather than by design, it is not accidental that their mood and thematic burdens tend towards tragedy: for me, reality is essentially a kind of cruel entropy relieved only by love and solidarity. *Alice Falling* (Sceptre, 2000) attends to issues of power and abuse (Michel Foucault is never far away from my writing); *Minding Children* (Sceptre, 2001), which I always think of as a kind of Gothic realist novel, was about childcare and child murder; *The Map of Tenderness* (Sceptre, 2002) considers end-of-life issues and euthanasia; *This is the Country* (Sceptre, 2005) riffs on the Celtic Tiger and capitalism – the dominant trope is that capitalism is a drug; and *Grace's Day* (Head of Zeus, 2018) is about the disintegration of a family around a childhood tragedy, but is also, among other things, a critique of the Green movement in its Irish incarnation.

The Map of Tenderness most nearly approaches the 'daily drama of the body' (Virginia Woolf, 'On Being Ill'). The plot centres on Joe, his girlfriend Suzie, his religious sister Mary and their father and mother – the latter is dying of Huntington's chorea, an illness which has a genetic component and is passed down by the mother. Joe and Mary have a fifty/fifty chance of inheriting the invariably-fatal disorder. But, for the purposes of this essay, it is important to note that, while writing the book, I was conscious of treating the mother's illness and the family's reactions as a metaphor for my own situation. Glancing back over my contemporaneous writing notes I find this entry:

> *Saturday, June 17, 2000*
> Problems with my left knee yesterday and had to have it injected. Consequently I woke early this morning and my head was full of thoughts about this book. As is often the case with steroid-induced thinking, not much came of it other than a general enthusiasm to start writing.

And later:

> *Tuesday, July 18, 2000*
> Inheritance. Joe inherits nothing except his disease.
> Scylla and Charybdis: Charybdis is changed into a whirlpool because she stole oxen from Hercules. Scylla is changed into a many headed monster that swallows sailors: she was at first a nymph of rare beauty. Her mother was Lamia who went mad and devoured children.

None of my other novels approaches the subject of illness directly, but I would argue that a cast of mind which sees the universe as a Manichean place full of pain is a direct consequence of, if not a response to, the sudden arrival in a child's life of a crippling disease. What seems certain to me is that the experience of entering into 'the night-side of life' (Sontag again) at such a young age, of being a relatively-helpless patient whose life was modulated by medical professionals and medication and who was dependent on parents very often for things like help sitting up in bed, had the effect, I believe, of making me aware of the physicality of the body in a way that normally resides in the unconscious for all of childhood. I think it accounts for such an early and determined drive to create worlds and plots and characters over whom I had at least partial control. That first period of enforced immobility (I was out of school for a year) at twelve years of age made me turn inwards and towards books; *the imagination was my emancipation.* Spending hours, days, weeks in bed, I began writing stories, poems and songs. It was the start of a lifelong habit (or indulgence) of writing on a tea tray. Over the years I have acquired more elaborate tea trays, including one with legs and a little drawer for pens. Coupled with the writing urge was an equal and correlative love of reading.

Curiously, I remember my first reading of Sylvia Plath. I can't now remember how I found her work, but I suspect my best friend gave me a copy of *Ariel*, and he probably got it from his elder sister. Plath's work spoke to me deeply – poems such as 'Ariel' with its startling opening line ('Stasis in darkness' in which I imagined myself both the child and the suffering listener:

The child's cry

Melts in the wall.
And I
Am the arrow,

The dew that flies
Suicidal, at one with the drive
Into the red

Eye, the cauldron of morning.

– (Plath, 36)

I did not, at the time, know the source of the pain that was apparent in her poetry, but I found it spoke to something in my own life. I understood a poem like 'Fever 103^0', for example, to be about the fevers that characterise Still's Disease: 'Your body/hurts me as the world hurts God ...' (Plath, 59). The slightly hallucinatory quality of much of her work attracted me too. It seemed to sit well with the strange states of steroid-medicated fever that I had to contend with, and that in due course would see their way into 'Q', as well as into the drug trip memories in *This is the Country*.

Place is not important to me *per se*, but landscape and cityscape and how people interact with their environment are. I find it difficult to write about locations with which I am not intimately familiar. Thus, for example, it has taken me many years of visiting Italy, learning the language and spending long periods of time there to feel comfortable enough to be able to write about it. My first four novels are located in Ireland; it is not until *Grace's Day* (2018) that I risked setting a book anywhere else. The first chapter ends with the sentence: 'There were three islands and they were youth, childhood and age, and I searched for my father in every one.' Those islands are in Ireland, England and Italy – three places that I have known very well. It is my first novel to name the settings.

All the other novels are set in fictional, usually unnamed places. *Grace's Day* centres on two sisters – Grace and Jeannie and their family. It opens on Castle Island, off the coast of West Cork, a beautiful empty rock facing the majesty of the Atlantic (though I imagine it further offshore than it actually is). The house where Grace and

Jeannie and their family live is, in reality, a ruin on the eastern shore. It looks onto a little pebble beach and the sound that separates it from Horse Island. This is Grace's habitat. But the novel moves on to London and eventually a second island – the Isle of Wight – where I spent many holidays as a teenager. I grew to love the chalky coast that fell into the sea after every storm, revealing fossils for the picking. I still have a fossilised sea-urchin that I found at my feet after a swim. Jeannie, the teenager who will grow up to be a geologist, is happiest here, collecting dinosaur bones and stones. The third and final island is Procida in the Bay of Naples, the most densely-populated rural area in Europe. It's the setting for the beautiful Massimo Troisi/Michael Bradford film *Il Postino* (The Postman). I fell in love with the place many years ago and have struggled to write about it ever since. It is the setting for the denouement of the novel, the polar opposite of the first island surrounded by our cold North Atlantic. The conflict of the ending is, I hope, counterpointed by the luxurious and communal life of the Mediterranean.

Another constant across all my writing – in fiction and in poetry – is the presence of the sea, which is almost a character in its own right in the fiction. I grew up in a house on Cork Harbour, so close to the sea in my early childhood that spray from the waves of northwesterly gales would splash against the windows; a house that was exactly at sea level and therefore subject to flooding in certain sea conditions. Swimming and messing about in neighbours' boats took up much of my summer holidays. I have always felt uncomfortable in places at a remove from the sea, and when I visit a new city I always try to find a way to see it from the water – whether a river, a lake or a bay. I feel I have a better understanding and engagement with the city once I have seen it from the offing.

I have a habit of listening to music while I write – not always, but particularly when I feel the need for inspiration. In particular, I listen to Scottish and Irish folk song, including Border Ballads and *sean-nós*. I like the Border Ballads for their brutal lyricism, a quality I try to cultivate in my own writing. The *sean-nós* I admire for the beauty of their imagery and how the songs key into states of mind. Take for example the classic 'Dónal Óg'. Like most *sean-nós*, it is a set of images rather than a narrative, typically (there are many versions) telling how Dónal promised that he would take the female narrator away over the sea, but then did not appear at the meeting point. Aside from that basic situation, the rest of the song expresses the girl's desolation – in other words, instead of a narrative, the song is concerned with a psychological state. The most famous verse is usually given as the last:

> Ó bhain tú thoir agus bhain tú thiar díom,
> Bhain tú an ghealach gheal is an ghrian díom,
> Bhain tú an croí seo bhí i lár mo chléibhe díom
> Is nach rí-mhór é m'fhaitíos gur bhain tú Dia díom.

> Oh you took the east and you took the west from me,
> You took the moon from me and you took the sun,
> You took the heart from deep in my breast,
> And great is my fear that you took God from me.

I read a good deal of history and philosophy, particularly political philosophy, as well as fiction, both short and long. I believe writers should read outside their own genre, and preferably they should read outside of fiction and poetry. I tend to think of the 'ideal reader' as someone who has read everything I've read and experienced everything I've experienced (i.e. myself!), but otherwise I find it difficult to believe in an abstract concept of 'the reader'. My wife, Liz, reads everything and if I have any concept of whom I'm writing for it must be her. Nor do I have any certainty as to how my writing begins. *Grace's Day*, for example, began for me (appropriately at dawn) as that sentence about the three islands. I don't know where it came from: the complete sentence was there in my head when I woke on a

July morning in 2008, insistently demanding to be noticed, like a bird tapping at the window. I wrote it down and as I wrote I became convinced that the voice was a woman's. I don't know why. Objectively, there is nothing in the words that determines a gender. It was just a hunch, an instinct. Maybe whatever brought the sentence to my head during the hours of sleep was part of a bigger dream. It's often like that for me, and that initial gift of a phrase gives me a voice in which to tell the story – a magical, and rare, moment in my working day.

Like most writers, I am at my keyboard early every morning; when a phrase like that presents itself, I try to be ready. Like most writers, I believe that anyone wishing to make a book – certainly a book of fiction – must be present to the imagination, must work daily whether the quality of the work is good or bad, and must be ready to seize the moment as it happens. I do not, however, carry a notebook and make constant notes as some writers do. Occasionally a whole phrase or a sentence will occur to me and I will make a note of it – often nowadays on my phone. But I do not spend my days searching for things to write down. Life itself is much too interesting.

Hedwig Schwall

WRITING:
THE 'BUSINESS' OF LIVING FULLY

'The making of art takes place in a borderland between self
and other' – *Siri Hustvedt* (quoted by Nuala O'Connor)

By way of coda or encoding, I want to provide some sort of
a synthesis of what I learned from reading these beautiful
texts.

First of all, I was often pleasantly surprised to find that
images can say more, and more precisely and concisely,
than lengthy explanations. Here, we find a kaleidoscope of
the most diverse extended metaphors to suggest what
writing fiction is like. To Mary Morrissy it is a road trip in
a bucking car, actively chasing an i-deer, whereas the
protagonist of Jan Carson's contribution finds herself
chased; Heather Richardson's character is in a middle
position, like a bee keeper: 'I spend most of my life
wandering through their buzzing'. Claire Kilroy uses the
image of a child entering a haunted house, while Debbie
Thomas zooms in on a talk show going on in the writer's

head. The theatre context reappears in Gerard Donovan: 'A novel hires and fires. Players audition, seem promising, fade'; Alan McMonagle selects worthy 'centres' for his novel from a multitude which 'shout and wave and make lots of theatrical gestures'. Wendy Erskine's image of writing is not an Aeolian harp but 'the arcade game Penny Falls'. Others use the hero questing for an idea(l) (Lia Mills), embarking on *imrama* (Celia De Fréine), or referring to Oisín's experience in the Land of Youth (Barry McCrea). Paul Lynch imagines the writer as Xenophon with his frost-bitten army on his wintry *Anabasis*, Dermot Bolger's idea is more sedentary: 'writing a novel is like opening up an imaginary hotel for the phantoms of your subconscious'; Paul Murray is inspired by William Gaddis' description of a novel being like having a friend in hospital, whom you hope will improve every day. Micheál Ó Conghaile compares the native Irish speaker writing in English to 'waking up in a friend's house and being on your own there ... You keep opening cupboards and drawers before you find exactly where things are'. Danny Denton pictures himself listening to an old radio keeping an ear peeled for a certain frequency where he can worship 'the music of what happens'. In Lucy Caldwell's universe writing is a matter of wells and stars which flow and ebb. While many writers use an extended metaphor to depict the relationship between the protagonist and her imagination, three write a complete short story: Jan Carson, Roisín O'Donnell and Danielle McLaughlin.

But why ask creative writers to write about writing? There is something contradictory about our need to explain literature, as Evelyn Conlon's contribution shows. Though willing to answer my invitation, she starts off with A.E. Housman's quote 'I could no more define poetry than a terrier can define a rat'. Likewise the late pope of German letters, Marcel Reich-Ranicki, famously stated that most authors 'know no more about literature than birds do about ornithology'.[1] But, as Anne Haverty puts it: 'Writers don't answer questions, they ask them'. They see, feel, hear, smell and taste in words; more precisely, they sound out, intuit, sense and probe. They *refine*, but they do not *define*. Instead, they blur the familiar and turn from functional expectation; they break the surface of social fashions in order to dive into the murky world of affects, to get in touch with what feeds our drives. The difficulty here is that you cannot simply hunt for the unknown: the writer must go halfway and allow herself to be hunted, and, as Claire Kilroy and Paul Murray show, haunted.[2] It is this detour via the unconscious which sharpens the senses. As I read the contributions to this book I felt a bit like Keats 'On First Looking into Chapman's Homer'. Chapman manages to transport the reader into another realm: his senses are so enlivened that he suddenly 'breathe[s]' Homer's world; his universe widens as 'a new planet swims into his ken'; his perception is charged with a new emotional energy, like 'stout Cortez' who looks 'with eagle eyes', while 'all his men' share in this new impetus as they 'Look'd at each other with a wild surmise –'. In this survey of contributions, I want to trace what roaming writers do in their own inner and outer worlds to intensify their perception of the world. My starting point is: what room does a writer need to set up this new roaming of their own?

While most contributors referred to a need for a retreat from family life, as children demand the full concentration which the writer needs for her art (Nuala O'Connor, Joseph O'Neill, Caitriona Lally, Geraldine Mills, Claire Kilroy, Lucy Caldwell), most also understood this 'room' as time to themselves – something which, as Sarah Moore Fitzgerald realises, is never given, it must be taken. Claire McGowan's title 'A Floor of One's Own' is a metonymy for many: any place which allows the writer to get in touch with the deeper self is fine, whether that be in a packed train (Billy O'Callaghan), a small car (Evelyn Conlon, Geraldine Mills), a bedroom with warm eiderdown (Bernard MacLaverty) fitted with 'elaborate tea-trays', even one with 'legs and a little drawer for pens' (William Wall), or any other room. For Mike McCormack the room may even be less important than the 'eighteen-inch square [sheet] of melamine' which has been the material support of his writing for nearly thirty years. Some need headphones to keep noise out (Sam Blake), others need noise to keep too much silence out (Roddy Doyle, Joseph O'Neill, Claire McGowan). Roddy Doyle, looking for the right music to calibrate his attention, found it in Arvo Pärt and other minimalists. One of Claire McGowan's favourite musical wallpapers is the soundtrack *Irish Coastal Experience*; Billy O'Callaghan needs the sea itself, which is normal 'when you're born within smelling-distance of water'. Gerard Donovan needs 'a wood of his own': catching the tone of the trees seething with wind inspires him with the voice of a killer protagonist. Mike McCormack too shows how a writer's surroundings find their way into a novel, as the boisterous pub life underneath his room pounded its way into his writing. A novel's tone is suggested by its surroundings.

The Other and the others: the matrix of art

So what happens in this special place? 'Strange work' is Paul Lynch's answer. Anne Haverty specifies this work as 'the struggle between the self in the world and the secret writing self'. These two 'selves' form the intrapersonal and, together with 'the politics of the interpersonal', comprise 'the matrix of art' (Anne Haverty). This matrix has four factors, situated on two axes: the 'social self' and the 'others' are on an axis of 'social interaction', while the 'Other' and 'the secret writing self' interact on the axis of the unconscious and subconscious. The two axes are connected in complex ways, barely hinted at by the dotted lines. Though all contributors to this book differ in their approach, there is a striking convergence in that almost everyone refers to these four factors. Below is a bare graphic representation of it; at the end I will insert the same scheme but populated with passages from the sixty-one contributions.

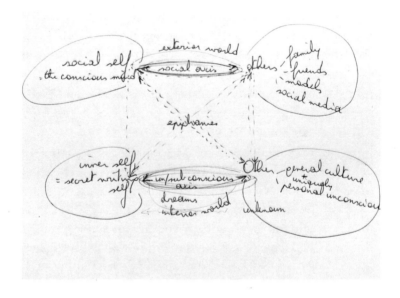

In Clare Boylan's *The Agony and the Ego: The Art and Strategy of Fiction Writing Explored*, the predecessor of this book, Malcolm Bradbury complained that 'criticism plainly lacks ... a substantive theory of creativity'.[3] He wanted to have the writer's 'instinct' explained, as well as the 'structure' of the writing process and 'modes' of how imagination turns 'instinct' into pattern. In this book the contributors replace 'instinct' with 'compulsion' to write. As to 'structure' they often mention the two relational axes, the social and the un/subconscious. The modes of the imagination are determined by the interaction between these two axes. For all of our contributors, the social 'I' is pleasure-focused and sensual; the I is mimetic in that it likes the things 'others' like – a fresh beer, a warm bed, a good sports match. Anne Haverty is rather jealous of people who enjoy these things, because she feels compelled to be involved with the Other (capital O) and the secret writing self. The Other refers to two realms, both suprapersonal: the culture in which one lives, and one's own unconscious. Both determine each person's life more than anything, yet they are invisible: the culture (so evident that we don't notice it) and our own unconscious (because we have only indirect access to it). Together our culture and our unconscious form the bubble in which each person lives, and it is *these* realms the writer wants to connect and explore. Because it is only in one's subconscious that one finds the unique self, and by extension one's unique voice.

To be a writer, says Alan McMonagle, is a matter of 'taking risks. It is a high wire act'. Two kinds of attention have to be juggled, one for the others and one for the Other. If the artist moves exclusively on the social axis this may be maddening: being hostaged by unrelenting family demands may cause 'cognitive disruption' (Claire Kilroy); if enthralled by social media one may be happy with mimetic babble, what Éilís Ní Dhuibhne calls 'verbal Coca Cola', but one's 'concentration span' may be fragmented (Claire McGowan) to the extent that one's brain turns into 'a demented flea' (Kevin Barry). On the other hand, if one is too deep into the unconscious one may be 'suffused with terror' (Anne Haverty). Yet this needs to be faced: writing is all about the 'ability to be with ourselves' (Paul Murray), which means to relate on both axes. To live in the writerly biotope is, ultimately, a matter of exploring the Other at work in the world, and for this one needs an emphatic and critical imagination. As Lia Mills puts it: 'everything hinges on the quality of attention you bring to the task'.

In what follows we will look at how authors calibrate this attention and will do so in four movements:

(1) the writer must escape the clutches of habit (the purely social self);

(2) to dive into the unconscious, where she must escape the clutches of its contradictoriness (the Other);

(3) which leads to the exhilarating play of exploring the subconscious world of dreams and actual fictionalizing work (the writing self);

(4) finally, under the title 'forms of responsibility', the interactions between writing and the community (the others) are highlighted.

Breaking the cocoon of comfort

For writers, the urge to write proves irrepressible. As Jennifer Johnston told Sophia Hillan '"If it's in you, you won't be able to stop it"'. The same goes for Claire Kilroy: 'I have a mind that needs writing'. With Caitriona Lally verbal language takes the form of an elemental force: 'if the words are there, they will push through'. To Patrick McCabe it's a need, and Mia Gallagher is reminded of John Cleese who told would-be actors that such a vocation is not a matter of wanting but of needing. Throughout the book, the word 'compulsion' is used: Lisa McInerney, Emer Martin and Catherine Dunne mention it and Paul Lynch notes that 'A book begins in the mind as an itch and the writer discovers a compulsion to scratch'.

Staying in the purely social dimension of life is a seductive idea; indeed, why not do the things demanded by 'common sense?' Better to cook, host, iron, clean, as these activities yield direct effect, unlike embarking on the creation of a fictional world which, after much effort and asocial behaviour, may refuse to co-operate. Or is this 'common sense' a *malin génie* which holds you from a more authentic calling? When Mary O'Donnell experiences her home as one which house-holds her, calling her to be distracted by chores, she sees the home as an uncanny Doppelgänger.

Physical work is one way to deflect the demands of the inner writer (as for Claire McGowan, Caitriona Lally, Éilís Ní Dhuibhne, Anne Haverty); another one is the comfort of routine. '[H]appiness writes white', Molly McCloskey quotes Henry de Montherlant, explaining: 'if one is too satisfied with life, too comfortable, then the tensions that give rise to writing just don't exist. The same goes for Roddy Doyle, who recognizes his own situation in Bob Dylan's memoir *Chronicles* (also lauded by Patrick McCabe): '"[T]hings had become too familiar, and I might have to disorientate myself" … when I start a new novel. I'm trying to rattle myself, or to knock myself off my own map'. '[I]nstead of the glib things that we initially thought we wanted to say', Dermot Bolger states, we should allow 'our subconscious minds to speculate and probe down to the awkward truths that we need to express'. The philosopher Rosi Braidotti, who sees the human being as basically a nomad, calls for a 'scrambling of the master-code', implying that both the ego and its culture have to be critically analysed and reconstituted.[4] Mia Gallagher does just this when she states that the writer should not 'just [be] … feeding the machine of capitalist-consumerism or my own lonely ego'. David Park endorses this: 'I do my best to avoid pretentiousness or expressions of ego in all its public forms … it requires my best self'. What the writer needs is a 'pure heart'; Eoin McNamee speaks of an 'elaboration of the soul'. In Lia Mills' wording, it is the full commitment of 'heart and soul' which provides 'the right engine of curiosity'. That engine is driven by fascination. It is on this wavelength that Lia Mills believes the reader will become linked in: 'what fascinates me about a character will hopefully fascinate unknown readers'.

Immersion and struggle: the drives of the unconscious

'The beginning is a baton pass from the unconscious, the part of the mind older than language. The tongue-tied writer awaits wearing a blindfold. A hand reaches into the dark and something shapeless is placed in your grip. Whatever it is, you've got to run with it ...' (Paul Lynch). While the writer 'envies' other people's 'ability to look forward simply and wholeheartedly to the next ... holiday ... what she really looks forward to is the next bout of writing. This looking forward is suffused with terror' (Anne Haverty). 'I regard myself as descending into chaos when I write, and trying to fashion matter out of it. I am frightened of chaos but ... Without writing, I am not living' (Claire Kilroy). 'When we write', Mia Gallagher quotes Ted Deppe, 'we go looking for trouble'. Paul Murray agrees: 'writing novels' means that 'you are using the best of yourself to create the most difficult, intractable problems you can think of, and then driving yourself crazy trying to solve them'. It is the story of the mire and the wire, the story of Baron Munchausen, recalled by Patrick McCabe, who maintained that while he was sinking in the marsh he could pull himself out by his own hair. If the mire is our unspoken fears and desires which can ambush and paralyze us, the wire is the thread of language, the traction of voice and story, which pull the characters through, or turn them into statues of humanity, mire fixed so that we admire them. It is this tension in 'structuring the world into sentences which reflects that confusion and allure ... that I am living' (Claire Kilroy). Likewise, Nuala O'Connor wants to write about 'mucky, confused people struggling through and gaining small triumphs and fucking up splendidly'.

It is striking that the three most important features of the unconscious identified by Freud recur in these testimonies: its compulsion to repeat, its contradictory signals and its indifference to the wellbeing of the 'social self'. This indifference is amply (and jokingly) illustrated by Danielle McLaughlin, whose story focuses on the difference between the social and the inner self. Each get a name: the former is 'the Other Woman', the latter 'Danielle McLaughlin'. Clearly the social person is the Caliban figure: she has to deal with practicalities. She may provide some material for the writing self, but it is the Ariel-like McLaughlin who is really in charge. At some point Danielle McLaughlin digs into the 'medical records from Other Woman … In doing this she was not motivated in any way by a concern for Other Woman. Truth was, she didn't give a shit about Other Woman'. To the writerly self, the social self is but 'a ready body of material to be harvested'. This is also true for Danny Denton, and for Rosemary Jenkinson: 'Writing is everything to me … Next to it, living is merely a hobby'. Likewise, a comfortable egocentric attitude only comes in the way of Gerard Donovan as he needs to empathize with his outsider protagonist Julius Winsome: 'I suspect [W. Somerset] Maugham is right about a certain indifference helping to bring about excellence'.

However, this indifference can become paralysing when the contradictions of the unconscious dominate the writer, leading to writer's block or depression. Gavin Corbett's contribution focuses on how he has to deal with 'this tempest of negativity in my head'. Belinda McKeon's description of oppositional forces in her drives illustrates 'how hard I had to *push* myself *not* to *avoid* the act of writing, even though it was the thing I always *wanted most* to do with my day' (my emphasis). Lia Mills shares the predicament: 'I was often at war with myself. I needed and wanted to write but had to struggle to do it, often feeling utterly unentitled, fraudulent – a toxic disempowerment that is the cruel opposite of the authority a writer, by definition, needs'. Alan McMonagle refers to Don DeLillo: 'what we are reluctant to touch often seems to contain the fabric of our salvation'. Glenn Patterson's brilliant piece on the one hand insists on the fact that 'quitting writing … [i]s absolutely real'. On the other hand, that same author treats this state of being drained with the distance of humour, insisting that he has 'quit writing 783 times', before discussing how he tries to cajole himself back into writing with 'a tactical' rather than a 'practical ... shower'. Claire McGowan can also laugh about the contradictoriness of one's urges: 'For years, even after I had a book deal, I wouldn't give my writing any proper space or time. I wrote ... in a chair that gave me chronic back pain'. Lucy Caldwell also writes about a moment when she felt completely depleted; and yet, on some unconscious level, a deep well must have been filling up at the time, because the writing started to flow again.

Striking that fine balance between being indifferent to your social ego and having confidence in your writerly self seems far from obvious. But Lia Mills indicates that 'reading other writers' is conducive to finding one's 'authority', one's voice (a topic on which Gerald Donovan elaborates in interesting ways). Writers seem to form a generous community 'that transcends time and space ... I can have conversations with the dead ... The magic of sentences reasserts itself'. (It is surprising how many contributors to this volume are inspired by Chekhov, Patrick Kavanagh and Bob Dylan while others find it in films (Patrick McCabe, Mary O'Donnell). I am reminded of Aby Warburg, the German art historian and cultural theorist, who found vital healing powers in art. When the best psychiatrists of his time could not help him he healed himself, and for him one insight was essential to the process: depression and mania are two sides of a coin. To accept a lifestyle which tips you from the (s)low to the high rhythm demands a kind of resilience which Warburg called *Besonnenheit*, 'thoughtfulness' (his translation of the Greek word *Sophrosyne*), denoting a talent to 'manage' the things that happen in the deep self.[5] This kind of wisdom is 'a compass for the soul'. Mia Gallagher gives a fine example of how art (visual and verbal) can offer her the wire out of the mire. '*Departure* ... was such a watershed; it was personal and revealing and I felt reluctant to show it to anyone when I'd finished it. ... [it did not] ... seem like play; more like channelling. I became a conduit for a voice, a stream of images and, most of all ... a handle on my unhappiness'. And when the inner breathing space opens up again and the voice picks up, Belinda McKeon senses her thoughts do not turn to dross but they soar, and 'you are going to be the channel, the long, sparking tram line, along which it shoots into itself, into its form'. As Emer Martin puts it: 'fiction is an extension of the spirit, the demonstration of our faith in the worth of each other and the value of our own existence'.

The fascination with the preconscious: phantasms, secrets and dreams
'A sixth sense? Perhaps not: maybe a dream-sense might be a better description. But it is, above all, a desire to bring something from the inchoate darkness of the dream world out into the light' (Catherine Dunne).
'... this game ... that happens in language is one I find deeply pleasurable, almost essential' (Anne Enright).

While the unconscious brings non-articulated matter, pure energy, fear and struggle, the preconscious brings 'secrets and dreams' (Bernie McGill) or 'serious play' (Mia Gallagher quoting Adam Wyeth, who sees this as a characteristic of creativity). The turn from doubt to confidence seems to occur when an 'associative process' (Molly McCloskey) morphs the mind into a mode of imagination which works, what McKeon calls the 'sparking tram line'. This is where the writerly self 'willingly cooperat[es] ... with the whirlpools of the subconscious' (Patrick McCabe), a place Catherine Dunne recognizes as 'that space where the conscious and the unconscious collide'. Is this a collision or a dovetailing of preconscious and actual work, the writing becoming a way of 'learning to tune into your subconscious' (Sam Blake), which happens when motifs 'coagulate'? Interestingly, the strongest motifs come from childhood, as Martina Devlin illustrates. This is underscored by Dermot Bolger, but before we go into his example I want to briefly hold up a beautiful word here, about 2500 years old, which sums up what keeps the writer's faculties together, causes the channel to form and the spark to fly: the phantasm. Aristotle mentions the phantasm as a set of images, often connected to objects from childhood, which form a personal iconography and reappear in varying forms which 'gladden the imagination'. The philosophers Giorgio Agamben, Jacques Lacan and others elaborate on these 'phantasmata'; the psychoanalyst Christopher Bollas calls them 'genera', because they resuscitate forgotten emotions and so generate a kind of timeline, a kind of preconscious diary, our destiny in pictures, objects and texts.[6] T.S. Eliot's 'objective correlative' is a helpful term here, as it indicates objects in real life which resonate with these preconscious emotions. Dermot Bolger's contribution gives a fine example of a phantasm/genera when he thinks of certain poems he read as an adolescent:

I didn't fully understand when I first encountered them at school but ... [they] have become signposts to my adult life: their lines re-emerging in my memory from across the decades to often help me survive moments of personal trauma.

Bolger's description offers the complete definition of a phantasm: something which is fascinating, exuding significance yet not releasing its meaning: that has to be teased out over the years, or appears suddenly in an epiphany; but even if the meaning never comes to light, its mere significance helps out in difficult moments, nudges the writer to stick to her guns, her pen or keyboard, her 'destiny', her unique way of life. Mary O'Donnell observes how the subconscious:

... actively seek[s] things that will nourish me creatively, intellectually, and in a less visible way. There is a seeking soul within all of us that beckons towards byways we had not expected to visit, but which we arrive at, explorers landing on new territory.

According to Lia Mills, it is 'an initiating idea. It could be character or conundrum, a place, atmosphere, or question – all stories and writers have different starting points. The idea stands up in the recesses of your mind and waves an invitation: do you want to come with me and do this thing?'

In Clare Boylan's collection of writers' testimonies, Jane Gardam explicitly links these iconic ideas to hinging moments in her creative life: 'With me the idea for a novel has always arrived with an image, which has often been the same one, of a child walking alone on a beach ... They were lucky encounters, colourplates I put away' (Boylan, 13–14). Phantasms can be verbal or visual; but, whether words or images, they work like magnets that make contents coagulate. So Nicola Pierce visiting an exhibition with a glass case holding a book opened on the line 'Home – there's magic in that little word' suddenly highlighted the theme of her new novel for her.

The short story Roisín O'Donnell wrote for this collection elucidates even more how the writer plays with the subconscious; this author's penchant for magic realism is ideal for describing such realms. In 'My Patron Saint', the protagonist's subconscious is personalized as her 'muse', named Francis. As in Danielle McLaughlin, the social self is so unimportant that she does not even get a name. Francis is not conducive to logical argument and academic discipline: 'Sometimes Francis' absence came as a relief. My essay grades improved'. The muse cannot be compelled by purpose, only works in 'incubation time' so Francis urges the writer '"let's sit on the bed or the sofa, or anywhere, but not the feckin desk"'. He cannot be controlled: 'This was the thing about Francis ... You couldn't cajole him or persuade him'. He takes nothing for granted but goes for playful variation: when the 'bemused' one tells him of an event 'he made me retell it from five different angles'. Lia Mills too indicates that writing gives space to a multiplicity of selves. Like Heather Richardson who felt ideas buzzing, Lia Mills finds herself in a busy place 'where the whole *I* of me lives. The real I, the plurality. Writing is where I am my most real, my most honest self; where all the voices are heard … where there are no rules and the life-supporting, life-giving condition is language'.

Writing as 'autogenesis': grappling with existence

'If my stories are at all a reflection of who I am – and I can't help but feel that my better ones are – then it is probably correct that they should come slowly and without certainty, that every sentence needs into be wrestled into place. I am not writing autobiography' (Billy O'Callaghan).

'All of your life is … how you transform the materials of your own life and experience into fiction' (Kevin Barry).

Several contributions in this book stress that writing literature is NOT a case of autobiography. In what follows I will discuss how the interactions between the two axes touch upon the role of knowledge, of the dream, of conflict and of 'existential happiness' as distinct from 'social happiness' in the making of fiction.

Often in interviews with writers the question arises as to why authors chose this or that theme. Some answer that they want to write about what they *know* (à la Jane Austen's 'four or five families in a country village') others about what they *don't* know. Most of the contributors to *The Danger and the Glory* say they write themselves into that which they *did not know they wanted to know*. Catherine Dunne observes 'my imagination had just given birth to a character I didn't even know I wanted to write about'; Lisa

McInerney and Emer Martin develop characters which are entirely opposed to their 'biographical self' to see where it brings them. For the contributors, 'knowing' has at least three modalities: firstly, the struggle to get out of the marmalade of mimetic behaviour demands *unknowing*; secondly, drifting on the uncertainties of unconscious impulses demands the sustained exercise of *not-knowing*; finally, when subconscious and craft grip into each other, the writer is rewarded with *new knowledge*. These different kinds of knowing are brought about by different states of mind, in which the ego's alertness is calibrated into variations of active, passive, receptive and medial. An author cannot 'will' a character into being, Catherine Dunne explains. 'It is … a state of being actively passive – not straining anxiously to capture something, but being alert'. Lucy Caldwell writes about 'the passive-receptive phase'; like her, many other authors observe that a story's hibernation is a vital part of the process. Things have to 'simmer in my mind', Micheál Ó Conghaile writes, but while for him a story's incubation time is often about four years, for Kevin Barry, Sam Blake, Celia de Fréine, Danny Denton, Martina Devlin, Catherine Dunne, Wendy Erskine, Sophia Hillan, it can be decades. To Barry McCrea, revisiting a place after many years is part and parcel of both his story's content and its production process. To Patrick McCabe the writer and his language are sparring partners, 'in a state of what might best be described as "lying in wait for yourself"'. This interactive relation is summed up by Bernard MacLaverty in the metaphor of breastfeeding: 'The baby's act of feeding stimulates the milk to arrive just as the act of writing stimulates words to come onto the page'.

As John Banville showed in 'Fiction and the Dream' (which triggered this collection), writers should assimilate (and simulate) the rhetorics of the dream. Kevin Barry says that writers should aim at being awake yet still 'puddled in dream-melt'; in this state of mind they may 'get to the place where we dream'. That writing and dreaming are often paralleled in this collection may become clear from three examples. Firstly, like people who find their deeper emotions via dreams, Dermot Bolger observes that writers 'start to discover things about ourselves, often in the guise of writing about some character who seems utterly different'. Secondly, like the dream which consists of manifest and latent contents, emotions turn into different versions which sediment in the 'finished' product. Thirdly, both dreams and literature offer phantasms, which always strike the receiver with significance while withholding their meaning. Witness the fascination of McCrea's diasporic protagonist when he returns to his country of birth; or that mentioned by Lucy Caldwell quoting from Louis MacNeice's beautiful poem 'Star-Gazer'.

But what fascinates us is not always as nice as MacNeice's stars. Bollas writes that genera (phantasms) are 'not always beautiful or wonderful occasions – many are ugly and terrifying but nonetheless profoundly moving because of the existential memory tapped'.[7] Alan McMonagle is plagued by nightmares; Lia Mills encounters a life-threatening reality but this sharpens her writerly attention: 'I was absolutely present in that illness, one big ball of apprehension: nervy, taking every thing in. … but there were powers I could summon – powers of suggestion, of association, of imagination and naming'. The fascination of what's difficult may take many forms, but for the writer its purpose is to fuel the right engine of curiosity, the 'very best attention' (Lia Mills). This engine is powered by conflict between the voices in the writerly self: the one who entertains and the one who challenges (Heather Richardson), the skilled professional one and the innocent, joyous one (Kevin Power); 'the me who dreams, imagines, intuits, and the me who observes, dissects, and crafts' (Catherine Dunne). Writing is always a struggle, 'the challenges of grappling with what Margaret Atwood calls "the slippery double"' (Catherine Dunne). In her 'private, unrelenting grappling with words' Siobhán Parkinson uses the same idea, only now there are more voices 'jostling ... in my own head'. To Nessa O'Mahony, writing is basically 'to wrestle with images that capture whatever existential crisis I'm currently grappling with'.

With her qualification 'existential' Nessa O'Mahony provides us with a keyword. In insisting on taking the unconscious axis into account, the writer is enriched, developing a language which is both more unique and has wider resonances than one limited to the social axis. Patrick McCabe stresses the uniqueness Gogol or Nabokov produce as they let the Other speak through them: each lives 'in his own looking-glass world, refracting the material through a mirror of his own making'. In doing this the writer is 'seeking and locating [his] ... own essential nature – one's personality, really'. Once the writer is properly at work, when the inner and outer worlds are mixing and mingling, when inklings find fixation in felicitous wording, the writer is 'ex-isting' (in its original Greek meaning, leaning out of oneself). She lets the Other (one's unconscious and one's own culture) do some of the work. This is the case with Geraldine Mills: 'Writing had somehow found me within myself. I wrote as if my life depended on it, not knowing that it did'. Dermot Bolger underscores this with Kavanagh's example: he 'could have been as happily unhappy as the ordinary countryman in Ireland', but he 'innocently dabble[d] in words and rhymes and finds that it is his life'. Dermot Bolger uses the verb 'to dabble' five times, thus stressing the important role of unintentionality in writing. It is this Other which brings the breath in a (literary) work. Aristotle had a name for this extra dimension, 'eudaimonia'. A combination of eu, Greek for good + daimon, it indicates that someone is living up to her unique challenges, represented by the 'daimon'.

Lia Mills finds this: 'Somewhere in that labyrinth of experience and observation, of dread and love and awe I came home to myself in writing. ... I was *happy* there ...'. Likewise Belinda McKeon feels steeped in 'the business of being alive'; Billy O'Callaghan senses he is 'authentically happening', 'whether the mornings flow or feel mired, I am for those few hours the *happiest* version of myself because that's the part of the day when whatever mask I feel the need to wear falls most easily away and I can get somewhere close to the truth of things' (my emphases). It is striking how many authors use the word 'happy' when they talk about the hardships their work brings. This leads me back to Anne Haverty who prefers writing which is 'suffused with terror' to the carefree holiday. Anne Haverty's distinction highlights the clear difference between 'social happiness' which is to be found on the social axis, and *eudaimonia*, the existential happiness described by the other contributors, which encompasses the unconscious axis. W.B. Yeats' correlative would have been 'Unity of Being', Nietzsche called it 'thorough health' or a wide, encompassing health (*'die große Gesundheit'*). One could call this 'happenness'; when the writers' four factors are all in interaction, realizing the unique cocktail of the author's energies in her work.

Yet dreams and phantasms never allow for a definitive interpretation. Writing was the rope to help William Wall out when bogged down: 'the imagination was my emancipation'; but the writer is 'not chasing easy': the fact that Billy O'Callaghan has no object in the sentence, merely an adverb, is telling. Likewise, Anne Enright talks of 'a fugitive sweetness there, that I seek out over and again'. This echoes with Patrick McCabe's evocation of writers '[a]s they strive for that endless, elusive note that defines who they are and where they belong'. Sara Baume is aware of the uniquely personal aspect of each work and that 'what constitutes an accomplishment' is mostly 'incomparable, and therefore impossible to measure'. But then she does find a fine criterion: 'Success, I realise, has the colour and consistency of condensation'. Caitriona Lally is not so sure. Part-time cleaner, part-time writer, she stresses the difficulty of assessing when a literary work is finished: 'When I write, I never know when I'm finished, when I should stop tweaking and honing my words, but when I clean, the endpoint is clear'.

Forms of responsibility

'The reader is as vital to the book as the writer' (Emer Martin).

'Language is a tool and a weapon, to be turned to any end: to nullify experience – or to transfuse it, and give it renewed meaning and life, and to create a space, textual and social, where none existed before. It is inherently personal, and social, and political. It must be all of these' (Neil Hegarty).

If the authors have successfully moved from social comfort to the existential experience of 'eudaimonia' or 'happenness', what does that mean to the community? The link is not a direct one. Like an Olympic swimmer in competition who focuses on the water, the air and his body, rather than on the public, authors focus on their writing. Yet, like sports champions, writers want to bring into existence some new aspect of humanity. In what follows we will look at three aspects of writing that are relevant to the community: direct criticism, careful articulation and an atmosphere conducive to empathy.

As the writer tries to break through her bubble of habit, her own (sub)culture, to find a wider frame of reference, she may hope that her work has the same effect on the community. To Evelyn Conlon this means that 'Because I am a citizen as well as a writer', she describes 'how the strictures of our society affected the ways we lived', expressing 'bafflement at the narrow view of what constituted a family'. Martina Devlin shows how a mere closed mind can 'ratchet up grievances'. She describes the decennia of useless violence deployed in the North: 'If civil rights had been extended when lobbying started – if British law had only been applied to Northern Ireland in exactly the same way as it was applied in any English, Scottish or Welsh city – there would have been virtually no support among the population for violence'.

While some writers analyse existing wrongs in a social reality, others offer remedies for personal traumas; some combine both. Paul Murray criticises aspects of globalization, especially the mental colonizing implemented by 'neoliberalism, or necro-capitalism'. But while the market creates this 'incessant distraction', leading 'the entire planet deathwards', literature can call a halt to this self-hurtling, as it allows both writer and reader to make space in themselves and re-open the inner playground where the many aspects of the self can return to existential happiness. Kevin Barry agrees: 'the daily or nightly reading of poetry is essential, not just for your development as a writer but for your development as a person'. More specifically it is the accuracy of literary language which helps, as it helps to articulate vague emotions. Joseph O'Neill stresses the 'care' that goes into his literary expression: 'An accurate sentence is the ideal. … I mean "accurate" in its etymological sense, "toward care" (*ad* + *cura*). An accurate sentence tends toward care – of language, of justice, of reality'. This ties in directly with Paul Murray's *cri de coeur* about the 'precipitous decline in public discourse' and 'the rise of hate speech' which 'seem to me to go hand-in-hand with the modern inability to pay attention, which is the first step towards empathy'. Which brings us to a third important factor in the writer-community relation, that authors create an atmosphere inviting people to empathize. To Neil Hegarty this means that the writer should develop an 'acute sensitivity to the presence of stories and histories not told, or redacted, or rejected, or dismissed' which is so typical for Northern Ireland, as we find illustrated in Anna Burns' work. But the south too has its gaps and silences: Emer Martin wants to rescue 'beggars and refugees' from oblivion, 'broken families adrift on a constricting planet; women prisoners'; Lisa McInerney puts characters from gang culture in the spotlight 'to try to understand them better'; Rosaleen McDonagh uses '[m]inority categories of people such as Irish Travellers/Roma and people with disabilities ... as active protagonists'. 'Playing with fiction', she works out 'a lived experience of racism, ableism and sexism'. Emer Martin goes one step further, seeing this empathy on a societal scale; she harks back to the function tragedy had in the Athenian community, when 'the Greeks recognized the cathartic element of performing tragedies in a shared setting'.

The inspiring community

'Fiction is a communal act' (Emer Martin).

But as Eoin McNamee knows, empathy is limited, which makes him wonder whether it is 'a sin' to use the misery of other people's lives to feed his fiction. Is he erecting a statue for those who would otherwise have been forgotten, or is he stealing their lives? With theft and stealth on the one hand, the imperative to tell and invest the self in the work on the other hand: do they balance? Do they transfigure each other? These questions contrast sharply with Seán O'Reilly's stunning story of a retired missionary. Though she was a compulsive diarist, writing down the details of her life among the poorest in many different cultures in order not to forget them, she was so humble that she did not think highly of 'the story of her life's journey, her very soul'.

With Emer Martin's *The Cruelty Men* the situation seems more straightforward as the author is thanked by someone who lived in a Magdalene Laundry for representing her troubles. Being aware of the difference between her own imagined knowledge and the woman's lived knowledge the author feels:

> moved and humbled. I knew then the story was bigger than me. It was outside of me. It had its own life. The book belonged to those who had suffered. Their courage and reliance was what inspired me to write it in the first place. Fiction is a communal act.

Emer Martin's objectification proved helpful as it made someone's trauma more manageable. She is aware of the fact that writers are the professionals of the imagination; as they translate dreams and inklings, ideals and nightmares into solid fiction they may one day provide the phantasms that will support some seeking souls. The writer 'spews images from fears, manufactures totems from dreams, and scaffolds our understanding with myth'.

The text's afterlife

'… a writer suffers at the desk for a result that is hard to define …' (Anne Enright).

To Catherine Dunne, characters are 'created by a silent agreement between writer and reader'. Gerald Donovan stands back even more, paring his fingernails after the work: 'In terms of the novel's organisation, any contest between the reader's perception and your intent as the novelist will produce a clear winner: perception'. Again, the writer's intentions are no match for the work's layeredness. Donovan further illustrates this by opposing two kinds of publications: the 'polished vanities' which are 'somehow pointless', and those in which the 'writing' remains vibrant. The text's life cannot be planned, '[i]t's what happens to it afterwards' – something Lucy Caldwell agrees with.

Lia Mills observed that long-dead writers can still be worthy partners in the Great Conversation: 'when I'm stuck, or lost, or in despair, there is a sure remedy in reading other writers'. Their work 'transcends time and space ... I can find their answers, freely given ... The magic of sentences reasserts itself'. Because some literary works are like a densely organized universe, they keep their appeal. And because a dense text does not aim at one issue or another, but to the complexity of human contexts, it proffers neither opinions nor meaning, only significant situations, labyrinths the reader must try out, engaging in the text with all the layers of his being.

Long after the author has gone, her work may still have the ability to respond. We notice this in the statement by Philippe Lançon, one of the journalists who worked for *Charlie Hebdo* and who survived the attack. Recently he published the Femina Award-winning book, *Le Lambeau*, on the event and his recovery. When asked about his attitude to the killers, he says that he read many articles about their motives, but never learned anything from journalism. 'I learn more from the novels by Joseph Conrad and Fjodor Dostoyeski. Terrorism is a problem of the community but also of the soul. And fiction writers are better than journalists in analyzing that'.[8]

This coda has given but a kaleidoscopic impression. There is so much in the contributions that they are worth reading and rereading, coming back to at different times, and in different moods: that way they can sink in properly, spark off ideas, inspire. I hope that the reader of these sixty-one texts will enjoy them as much as I did, and continue to do so.

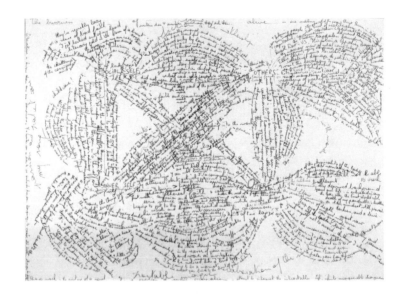

NOTES

1   'Die meisten Schriftsteller verstehen von der Literatur nicht mehr, als ein Vogel von der Ornithologie'. https://www. stern.de/kultur/buecher/zum-tod-von-marcel-reich-ranicki-literaturpapst-mit-jahrhundert-biografie-3049874.html

2   Throughout this text I refer to the writer as 'she' and 'her' since the majority of the contributions are by women.

3   Clare Boylan (ed.), *The Agony and the Ego: The Art and Strategy of Fiction Writing Explored* (Harmondsworth, Penguin, 1993), p. 62.

4   Rosi Braidotti, *Metamorphoses: Towards a materialist theory of becoming* (Cambridge/Malden, Polity, 2002), p. 124.

5   Davide Stimilli, 'L'énigme de Warburg', *Revue française de psychanalyse* 79 (2015, 4), pp 1100–114. See also 'Daimon and Nemesis', *Anthropology and Aesthetics* 44 (2003, Autumn), 99–112.

6   In Clare Boylan's book Marina Warner admires Italo Calvino for the way in which he concentrates on this very private album: 'in *Six Memos for the Next Millennium* … [Calvino] describes how he used to pore over comic strips obsessively before he could read … He was trying to create … "a fantastic iconology"' (Boylan, p. 32).

7   Christopher Bollas, *The Shadow of the Object: Psychoanalysis of the Unthought Known* (NYC, Columbia University Press, 1987), 29.

8   Interview in *De Standaard Weekblad*, 3 November 2018, nr 370; 28.

John Banville's seventeen novels have met with worldwide acclaim and won many prizes, among which the Booker, the James Tait Black Memorial Prize, the Guardian Fiction Prize, the Franz Kafka Prize, the Austrian State Prize for European Literature and the Prince of Asturias Award for Literature. Under the pen-name Benjamin Black he has written a number of crime novels, for which he received the RBA Prize for Crime Fiction. He is also a screenwriter, playwright and book reviewer for the *New York Review of Books* and *The Guardian.*

Kevin Barry is the author of the novels *Beatlebone, City of Bohane* and *Night Boat to Tangier.* He has also written two short story collections, *Dark Lies the Island* and *There are Little Kingdoms.* He has won the IMPAC Award, the Goldsmiths Prize, the Sunday Times EFG Short Story Prize, the EU Prize for Literature, the Rooney Prize and many others. He has been translated into 18 languages, and his stories have appeared in *The New Yorker, Granta, The Stinging Fly* and elsewhere. He also writes plays and screenplays, and he is co-editor and publisher of the annual anthology, *Winter Papers.* He lives in County Sligo.

Sara Baume's debut novel, *Spill Simmer Falter Wither,* won the Geoffrey Faber Memorial Prize and has been widely translated. Her second novel, *A Line Made by Walking,* was shortlisted for the Goldsmiths Prize. She lives in West Cork and works as a visual artist as well as a writer.

Sam Blake is a pseudonym for Vanessa Fox O'Loughlin, the founder of The Inkwell Group publishing consultancy and the award-winning online writing magazine Writing.ie. She is Ireland's leading literary scout. Vanessa started writing fiction when her husband set sail across the Atlantic for eight weeks and she had an idea for a book. *Little Bones,* the first in her bestselling Cat Connolly crime trilogy, was a No 1 bestseller and shortlisted for Irish Crime Novel of the Year.

Born in Dublin in 1959, Dermot Bolger's fourteen novels include *The Journey Home, The Family on Paradise Pier, The Lonely Sea and Sky* and *An Ark of Light.* His debut play, *The Lament for Arthur Cleary,* received the Samuel Beckett Award. His numerous other plays include *The Ballymun Trilogy* and an adaptation of *Ulysses,* staged by the Abbey Theatre, who will stage his latest play, *Last Orders at the Dockside*, in 2019. A poet, his ninth collection, *The Venice Suite: A Voyage through Loss*, appeared in 2012 and his New and Selected Poems, *That Which is Suddenly Precious*, in 2015.

Born in Belfast in 1981, LUCY CALDWELL is the author of three novels, a collection of short stories, several theatre and radio dramas, and the editor of *Being Various: New Irish Short Stories* (Faber, 2019). Her many awards include the Rooney Prize for Irish Literature, the Dylan Thomas Prize and a Major Individual Artist Award from the Arts Council of Northern Ireland. Her website is www.lucycaldwell.com and she tweets at @beingvarious.

JAN CARSON is a writer and community arts facilitator based in East Belfast. Her debut novel, *Malcolm Orange Disappears* and short story collection, *Children's Children*, were published by Liberties Press. A micro-fiction collection, *Postcard Stories* was published by the Emma Press in 2017. Jan's novel *The Fire Starters* was published by Doubleday in 2019. Her stories have appeared in journals such as *Banshee*, *The Tangerine* and *Harper's Bazaar* and on BBC Radio 3 and 4. In 2018 Jan was the Irish Writers Centre's inaugural Roaming Writer in Residence on the trains of Ireland.

EVELYN CONLON, described as 'one of Ireland's major truly creative writers' is a novelist, short story writer, radio essayist and compiler of anthologies. Her work has been described by turn as poetic, acerbic, spare and beautifully descriptive. 'She wears her attention to detail and research as the lightest of cloaks'. Her work often deals with people who are between places, crossing borders both real and imagined. It has been widely anthologised and translated, most recently into Chinese. She lives in Dublin – www.evelynconlon.com.

GAVIN CORBETT was born in the west of Ireland and grew up in Dublin, where he lives. He has published three novels: *Innocence* (2003), *This Is the Way* (2013), and *Green Glowing Skull* (2015) – and a book of photographs with text, *The Giving Light* (2017). *This Is the Way* was named Kerry Group Irish Novel of the Year in 2013. He has been writer-in-residence at Trinity College Dublin, University College Dublin and at Temple Bar Gallery and Studios. He's currently a Teacher Fellow in the Department of Creative Writing at University College Dublin.

CELIA DE FRÉINE writes in Irish and English. She was born in Newtownards and now divides her time between Dublin and Connemara. Her poetry has won many awards, including the Patrick Kavanagh Award (1994) and Gradam Litríochta Chló Iar-Chonnacht (2004). Her most recent collection is *cuir amach seo dom : riddle me this* (Arlen House, 2014). Her plays have won many awards and are staged regularly by Umbrella Theatre Company. *Ceannródaí*, her biography of Louise Gavan Duffy (LeabhairCOMHAR, 2018) was nominated for an An Post Irish Book Awards in 2018 – www.celiadefreine.com.

DANNY DENTON is a writer from Cork. His first novel, *The Earlie King & the Kid in Yellow*, was published by Granta Books in 2018. Among other publications, his work has also appeared in *The Stinging Fly, Southword, Granta, Winter Papers, Tate, Etc, The Guardian, The Irish Times, Architecture Ireland* & *The Big Issue*. He is currently writer-in-residence for Cork County Libraries and guest-edits *The Stinging Fly* in Summer 2019.

Author and journalist MARTINA DEVLIN has written ten books, from non-fiction to novels including *About Sisterland* and *The House Where It Happened*. Her latest is a short story collection, *Truth & Dare*. Prizes include the Royal Society of Literature's V.S. Pritchett Prize and a Hennessy Literary Award, and she has been shortlisted three times for the Irish Book Awards. She writes a weekly current affairs column for the *Irish Independent* and has been named National Newspapers of Ireland commentator of the year. She is vice-chair of the Irish Writers Centre and a Ph.D candidate at Trinity College Dublin.

GERARD DONOVAN's third novel, *Julius Winsome*, received worldwide critical acclaim and has been translated into a dozen languages. *The New Yorker* observed: 'Donovan delivers with devastating force'. A bestseller in Germany, it will be appearing as a major motion picture. Donovan attended Jesuit College, Galway, NUI Galway, and studied music at DIT. He is a graduate of The Johns Hopkins Writings Seminars. His first novel, *Schopenhauer's Telescope*, won the Kerry Group Irish Fiction Award.

RODDY DOYLE was born in Dublin in 1958. He is the author of eleven novels, among which *The Commitments* (1987), *The Snapper* (1990), *Paddy Clarke Ha ha ha* (1993), for which he won the Booker Prize, *The*

Woman Who Walked Into Doors (1996), *A Star Called Henry* (1999) and, most recently, *Smile* (2017). A feature film, *Rosie*, for which he wrote the screenplay, had its world premiere at the Toronto International Film Festival, in September 2018. He is co-founder and chairperson of *Fighting Words* (founded in 2009), an organisation which provides free mentoring in creative writing to children and young people.

CATHERINE DUNNE is the author of ten published novels. Her one work of non-fiction, *An Unconsidered People,* is a social history that explores the lives of Irish immigrants in London in the 1950's. Among her novels are: *The Things We Know Now*, which won the Giovanni Boccaccio International Prize for Fiction in 2013 and was shortlisted for Novel of the Year at the Irish Book Awards. *The Years That Followed* was published in 2016 and was longlisted for the International Dublin Literary Award. She is this year's recipient of the Irish PEN Award for Contribution to Irish Literature.

ANNE ENRIGHT was born in Dublin in 1962 and stayed. She has written six novels, two books of short stories and a book of essays about motherhood. Key awards were The Man Booker Prize (2007) – which brought her work to global attention – The Andrew Carnegie medal for Excellence in Fiction (2012) and the Irish Novel of the year (2008 and 2016). Anne was the inaugural Laureate for Irish Fiction (2015–2018) and has recently been appointed Professor of Fiction at UCD.

WENDY ERSKINE lives in Belfast. Her debut collection of short stories, *Sweet Home,* was published by The Stinging Fly Press in September 2018. Her writing has also appeared in issues of *The Stinging Fly*, in *Stinging Fly Stories* (2018), *Winter Papers* (2018), and *Female Lines: New Writing by Women from Northern Ireland* (New Island Books, 2017), and on BBC Radio 4. In 2019 one of her stories appeared in *Being Various: New Irish Short Stories* (Faber).

MIA GALLAGHER is the author of two acclaimed novels: *HellFire* (Penguin, 2006), awarded the *Irish Tatler* Literature Award 2007; and *Beautiful Pictures of the Lost Homeland* (New Island, 2016), longlisted for the 2016 Republic of Consciousness Award. Her debut short story collection *Shift* (New Island, 2018) was shortlisted for the Irish Book Awards 2018. She also writes non-fiction, writes for the stage and is a contributing editor to the *Stinging Fly*. In 2018 she was elected to Aosdána, an affiliate of Irish artists recognised for their contribution to Irish culture.

ANNE HAVERTY, born in Tipperary and educated at TCD and the Sorbonne, is a fiction writer and a poet. While *One Day as a Tiger* (1997, Rooney Prize and shortlisted for the Whitbread/Costa) and *The Free and Easy* (2006) portray contemporary Ireland, *The Far Side of a Kiss* (2000) is set in the London of 1820. Her biography, *Constance Markievicz: Irish Revolutionary*, is considered a classic. Her poetry collection *The Beauty of the Moon* (1999, a Poetry Book Society Recommendation) was followed by *A Break in the Journey* (2018). Anne Haverty has been Visiting Professor at the Adam Mickiewicz University in Poznan and Writing Fellow at TCD; she is a member of Aosdána.

NEIL HEGARTY grew up in Derry. He studied English literature at Trinity College Dublin, where he received his Ph.D. Neil's debut novel *Inch Levels* (Head of Zeus) was published in 2016 and was shortlisted for the Kerry Group Novel of the Year award in 2017. A French edition of the novel will be published by Gallimard in 2019. Neil's second novel *Jewel* will be published in 2019. Neil has also published widely in non-fiction. His titles include *Frost: That Was the Life That Was* (WH Allen), the authorised biography of David Frost; *The Story of Ireland* (BBC Books), which accompanies the BBC/RTÉ television history of Ireland; and *The Secret History of our Streets* (BBC Books), a social history of twentieth-century London. His short fiction and essays have appeared in the *Stinging Fly*, *Tangerine*, *Dublin Review* and elsewhere; and he is a regular reviewer for the *Irish Times*.

Dr SOPHIA HILLAN, author of *The Cocktail Hour* (Arlen House 2018), was Associate Director of Queen's University Belfast's Institute of Irish Studies (1993–2003) and Director of QUB's Irish Studies Summer School (2003–2005). She is also the author of *May, Lou and Cass: Jane Austen's Nieces in Ireland* (Blackstaff Press, 2011) and of two novels, *The Friday Tree* (Ward River, 2014) and *The Way We Danced* (Ward River, 2016). Her work on Michael McLaverty includes *In Quiet Places* (Poolbeg, 1989), *The Silken Twine* (Poolbeg, 1992) and *The Edge of Dark* (Academica Press, 2000).

ROSEMARY JENKINSON was born in Belfast and is an award-winning playwright and short story writer. Her plays include *The Bonefire* (winner of the Stewart Parker BBC Radio Award), *Basra Boy, White Star of the North, Planet Belfast, Here Comes the Night, Michelle and Arlene, Lives in Translation* and *I Shall Wear Purple*. She has published three collections of short stories: *Contemporary Problems Nos. 53 & 54, Aphrodite's Kiss,* and *Catholic Boy* (Doire Press). She was Artist-in-Residence at the Lyric Theatre in 2017 and recently received a Major Individual Artist Award from the Arts Council of Northern Ireland.

CLAIRE KILROY's debut novel *All Summer* was described in *The Times* as 'compelling ... a thriller, a confession and a love story framed by a meditation on the arts', and was awarded the 2004 Rooney Prize for Irish Literature. Her second novel, *Tenderwire,* was shortlisted for the 2007 Irish Novel of the Year and the Kerry Group Irish Fiction Award. It was followed, in 2009, by the highly acclaimed novel, *All Names Have Been Changed* and *The Devil I Know* in 2012. Educated at Trinity College, she lives in Dublin.

CAITRIONA LALLY is the 2018 recipient of the Rooney Prize for Irish Literature. Her debut novel, *Eggshells,* was published in 2015. It was shortlisted for the Newcomer Award at the Bord Gáis Energy Irish Book Awards and the Kate O'Brien Award. She lives in Dublin with her young family and is currently trying to finish her second novel.

PAUL LYNCH is the author of three internationally acclaimed novels – *Grace,* winner of the Kerry Group Irish Novel of the Year 2018 and a finalist for the Walter Scott Prize and the William Saroyan International Prize for Writing; *The Black Snow,* winner of France's Prix Libr'à Nous for Best Foreign Novel; and *Red Sky in Morning,* a finalist for France's Prix du Meilleur Livre Étranger (Best Foreign Book Prize). His fourth novel, *Beyond The Sea,* will be published in 2019. *Libération* has called Lynch 'one of the great Irish writers of today'. He lives in Dublin with his wife and two children

Belfast man, BERNARD MACLAVERTY, lives in Glasgow. He has published five collections of short stories and five novels, the latest of which, *Midwinter Break,* won Novel of the Year in the Irish Book Awards 2017. He has written versions of his fiction for other media – radio plays, television plays, screenplays, libretti for Scottish Opera. He is a member of Aosdána.

EMER MARTIN's first novel, *Breakfast in Babylon,* won the 1996 Book of the Year in her native Ireland at the prestigious Listowel Writers'

Week. *More Bread Or I'll Appear*, her second novel, was published internationally in 1999. Her third novel, *Baby Zero*, was published in the UK and Ireland in March 2007, and released in the US in 2014. *The Cruelty Men* is her latest novel, published in June 2018. Martin studied painting in New York and has had two sell-out solo shows of her paintings at the Origin Gallery in Harcourt Street, Dublin. In 2000 she was awarded the Guggenheim Fellowship.

Born in Clones, Co. Monaghan in 1955, PATRICK MCCABE has published many novels including *The Dead School*, *The Butcher Boy* and *Breakfast on Pluto*, the latter two of which were made into movies with Neil Jordan. His novel, *Heartland*, was published in April 2018 by New Island and his new novel, *The Big Yaroo* is due from the same publisher in September 2019. He is a member of Aosdána.

MOLLY MCCLOSKEY is the author of four works of fiction. Her most recent novel, *When Light is Like Water* (published in the US as *Straying*), is set between Ireland, Kenya, and the US. Her short stories have appeared in many anthologies, including Faber's *Town & Country: New Irish Short Stories*, and *The Long Gaze Back: An Anthology of Irish Women Writers*. She is also the author of the memoir *Circles Around the Sun: In Search of a Lost Brother*. She contributes regularly to the *Dublin Review* and *The Guardian*, and has written essays on a range of subjects, including the Guantanamo military commissions. Born in Philadelphia, she lived for 25 years in Ireland, and is a citizen of both Ireland and the US.

MIKE MCCORMACK is the author of two collections of short stories *Getting it in the Head* and *Forensic Songs*, and three novels *Crowe's Requiem*, *Notes from a Coma* and *Solar Bones* which was published in 2016. In 1996 he was awarded the Rooney Prize for Literature and *Getting it in the Head* was chosen as a *New York Times* Notable Book of the Year. In 2006 *Notes from a Coma* was shortlisted for the Irish Book of the Year Award. In 2016 *Solar Bones* was awarded the Goldsmiths Prize and the Bord Gais Energy Irish Novel of the Year and Book of the Year; it was also long-listed for the 2017 Man Booker Prize. In 2018 it was awarded the International Dublin Literary Award. He teaches creative writing at NUI Galway and is a member of Aosdána.

BARRY MCCREA's most recent book, *Languages of the Night*, won the René Wellek prize for the best book of 2016. He is the author of *In the*

Company of Strangers, a study of family and narrative structure in Dickens, Arthur Conan Doyle, Joyce, and Proust. His novel, *The First Verse,* won the 2006 Ferro-Grumley prize for fiction. He is currently completing a trilogy of novels set in Dublin from 1982 to the present. He holds a Chair in modern literature at the University of Notre Dame.

Playwright ROSALEEN MCDONAGH is a frequent contributor to Sunday Miscellany on RTÉ Radio 1 and also a columnist for *The Irish Times.* Rosaleen is a performer and member of Aosdána and a board member of Pavee Point and Project Art Centre. Theatre work includes *The Baby Doll Project, She's Not Mine,* and *Rings. Mainstream* was produced in 2017. Colum McCann's novel *Zoli,* a fictionalised narrative of the Roma poet Papusza, will be adapted by Rosaleen for production in 2019 with Fishamble Theatre Company. She has worked with Graeae Theatre Company; Tutti Theatre Company in Adelaide, Australia have invited Rosaleen to be writer in residence at the Adelaide Theatre Festival 2019. Rosaleen holds a BA and two M.Phil's from Trinity College Dublin. Rosaleen is currently a Ph.D candidate in Northumbria University. Rosaleen has cerebral palsy. She is a member of the Traveller Community.

BERNIE MCGILL is the author of *Sleepwalkers,* a collection of stories short-listed in 2014 for the Edge Hill Short Story Prize, and of the novels *The Butterfly Cabinet* and *The Watch House.* She has been published in the UK, the US and in translation in Italy and in The Netherlands. Her short fiction has appeared in acclaimed anthologies *The Long Gaze Back, The Glass Shore* and *Female Lines.* She is currently Writing Fellow with the Royal Literary Fund, based at the Seamus Heaney Centre, Queen's University, Belfast – www.berniemcgill.com.

CLAIRE MCGOWAN was born in Northern Ireland and moved to England to study at Oxford University. After living in France and China, she settled in London. She is the author of the Paula Maguire crimes series, and several other novels under the name Eva Woods. She has also written plays, scripts, and short stories, and a radio drama broadcast on Radio 4 in 2019. She was awarded the Nickelodeon International Writing Fellowship in 2018, and as part of that spent time living in Los Angeles.

LISA MCINERNEY's work has featured in *Winter Papers, The Stinging Fly, Granta, The Guardian*, BBC Radio 4 and various anthologies. Her story 'Navigation' was longlisted for the 2017 *Sunday Times* EFG Short Story Award. Her debut novel *The Glorious Heresies* won the 2016 Baileys Women's Prize for Fiction and the 2016 Desmond Elliott Prize. Her second novel, *The Blood Miracles*, won the 2018 RSL Encore Award.

BELINDA MCKEON was born in Longford and attended Trinity College, Dublin and University College Dublin. From 2000 to 2010 she worked for *The Irish Times*, writing on theatre, literature and the arts. Her first novel, *Solace*, won the Geoffrey Faber Memorial Prize and the *Sunday Independent* Best Newcomer Award and was named Bord Gáis Energy Irish Book of the Year in 2011. Her second novel, *Tender*, was shortlisted for Novel of the Year at the 2015 Irish Book Awards. She currently lives in Newburgh, New York and is Assistant Teaching Professor in Creative Writing at Rutgers University.

DANIELLE MCLAUGHLIN's stories have appeared in newspapers and magazines such as *Inaque* in 2016. In 2017, she was a Visiting Fellow at the Oscar Wilde Centre, Trinity College, Dublin, where she led workshops for students on the M.Phil in Creative Writing. She is UCC Writer-in-Residence 2018–2019. Together with Madeleine D'Arcy, she co-runs Fiction at the Friary, a free monthly fiction event in Cork which takes place at the Friary Bar, North Mall on the last Sunday of every month.

ALAN MCMONAGLE has written for radio and published two collections of short stories (*Psychotic Episodes* (Arlen House, 2013) and *Liar Liar* (Wordsonthestreet, 2008). *Ithaca*, his first novel, was published by Picador in 2017 as part of a two-book deal and was longlisted for the Desmond Elliott Award for first novels and shortlisted for an Irish Book Award. He lives in Galway.

EOIN MCNAMEE is the author of eight novels including *Resurrection Man* and the *Blue Trilogy*. His latest novel is *The Vogue*.

GERALDINE MILLS is a poet and short story writer from County Galway. She has published four collections of poetry, three of short stories and a children's novel. She has been awarded many prizes and bursaries including the Hennessy/*Sunday Tribune* New Irish

Writer Award, two Arts Council Bursaries and a Patrick and Katherine Kavanagh Fellowship. Her fiction and poetry are taught in US universities in St Louis, Connecticut, Emory and Atlanta, and on the Emerson College, Massachusetts summer course held in Ballyvaughan, Co Clare. Her fifth poetry collection, *Bone Road*, is forthcoming from Arlen House.

LIA MILLS writes novels, short stories, essays and an occasional blog. Her most recent novel, *Fallen*, was the 2016 Dublin/Belfast Two Cities One Book festival selection. She has been an invited contributor to anthologies such as *The Long Gaze Back* (edited by Sinéad Gleeson) and *Beyond the Centre: Writers on Writing* (edited by Declan Meade). Her work has appeared in, among others, *The Dublin Review, The Stinging Fly, The Irish Times* and *The Dublin Review of Books*. She is currently working on a collection of short stories.

SARAH MOORE FITZGERALD is a professor of teaching and learning at the University of Limerick and a member of the Creative Writing teaching team. An academic, researcher and novelist, Sarah's four novels are *Back to Blackbrick, The Apple Tart of Hope, A Very Good Chance,* and *The List of Real Things*. Her work has been shortlisted for several literary prizes including the CBI book of the year and the Waterstones Prize. In 2016 she won the Jack Harte award. Her work has been adapted for the stage and performed in Edinburgh and London. Sarah is also founder of UL's Creative Writing Winter School https://smoorefitzgerald.wixsite.com/ulcwwinterschool.

MARY MORRISSY is the author of three novels, *Mother of Pearl, The Pretender* and *The Rising of Bella Casey* and two collections of stories, *A Lazy Eye* and most recently, *Prosperity Drive*. Her short fiction has been anthologised widely and won her a Hennessy Award in 1984. In 1995 she was awarded the prestigious US Lannan Foundation Award. She is Associate Director of Creative Writing at University College Cork and a member of Aosdána.

PAUL MURRAY was born in Dublin in 1975. He has written three novels: his first, *An Evening of Long Goodbyes*, was shortlisted for the Whitbread First Novel Prize in 2003 and nominated for the Kerry Group Irish Fiction Award. His second novel *Skippy Dies* was longlisted for the 2010 Booker Prize and shortlisted for the 2010 Costa Prize, the Bollinger Everyman Wodehouse Prize for Comic Fiction and the National Book Critics Circle Award for Fiction. It was also #3 on *Time* magazine's top ten works of fiction from 2010. His latest novel, *The Mark and the Void*, was one of *Time*'s top ten best fiction books for 2015, and joint winner of the Bollinger Everyman Wodehouse Prize in 2016.

Éilís Ní Dhuibhne was born in Dublin and is a graduate of UCD. Her novel *The Dancers Dancing* was shortlisted for the Orange Prize for Fiction. In 2015 she was awarded the Irish PEN award for an outstanding contribution to Irish literature, and in 2016 she was given a Hennessy Hall of Fame award for lifetime achievement. Her latest novel for young people, *Aisling*, was published in 2015, and her collection of short stories, *The Shelter of Neighbours*, was published in 2012. She was elected to Aosdána in 2004. She is a current ambassador for the Irish Writers' Centre, and President of the Folklore of Ireland Society.

Billy O'Callaghan, from Cork, is the author of three short story collections and two novels, the latest of which, *My Coney Island Baby* (Jonathan Cape/Harper, 2019) has been translated into eight languages. He won an Irish Book Award in 2013 and was a finalist for the 2016 Costa Short Story Award, and his stories have appeared in such journals as *Agni*, *The Chattahoochee Review*, *The Kenyon Review*, *London Magazine*, *Ploughshares*, *Salamander* and *The Saturday Evening Post*. A new collection, *The Boatman and Other Stories*, is forthcoming from Jonathan Cape/Harper in 2020.

Micheál Ó Conghaile was born in Inis Treabhair in Connemara in 1962. He established the publishing company Cló Iar-Chonnacht (CIC) in 1985. A prolific writer, he has published poetry, short stories, a novel, plays, and a novella, and has also done some translation work and edited several books. In 1997 the Irish American Cultural Institute awarded him the Butler Literary Award and he won the Hennessy Irish Writer of the Year Award. A member of Aosdána, his works have been translated into various languages, including Romanian, Croatian, Albanian, Slovenian, German, Bengali, Polish, Macedonian, Arabic and English. He was writer in residence at Queen's University, Belfast and at the University of Ulster Coleraine between 1999–2002. His selected short stories, *The Colours of Man*, was published in 2012 and Mercier Press published his *Colourful Irish Phrases* in 2018.

NUALA O'CONNOR lives in County Galway. Her short story 'Gooseen' won the UK's 2018 Short Fiction Prize, was published in *Granta* and was shortlisted for Story of the Year at the Irish Book Awards. Nuala's third novel, *Miss Emily*, about the poet Emily Dickinson and her Irish maid was shortlisted for the Eason Book Club Novel of the Year 2015 and longlisted for the 2017 International DUBLIN Literary Award. Her fourth novel, *Becoming Belle*, was published to critical acclaim in September 2018. She is currently writing a novel about Nora Barnacle, wife of James Joyce – www.nualaoconnor.com.

Monaghan-born MARY O'DONNELL is one of Ireland's best known contemporary authors. Her poetry collections include *Unlegendary Heroes* and *Those April Fevers* (Ark Publications). Four novels include *Where They Lie* (2014) and a best-selling debut novel *The Light Makers*, reissued last year by 451 Editions. A volume of essays, *Giving Shape to the Moment: the Art of Mary O'Donnell, Poet, novelist, short-story writer* appeared from Peter Lang (Zurich) last June, and her latest collection of stories, *Empire* (Arlen House) was published in 2018. She is a member of Aosdána, Ireland's multi-disciplinary arts academy – www.maryodonnell.com.

ROISÍN O'DONNELL was the winner of the Irish Book Award for Short Story of the Year 2018. Her debut short story collection, *Wild Quiet*, was published in 2016 and was shortlisted for the Kate O'Brien Award and the International Ruberry Book Award and longlisted for the Edge Hill Short Story Prize. Roisín's stories have been published internationally. Two of her stories were selected for inclusion in major anthologies of Irish women's writing, *The Long Gaze Back* and *The Glass Shore*, both of which won Irish Book Awards. She has family roots in Derry city and now lives in County Meath.

NESSA O'MAHONY is a Dublin-born writer. She has published four books of poetry and is a recipient of three literature bursaries from the Arts Council. She produces and presents a podcast for writers called The Attic Sessions. Her debut crime novel, *The Branchman*, was published by Arlen House in 2018. Her fifth poetry collection, *The Hollow Woman on the Island*, was published by Salmon Poetry in 2019.

JOSEPH O'NEILL was born in Cork and grew up in The Netherlands. A former barrister, his books include four novels, most recently *The*

Dog (longlisted for the Booker prize; shortlisted for the Bollinger Everyman Wodehouse Prize for comic fiction) and *Netherland*, for which he received the PEN/Faulkner Award for Fiction and the Kerry Group Irish Fiction Award. He has published a family history, *Blood-Dark Track*, and a book of short stories, *Good Trouble*, appeared in 2018.

Born in Derry, SEAN O'REILLY is the author of the short story collection, *Curfew*, and the novels, *Love and Sleep*, *The Swing of Things* and *Watermark*. His latest book is *Levitation*. He leads the *Stinging Fly* Writing Workshop in Dublin. He is a member of Aosdána.

DAVID PARK is the author of nine novels and two collections of short stories. His first novel *The Healing* (Jonathan Cape, 1992) won the Authors' Club First Novel Award. *The Truth Commissioner* (Bloomsbury, 2008) was awarded the Ewart-Biggs Memorial Prize and adapted for film; *The Light of Amsterdam* (Bloomsbury, 2012) was shortlisted for the IMPAC Award and *The Poets' Wives* (Bloomsbury, 2014) was Belfast's One City One Book. He has received a Major Artist Award from the Arts Council of Northern Ireland and the American Ireland Fund Literary Award. *Travelling in a Strange Land*, published in March 2018 by Bloomsbury, was shortlisted for the Irish Novel of the Year and won the Novel of the Year Award in 2019. His work has been published widely in translation.

SIOBHÁN PARKINSON studied at Trinity College Dublin. After a year in Germany, she came back to Trinity to do her Ph.D (on the poetry of Dylan Thomas). She has written over 25 books for children and was Ireland's first children's laureate (2010–2012). She is currently publisher of Little Island Books, a small children's publishing house she set up in 2010; it is now established as a leading children's publisher in Ireland. Her most recent books are a children's novel, *Miraculous Miranda* (Hodder, 2016) and a non-fiction title, *Rocking the System* (Little Island, 2018). She is currently working on an Irish-language historical novel.

GLENN PATTERSON is the author of three works of non-fiction and ten novels, most recently *Gull* (2016). He is co-writer (with Colin Carberry) of *Good Vibrations* (BBC Films), which the pair adapted for stage at the Lyric Theatre Belfast in September 2018. He has written plays for Radio 3 and Radio 4 and with composer Neil Martin he wrote *Long Story Short: the Belfast Opera* in 2016. His novel *The Mill for*

Grinding Old People Young was One City One Book choice for Belfast in 2012. He is director of the Seamus Heaney Centre at Queen's University, Belfast.

Former ghost-writer, NICOLA PIERCE's first children's novel, *Spirit of the Titanic*, was published in 2011. *City of Fate*, her second novel, about World War II's Battle of Stalingrad, was shortlisted for the 2015 Warwickshire School Library Service Award. *Behind the Walls*, about the Siege of Derry, was published in 2015, a prequel to her 2016 novel, *Kings of the Boyne*, which was shortlisted for the 2017 LAI (Literary Association Ireland) Children's Book Award. Her latest book, for adults, *Titanic True Stories*, was published in April 2018. She is currently working on her fifth children's novel.

KEVIN POWER is the author of *Bad Day in Blackrock* (2008) and the winner of the 2009 Rooney Prize for Irish Literature. He has written fiction and criticism for various newspapers and journals. He graduated with a Ph.D from UCD in 2013 and now teaches on the M.Phil in Creative Writing at Trinity College Dublin. His new novel will be published by Simon & Schuster UK in 2020.

HEATHER RICHARDSON is a writer and artist who works across a spectrum from prose and poetry to visual art. She is particularly interested in the places where these disciplines overlap, and her most recent work is in the form of narrative textiles. Her poetry and short stories have been published in the UK, Ireland and Australia. She is the author of two historical novels, *Magdeburg* (Lagan Press, 2010) and *Doubting Thomas* (Vagabond Voices, 2017). Her narrative textile piece 'A dress for Kathleen' was exhibited at the Linen Biennale Northern Ireland in 2018.

DEBBIE THOMAS has written five middle-grade novels for children. After training as a BBC radio journalist, she worked for ten years in Bangladesh and South Africa for international aid agencies before moving to Ireland. She is the Writer in Residence at Crumlin Children's Hospital and an Ireland committee member of the International Board on Books for Young People that fosters intercultural understanding through children's books. She works for an organisation supporting people with leprosy in Nepal.

WILLIAM WALL has published six novels, most recently *Grace's Day* (2018) and *Suzy Suzy* (2019), three collections of short fiction including *Hearing Voices Seeing Things* (2016) and *The Islands* (2017), and four collections of poetry including *Ghost Estate* (2011) and *The Yellow House* (2017). He was the first European to win the Drue Heinz Literature Prize, and he has won numerous other awards. His 2005 novel *This is the Country* was longlisted for the Man Booker Prize. He holds a Ph.D from UCC. His work has been widely translated and he translates from Italian – www.williamwall.net.

FINTAN O'TOOLE was educated at UCD. He is an author, literary critic and columnist with *The Irish Times*. He has written political commentary on the rise, fall and aftermath of Ireland's Celtic Tiger, on political corruption in Ireland and on Brexit. He has won numerous prizes for his work, among which the European Press Prize (Commentator Award, 2017), the Orwell Prize for Journalism (2017) and the NewsBrands Ireland Journalism Awards Broadsheet Columnist of the Year (2017 and 2018).

HEDWIG SCHWALL is General Director of the Leuven Centre for Irish Studies (LCIS) and Project Director of the European Federation of Associations and Centres of Irish Studies (EFACIS) – www.efacis.eu. She is literature editor of *RISE*, the *Review of Irish Studies in Europe* and special editor of the issue 'Irish Textiles: (t)issues in communities and their representation in art and literature' (2018). She publishes in and reviews for several journals in Irish Studies. In her research she focuses on contemporary Irish literature as well as on European art, often using psychoanalytic theory and contemporary philosophy.